Opposite and above: Two interpretations of Nicolo Paganini at different periods of his life. Opposite is the Eugene Delacroix oil painting done around 1832, from the Phillips Collection, Washington, D.C.; above is the Ingres sketch done around 1819.

Fiddlers in Fiction

Murray J. Levith

PAGANINIANA
ISBN 0-87666-616-0
Z-27

Cover design after an original poster titled
Music, *by VAAP, the copyright agency of the*
USSR.

Paganiniana Publications, Inc.
Box 427 • Neptune, NJ 07753

CONTENTS

ACKNOWLEDGMENTS

University of Chicago Press for permission to reprint "Councillor Krespel" by E. T. A. Hoffmann, translated by Leonard J. Kent and Elizabeth C. Knight, from *Selected Writings of E. T. A. Hoffmann.* Copyright 1969.

Roy Publishers, Inc. for permission to reprint "The Poor Fiddler" by Franz Grillparzer, translated by E. B. Ashton, from *The Blue Flower,* edited by Hermann Kesten. Copyright 1946.

Thomas Y. Crowell for permission to reprint "Albert" by Leo Tolstoy, translated by Nathan Haskell Doyle, from *A Russian Proprietor.* Copyright 1887.

"Rothschild's Fiddle" by Anton Chekhov, translated by Marian Fell, is reprinted by permission of Charles Scribner's Sons from *Russian Silhouettes.* Copyright 1915 Charles Scribner's Sons.

"The Fiddle," taken from *The Old Country* by Sholom Aleichem. Copyright 1946, 1974 by Crown Publishers, Inc. Used by permission of Crown Publishers, Inc.

Princeton University Press for permission to reprint "The Fiddler" by Herman Melville, from *The Apple-Tree Table.* Copyright 1922.

American Play Company, Inc. for permission to reprint "100 Percent Man" by Damon Runyon, from *Runyon First and Last.*

Estate of Paul Goodman for permission to reprint "The Birthday Concert" by Paul Goodman, from *Adam and His Works.*

"The Resemblance Between a Violin Case and a Coffin" by Tennessee Williams, from *Hard Candy.* Copyright 1954 by Tennessee Williams. Reprinted by permission of New Directions Publishing Company.

"The Wasp" by permission of Herbert Kubly.

"Harry Belten and the Mendelssohn Violin Concerto" by permission of Barry Targan.

To my mother,
who chased me around the dining-room table
to get me to practice

INTRODUCTION

The idea for this collection came to me some years ago when I was attending a graduate seminar in music at Syracuse University. "Survey of Contemporary String Literature" was taught by a number of distinguished musicians: violinist Joseph Fuchs, composer Quincy Porter, former assistant conductor and concertmaster of the Boston Symphony, Richard Burgin, Louis Krasner (who introduced the Alban Berg and Arnold Schoenberg violin concertos), the Hungarian Quartet, and Rudolph Kolisch of the celebrated Kolisch Quartet, among others.

The most striking thing about the seminar—besides the music, to be sure—was the wonderful storytelling that went on in class. Each artist was an encyclopedia of anecdotes about his fellows, past and present. And tales were told with skill and relish.

Even we students got into the act and inadvertently spiced the stories. When Rudolph Kolisch spoke of his lively times in Vienna playing chamber music with Schoenberg, one of us asked whether Schoenberg was a good 'cellist. "Terrible," Kolisch answered in his gruff German-English. A lengthy and rather embarrassed *fermata* followed this shocking bit of information. At last, another student attempted to heal the wounded atmosphere. "How do you mean?" he questioned, "Terrible in technique? Terrible in ensemble playing?" "Ach," understood Kolisch, lighting up, "*Marvelous* terrible!"

I wondered if there were many tales about fiddlers by professional storytellers. I knew of a few. Along the way of my research I discovered a great number. Remarkable was the exceptional literary quality of the majority of the stories I found. The stature of the authors who wrote fiddlers into fiction may have accounted for this: great American writers like Herman Melville and Tennessee Williams, great European writers like E. T. A. Hoffmann, Sholom Aleichem, Thomas Hardy. True, some stories read were horrible— little more than sentimental clichés or of-the-moment drivel. Horatio Alger, for example, wrote about *The Young Musician,* and,

Opposite: Marc Chagall's *THE GREEN VIOLINIST,* from the collection of the Solomon R. Guggenheim Museum, New York.

although the film version of "Humoresque" is a classic, Fannie Hurst's story on which it is based is not.

This anthology has broad narrative range. From the relatively straight-forward allegories of, say, Anton Chekhov in "Rothschild's Fiddle" or Thomas Bailey Aldrich in "The Little Violinist," to the ambitious and richly complex novellas "Albert" by Leo Tolstoy and "The Poor Fiddler" by Franz Grillparzer, a wide spectrum of styles and thematic densities is represented herein. I have tried to be selective with an eye to variety and interest.

One story in the collection warrants a special note. I was a sort of unofficial technical advisor and consultant during the composition of "Harry Belten and the Mendelssohn Violin Concerto." Its author, Barry Targan, is my violin student. Arleen Targan, the writer's wife, executed the marvelous illustrations to be seen throughout *Fiddlers in Fiction.*

Thanks for help with this project go to my wife Tina, Skidmore College, Gillian Lewis (friend and reference librarian), and my various student assistants—especially Lynn Armentrout and Pamela Nelson. Finally, very special thanks and gratitude are due my violin teacher of long ago, Markus Klein, who, with the patience of a saint and my strong-willed parents, taught me to play the violin.

Murray J. Levith
Skidmore College
Saratoga Springs,
New York

"Councillor Krespel" (1816) is one of the famous *Tales of Hoffmann,* and the basis for the third act of Jacques Offenbach's opera. Ernst Theodor Amadeus Hoffmann was actually born E. T. *W.* (for Wilhelm), but the writer assumed the *A.* in honor of his admired Mozart. Like Mozart, Hoffmann studied violin and harpsichord from an early age. A man of many talents, he was at various times lawyer, artist, composer, music critic, opera director, and novelist. His fiction is distinguished by interest in the supernatural and grotesque. "Councillor Krespel," an excellent character study, is thought to be based on a historical personage, Johann Berhard Crespel (1747-1813), with elements of autobiography mixed in.

Councillor Krespel

by E. T. A. Hoffmann
Translated by Leonard J. Kent and Elizabeth C. Knight

Councillor Krespel was one of the most eccentric men I ever met in my life. When I went to H——, where I was to live for a time, the whole town was talking about him because one of his craziest schemes was then in full bloom. Krespel was renowned as both an accomplished jurist and a skilled diplomat. A reigning German Fürst—one of no great significance—requested that he draw up a memorandum for submission to the Imperial Court establishing his legal claim to a certain territory. The suit was crowned with unusual success, and because Krespel had once complained that he could never find a house which properly suited him, the Fürst, who decided to reward him for services rendered, agreed to assume the cost of building a house which Krespel might erect according to his own desires. The Fürst also offered to purchase any site that pleased Krespel, but Krespel rejected this offer, insisting that the house should be built in his own garden, which was located in a very beautiful area outside the town gates. Then he bought all kinds of building materials and had them delivered there; thereafter he could be seen all day long, dressed in his peculiar clothes—which he always made himself according to his own specific theories— slaking lime, sifting sand, stacking building stones in neat piles, and so on. He had not consulted an architect, nor had he drawn any formal plan. One fine day, however, he called on a master mason in H—— and asked him to appear at his garden at dawn the next day with all of his journeymen and apprentices, many of his laborers, and so on, to build his house for him. Naturally, the mason requested the architect's plan and was more than a little astonished when Krespel replied that there was no need for a plan and that everything would turn out very well without one.

When the mason and his men arrived the next morning, they discovered that an excavation had been dug in a perfect square. "This is where the foundation of my house is to be laid," Krespel said, "and the four walls are to be built up until I tell you that they are high enough."

"Without windows and doors, without partition walls?" the mason interrupted as if shocked by Krespel's crazy notions.

"Do what I tell you, my good man," Krespel replied very calmly. "The rest will take care of itself."

Only the promise of generous payment induced the builder to proceed with this ridiculous building; but never was there one erected under more merry circumstances. The workmen, who laughed continually, never left the site, as there was an abundance of food and drink on hand. The walls went up with unbelievable speed, until Krespel one day shouted, "Stop!" When trowels and hammers were silenced, the workmen descended from the scaffolding and circled around Krespel, every laughing face seemed to ask "So, what's next?"

"Make way!" cried Krespel, who then ran to one end of the garden and paced slowly toward his square building. When he came close to the wall he shook his head in dissatisfaction, ran to the other end of the garden, and again paced toward the wall, with the same result. He repeated this tactic several times until finally, running his sharp nose hard against the wall, he cried, "Come here, come here, men. Make me a door right here!" He specified the exact dimensions to the inch, and his orders were carried out. Then he walked into the house and smiled with pleasure as the builder remarked that the walls were precisely the height of a well-constructed two story house. Krespel walked thoughtfully back and forth inside. The builders, hammers and picks in hand, followed behind him; and whenever he cried "Put a window here, six by four; and a little window here, three by two!" space was immediately knocked out.

I arrived at H—— at this stage of the operation, and it was very entertaining to see hundreds of people standing around in the garden, all cheering loudly when stones flew out and still another window appeared where it was least expected. Krespel handled the rest of the construction and all other necessary work in the same way. Everything had to be done on the spot, according to his orders of the moment. The comic aspect of the whole project, the growing conviction that everything was turning out better than could possibly have been expected, and above all, Krespel's generosity—which, indeed, cost him nothing—kept everyone in good humor. The difficulties intrinsic in this peculiar method of building were thus overcome, and in a short time a completely finished house was standing, presenting a most unusual appearance from the outside—no two windows being alike, and so on—but whose interior arrangements aroused a very special feeling of ease. Everyone who went there bore testimony to this, and I felt it myself when I grew better acquainted with Krespel and was invited there. Up to that time I had not spoken with this strange man. He had been so preoccupied with his building that he had not even once come to Professor M——'s house for lunch, as had always been his wont on Tuesdays. Indeed, in response to an explicit invitation, he replied that he would not set foot outside his new home before the housewarming took place. All his friends and acquaintances looked forward to a great feast, but Krespel invited no one except the masters, journeymen, apprentices, and laborers who had built his house. He entertained them with the most splendid dishes. Masons' apprentices, without thinking of possible consequences, gorged themselves on partridge pies; carpenters' boys joyfully planed roast pheasants; and hungry laborers for once labored on choicest morsels of *truffes fricassées*. In the evening their wives and daughters arrived, and a great ball began. Krespel waltzed a little with the builders' wives and then sat down with the town musicians, took up his fiddle, and conducted the dance music until daybreak.

On the Tuesday following this festival, which established Krespel as a friend of the people, I finally met him, to my no small pleasure, at Professor M——'s. It would be impossible to imagine anything stranger than Krespel's behavior. His movements were so stiff and awkward that he looked as if he would bump into or damage something at any moment. But he didn't, and it was soon obvious that he wouldn't, for the mistress of the house did not bother to turn a shade paler when he stumbled around the table set with beautiful cups or maneuvered in front of a great full-length mirror, or seized a vase of exquisitely painted porcelain and swung it around in the air as if to let the colors flash. In fact, before lunch Krespel scrutinized everything in the Professor's room most minutely. He even climbed up one of the upholstered chairs to remove a picture from the wall and then rehung it, while chattering incessantly and with great emphasis. Occasionally—it was most especially noticeable at lunch—he jumped from one subject to another; then, unable to abandon some particular idea, he returned to it over and over again, got himself completely enmeshed in it, and could not disentangle his thoughts until some fresh idea caught him. Sometimes his voice was harsh and screeching, sometimes it was slow and singsong; but never was it in harmony with what he was talking about. We were discussing music and praising a new composer when Krespel smiled and said in his musical voice, "I wish that the black-winged Satan would hurl that damned music mutilator ten thousand million fathoms deep into hell's pit!" Then, he burst out wildly and screechingly, "She is heaven's angel, nothing but pure God-given harmony—the light and star of song!" and tears formed in his eyes. One had to recall that an hour before he had been talking about a celebrated soprano.

As we were eating roast hare I noticed that Krespel carefully removed every particle of flesh from the bones on his plate and asked especially for the paws, which the Professor's five-year-old daughter brought to him with a friendly smile. The children had cast many friendly glances at Krespel during dinner, and now they got up and moved near to him, but with a respectful shyness, staying three paces away. "What's going to happen now?" I thought to myself. The dessert was brought in; then Krespel took from his pocket a little box in which there was a tiny steel lathe. This he immediately screwed to the table, and with incredible skill, made all kinds of little boxes and dishes and balls out of the bones, which the children received with cries of delight.

Just as we were rising from the table, the Professor's niece asked, "What is our Antonia doing now, dear Councillor?"

Krespel made a face like someone biting into a sour orange who wants to look as if it were a sweet one; but soon his expression changed into a horrifying mask and his laugh was bitter and fierce as he answered with what seemed to me to be diabolical scorn, "Our? *Our* dear Antonia?" he asked in his languid, unpleasant singing tone. The Professor quickly intervened; in the reproving glance he threw at his niece, I read that she had touched a chord which must have jarred discordantly within Krespel.

"How is it going with the violins?" the Professor asked gaily, taking the Councillor by both hands.

Then Krespel's face lightened, and he answered in his firm voice, "Splendidly, Professor, only this morning I cut open that marvelous Amati I told you about recently that fell into my hands through a lucky accident. I hope that Antonia has carefully taken the rest of it apart."

"Antonia is a good child," the Professor said.

"Yes, indeed, that she is," Krespel screamed, quickly turning around, simultaneously grabbing his hat and stick, and rushing out through the door. I saw in the mirror that there were tears in his eyes.

As soon as the Councillor had left, I insisted that the Professor tell me immediately what Krespel was doing with violins, and especially about Antonia. "Well," the Professor said, "As the Councillor is in general a very remarkable man, he has his own mad way of constructing violins."

"Constructing violins?" I asked in astonishment.

"Yes," continued the Professor. "In the opinion of those who know what it is all about, Krespel makes the best violins that can be found nowadays. Formerly, if one turned out very well, he would allow others to play it; but that has been over for a long time now. When Krespel has made a violin, he plays it himself with great power and with exquisite expression, for an hour or two, then he hangs it up with the rest and never touches it again, nor does he allow anyone else to touch it. If a violin by any of the eminent old masters is on the market, the Councillor buys it, at any price asked. But, as with his own violins, he plays it only once, then takes it apart in order to examine its inner structure, and if he thinks that he has not found what he has been looking for, he flings the pieces into a large chest which is already full of dismantled violins."

"But what's this about Antonia?" I asked suddenly and impetuously.

"Well, now," continued the Professor. "Well, now, that is something that might make me detest the Councillor if I were not convinced of his basic good nature; indeed, he is so good that he errs on the side of weakness, and there must be some hidden explanation behind it all. When he came here to H—— several years ago, he lived like an anchorite, with an old housekeeper in a gloomy house in —— Street. Soon his eccentricities aroused the curiosity of his neighbors, and as soon as he noticed this, he sought and made acquaintances. Just as in my house, people everywhere grew so accustomed to him that he became indispensable. Despite his coarse appearance, even the children loved him, without becoming pests; for in spite of this friendliness, they retained a certain respect for him that protected him from any undue familiarities. You saw for yourself today how he is able to win the hearts of children with various ingenious tricks. We all took him for a confirmed bachelor, and he never contradicted this impression.

"After he had been here for some time, he went away, no one knew where, and returned after several months. On the evening following his return his windows were lighted up more brightly than usual, and this attracted the attention of the neighbors, who soon heard a surpassingly lovely female voice singing to the accompaniment of a piano. Then the sound of a violin struck up and challenged the voice to a dazzling and fiery contest. One immediately knew that it was Krespel playing. I myself mingled with the large crowd which had gathered in front of the Councillor's house to listen to this wonderful concert; and I must confess that the singing of the most famous soprano I had ever heard seemed feeble and expressionless compared with that voice and the peculiar impression it made, stirring me to the depths of my soul. Never before had I had any conception of such long-sustained notes, of such nightingale trills, of such crescendos and diminuendos, of such surging to organ-like strength and such diminution to the faintest whisper. There was no one who was not enthralled by the magic, and when the singer stopped, only gentle sighs interrupted the profound silence.

"It must have been midnight when we heard the Councillor talking violently. Another masculine voice could be heard which, to judge from its tone, seemed to be reproaching him; and at intervals the voice of a girl complained in disjointed phrases. The Councillor shouted more and more loudly until he finally fell into that familiar singsong voice of his. He was interrupted by a loud scream from the

girl, and then all grew deathly silent until, suddenly, there was a commotion on the stairs, and a young man rushed out sobbing, threw himself into a carriage waiting nearby, and drove quickly away.

"The Councillor seemed to be very cheerful the next day, and no one had the courage to question him about what had happened the previous night; but the housekeeper, upon being questioned, said that the Councillor had brought home with him a very young lady, as pretty as a picture, whom he called Antonia, and it was she who had sung so beautifully. A young man, who had treated Antonia very affectionately and must have been her fiancé had also come along with them. But, because the Councillor had insisted upon it, he had had to leave quickly. The relationship between Antonia and the Councillor is still a secret, but it is certain that he tyrannizes the poor girl in a most hateful fashion. He watches her as Doctor Bartolo watched his ward in *The Barber of Seville;* she hardly dares to be seen at the window. And if she can occasionally prevail upon him to take her into society, his Argus eyes follow her and he will not permit a musical note to be played, let alone allow her to sing. Indeed, she is no longer permitted to sing in his home either. Antonia's singing on that night has become something of a legend, something romantic that stirs the imagination of the townsfolk; and even the people who did not hear her, often say, when a singer performs here, 'What sort of miserable caterwauling is that? Only Antonia knows how to sing.' "

You know that such fantastic events are my special weakness, and you can easily guess how imperative it was for me to become acquainted with Antonia. I had often heard the popular comments about her singing, but I had no idea that the glorious Antonia was living in the town, held captive by the mad Krespel as if by a tyrannical sorcerer. Naturally, I heard Antonia's marvelous singing in my dreams the following night, and when she most touchingly implored me to save her in a superb adagio (which, absurdly enough, I seemed to have composed myself), I determined, like a second Astolpho, to break into Krespel's house as into Alzinen's magic castle, and deliver the queen of song from her shameful bonds.

It all came out differently from what I had imagined. As soon as I had seen the Councillor once or twice and avidly discussed with him the best structure of violins, he himself invited me to call on him at his house. I did so, and he showed me his treasury of violins. At least thirty of them were hanging in a closet, and one of them, conspicuous because it bore the marks of great antiquity (a carved lion's head, and so on), was hanging higher than the rest, crowned with a wreath of flowers that seemed to make it a queen over the others.

"This violin," Krespel said when I asked him about it, "this violin is a very remarkable and wonderful piece by an unknown master, probably of Tartini's time. I am completely convinced that there is something peculiar about its inner construction and that if I take it apart I will discover a secret I have been looking for, but—laugh at me if you like—this dead thing, which depends upon me for its life and its voice, often speaks to me by itself in the strangest manner. When I played it for the first time, it seemed as if I was but the hypnotist who so affects his somnambulist that she verbally reveals what she is able to see within herself. Do not suppose that I am idiotic enough to attribute even the slightest importance to ideas so fantastic in nature, but it is peculiar that I have never succeeded in convincing myself to dismantle that inanimate and dumb object. Now I am pleased that I have never dismantled it; since Antonia's arrival I occasionally use it to play something to her. She is extremely fond of it—extremely."

This was said by Krespel with obvious emotion, and I was encouraged to ask, "My dear Councillor, will you not one day play in my presence?" But his face assumed his sweet-sour expression, and he said in that slow singsong way of his, "No, my dear Herr Studiosus!" And this ended the business; I had to continue looking at all sorts of curiosities, frequently childish ones. Ultimately he thrust his hand in a chest and withdrew from it a folded paper, which he then pressed in my hand, while most seriously saying, "You are a lover of art. Take this present as a true keepsake and value it above all else in the world."

Saying this, he softly clutched both my shoulders and shoved me towards the door, embracing me on the threshold. Actually, I was symbolically thrown out of the house.

When I opened the paper I discovered a piece of an E string which was about an eighth of an inch in length; and alongside the string was written, "From the E string of the violin used by the deceased Stamitz when he played his last concert."

This unfriendly dismissal at the mention of Antonia suggested that I would never succeed in seeing her; but this was not so, for when I visited the Councillor for the second time I found Antonia in his room, helping him put a violin together. Antonia did not make a strong impression at first sight, but I soon found it impossible to resist her blue eyes, her sweet rosy lips, and her singularly

17

delicate and lovely figure. She was very pale, but if anything was said which was witty and amusing, a fiery blush suffused her cheeks, only to fade to a faint pink glow.

I talked to her without restraint, and I noticed none of those Argus-like glances that the Professor had attributed to Krespel; on the contrary, the Councillor remained absolutely his usual self and even seemed to approve of my conversing with Antonia. And so I often visited the Councillor; and as we grew more familiar, our little circle assumed a warm intimacy which gave the three of us great pleasure. The Councillor continued to entertain me with his eccentricities, but of course it was really Antonia, with her irresistible charm, who drew me there and led me to tolerate a good deal which my impatient nature would otherwise have found unbearable. The Councillor's eccentric behavior was sometimes in bad taste and tedious, and what I found particularly irritating was that as soon as I steered the conversation to music, especially singing, he would interrupt me in his singsong voice, a diabolical smile upon his face, and introduce some irrelevant, often coarse subject. I realized from the great distress in Antonia's eyes at such moments that his sole purpose was to preclude my asking her to sing. I did not give up. The obstacles which the Councillor threw in my way only strengthened my resolution to overcome them. If I was to avoid dissolving in fantasies and dreams about her singing, I had to hear her sing.

One evening Krespel was in an especially good mood. He had been taking an old Cremona violin apart and had discovered that the sound post was so fixed that it was about half a line more oblique than was customary—an important discovery of great practical value! I was successful in getting him to talk very fervently about the true art of violin playing. Krespel mentioned that the style of the old masters had been influenced by that of the truly great singers—Krespel happened just then to be talking about this—and naturally I commented that the practice was now reversed and that singers imitated the leaps and runs of the instrumentalists.

"What is more senseless than this?" I cried, leaping from my chair, running to the piano, and opening it quickly. "What can be sillier than such absurd mannerisms, which instead of being music sound like the noise of peas rattling across the floor!"

I sang several of the modern *fermatas* that run back and forth and hum like a well-spun top, accompanying myself with a few chords. Krespel laughed excessively and cried, "Ha, ha! I seem to hear our German-Italians, or our Italian-Germans, starting some aria by Pucitta or Portogallo, or by some other *maestro di capella,* or rather *schiavo d'un primo uomo."*

"Now," I thought, "is the moment"; and turning to Antonia I asked, "Isn't that right? Antonia knows nothing of such squealing?" And I immediately began one of the beautiful soul-stirring songs by old Leonardo Leo. Antonia's cheeks flushed, her eyes flashed with a newly awakened radiance. She sprang to the piano and parted her lips. But at that very instant Krespel pushed her away, seized me by the shoulders, and shrieked in his shrill tenor voice, "My dear boy, my dear boy!" Then, grasping my hand while bowing most courteously, he led me immediately away, saying in his soft singsong way, "In truth, my esteemed and honorable sir, in truth it would be a breech of courtesy and good manners if I were to express my wish loudly and clearly that you should have your neck softly broken by the scorching claws of the devil who would, one could say, dispose of you quickly; but putting that aside for the moment, you must admit, my dear, dear sir, that it is growing very dark, and since there are no lamps lighted today, you might risk damaging your precious legs, even if I did not kick you out right now. Be good and go home in safety and think kind thoughts of me, your true friend, if it so happens that you never—do you understand me?—if you never happen to find him at home again."

He thereupon embraced me and, grasping me firmly, slowly turned me towards the door so that I could not get another look at Antonia. You must admit that in my situation I could hardly beat up the Councillor, which he really deserved. The Professor enjoyed a good laugh at my expense and assured me that my break with the Councillor was absolutely permanent. Antonia was too precious to me, too sacred, I might say, for me to play the part of the languishing *amoroso* who stands gazing up at her window or fills the role of the lovesick adventurer. I left H—— completely shattered, but as usually happens in such cases, the brilliant colors of the picture painted by my imagination grew dim, and Antonia— yes, even her singing, which I had never heard—glimmered in my recollection like a gentle, consoling light.

Two years later, when I had settled in B——, I undertook a trip through Southern Germany. The towers of H—— rose up in the hazy red glow of the evening; as I drew nearer, I was oppressed by an indescribable feeling of anxiety which lay upon my heart like a heavy weight. I could not breathe; I had to get out of the carriage and into the open air, but the oppressiveness increased until it became physically agonizing. I soon seemed to hear the strains of a solemn chorale floating on the air. The sound grew more distinct, and I could distinguish men's voices singing a hymn.

"What's that? What's that?" I cried, as it pierced my breast like a burning dagger.

"Can't you see?" said the postillion next to me. "They're burying someone over there in the churchyard."

We were, in fact, close to the churchyard, and I saw a circle of people clad in black standing around a grave which was being filled. Tears welled in my eyes; I felt somehow that all the joy and happiness of my life were being buried in that grave. Moving quickly down the hill, I could no longer see into the churchyard. The hymn was over, and not far from the city gate I could see some of the mourners returning from the funeral. The Professor, his niece on his arm, both in deep mourning, passed close-by without noticing me. The niece had her hankerchief pressed to her eyes and was sobbing convulsively. It was impossible for me to go into town; therefore, I sent my servant with the carriage to the inn where I usually stay, while I hurried off to the neighborhood so familiar to me in an effort to shake off my mood, possibly due to something physical, perhaps the result of becoming overheated on the journey.

When I arrived at the avenue leading to a park, a most extraordinary spectacle took place. Councillor Krespel was being guided by two mourners, from whom he appeared to be trying to escape by making all kinds of strange leaps and turns. As usual, he was dressed in the incredible grey coat he had made himself, but from his small three-cornered hat, which he wore cocked over one ear in a military manner, a mourning ribbon fluttered this way and that in the breeze. A black sword belt was buckled around his waist, but instead of a sword, a long violin bow was tucked beneath it. A cold shiver ran through me. "He is mad," I thought as I slowly followed them. The men conducted him as far as his house, where he embraced them, laughing loudly. They left him, and then his glance fell on me, for I was now standing very close to him. He stared at me fixedly for some time, then called in a hollow voice, "Welcome, Herr Studiosus! You do, of course, understand everything about it." With this he seized me by the arm and dragged me into the house, up the stairs, and into the room where the violins hung. They were all draped in crepe; the violin by the old master was missing; in its place there hung a wreath of cypress. I knew what had happened.

"Antonia! Antonia!" I cried inconsolably. The Councillor, his arms folded, stood beside me as if paralyzed. I pointed to the cypress wreath.

"When she died," he said very solemnly and gloomily, "the sound post of that violin broke with a resounding crack and the soundboard shattered to pieces. That faithful instrument could only live with her and through her; it lies beside her in the coffin; it has been buried with her." Deeply shaken, I sank into a chair, but the Councillor began singing a gay song in a hoarse voice. It was truly horrible to see him hopping about on one foot, the crepe (he was still wearing his hat) flapping about the room and against the violins hanging on the walls; indeed, I could not repress a loud shriek when the crepe hit me during one of his wild turns. It seemed to me that he wanted to envelop me and drag me down into the black pit of madness. Suddenly he stopped gyrating and said in his singsong fashion, "My son, my son, why do you shriek like that? Have you seen the Angel of Death? He's usually seen before the funeral"; and suddenly stepping into the middle of the room, he drew the bow from his belt; and having raised it above his head in both hands, he broke it into a thousand pieces. Then he cried with a loud laugh, "Now you imagine that the staff has been broken over me, don't you, my son? But it's not so. Now I am free, free. I am free! I will no longer make violins—no more violins—hurrah! No more violins!" This he sang to a hideously mirthful tune, again jumping about on one foot. Aghast, I tried to get out of the door quickly, but the Councillor held me tightly and said quietly, "Stay here, Herr Studiosus, and don't think I am mad because of this outpouring of agony which tortures me like the pangs of death. It is all because only a short while ago I made a nightshirt for myself in which I wanted to look like Fate or like God."

The Councillor continued this frightening gibberish until he collapsed in utter exhaustion. The ancient housekeeper came to him when I called, and I was glad when I once more found myself in the open air.

Not for a moment did I doubt that Krespel had become insane, but the Professor held to the contrary. "There are men," he said, "from whom nature or some peculiar destiny has removed the cover beneath which we hide our own madness. They are like thin-skinned insects whose visible play of muscles seem to make them deformed, though in fact, everything soon returns to its normal shape again. Everything which remains thought within us becomes action in Krespel. Krespel expresses bitter scorn in mad gestures and irrational leaps, even as does the spirit which is embedded in all earthly activity. This is his lightning rod. What comes from the earth, he returns to the earth, but he knows how to preserve the divine. And so I believe that his inner consciousness is well, despite the apparent madness which springs to the surface. Antonia's sudden death weighs very heavily upon him, but I bet that tomorrow he'll be jogging along at his donkey trot as usual."

It happened that the Professor's prediction was almost exactly fulfilled. The next day the Councillor seemed to be completely himself again, but he declared that he would never again construct a violin, or play one. As I later learned, he kept his word.

The Professor's theories strengthened my private conviction that the carefully concealed, yet highly intimate nature of the relationship between Antonia and the Councillor, and even her death, had been marked by guilt, which could not be expatiated. I did not want to leave H—— without confronting him with this crime of which I suspected him; I wanted to shake him to the depths of his soul and so compel him to make an open confession of his horrible deed. The more I thought about the matter, the more I convinced myself that Krespel must be a scoundrel, and as the thoughts in my mind grew more fiery and forceful they developed into a genuine rhetorical masterpiece. Thus equipped, and in great agitation, I ran to the Councillor's. I found him calmly smiling, making toys.

"How is it possible," I began the assault, "for you to find a moment's peace in your soul when the memory of your terrible deed must torture you like a serpent's sting?"

Krespel looked at me in astonishment, put his chisel aside, and said, "What do you mean my dear fellow? Do have a seat please, on that chair."

But I grew more and more heated, and I accused him directly of having murdered Antonia and threatened him with the retribution of the Eternal. In fact, as a recently qualified court official imbued with my profession, I went so far as to assure him that I would do everything possible to bring the matter to light and to deliver him into the hands of an earthly judge. I was considerably taken aback, however, when at the conclusion of my violent and pompous harangue, the Councillor fixed his eyes upon me serenely, without uttering a word, as if waiting for me to continue. Indeed, I did try to do so, but it all sounded so clumsy and so utterly silly that I almost immediately grew silent again.

Krespel luxuriated in my perplexity; a malicious and ironical smile darted across his face. Then he became very serious and spoke to me in a solemn voice: "Young man, you may take me for a madman; I can forgive you for that. We are both confined to the same madhouse, and you accuse me of imagining that I am God the Father because you consider yourself to be God the Son. But how dare you presume to force your way into the life of another person to uncover hidden facts that are unknown to you and must remain so? She is dead now and the secret is revealed."

Krespel rose and paced back and forth across the room several times. I ventured to ask for an explanation; he stared at me with fixed eyes, grasped my hand, and led me to the window. After opening both casements, he propped his arms on the sill, leaned out, and looking down into the garden, he told me the story of his life. When he had finished, I left him, deeply moved and ashamed.

The facts of his relationship with Antonia were as follows: About twenty years ago the Councillor's all-consuming passion for hunting out and buying the best violins by the old masters had led him to Italy. He had not at that time begun to make violins himself, nor, consequently, had he begun to take them apart. In Venice he heard the famous singer Angela ———i, who at that time was triumphantly appearing in the leading roles in the Theatro di S. Benedetto. His enthusiasm was kindled, not only because of her art, which Signora Angela had developed to absolute perfection, but by her angelic beauty as well. The Councillor sought her acquaintance, and despite his uncouthness, he succeeded, primarily by his bold and most expressive violin playing, in winning her entirely for himself.

In a few weeks their close intimacy led to marriage, which was kept a secret because Angela did not wish to part from the theater nor surrender the name under which she had become famous nor add the awkward name of Krespel to it. With the most extravagant irony, the Councillor described the very peculiar way Angela plagued and tortured him as soon as she became his wife. Krespel felt that all the selfishness and all the petulance which resided in all the primadonnas in the world were somehow concentrated in her little body. When he once tried to assert his own position, Angela turned loose on him a whole army of *abbates, maestros, academicos* who, ignorant of his true relationship, found in him a completely intolerable and uncivilized admirer who was beyond adapting himself to the Signora's delightful whims. Right after one of these tumultuous scenes, Krespel fled to Angela's country house, trying to forget the suffering the day had brought by improvising on his Cremona violin. He had not been playing long, however, when the Signora, who had followed hard after him, stepped into the room. She was in the mood for playing the affectionate wife, so she embraced the Councillor with sweet languishing glances and laid her head on his shoulder. But the Councillor, who was lost in the world of his music, continued playing until the walls resounded, and it so happened that he touched the Signora a little ungently with his arm and the bow. Blazing into fury, she sprang back, shrieking *"bestia tedesca!"* snatched the violin from his hands, and smashed it into a thousand pieces on the marble table. The Councillor stood like a statue before her; but then, as if waking from a dream, he seized the Signora with the strength of a giant and flung her out of the window of her own country house, after which, without troubling himself about the matter any further, he fled to Venice, then Germany.

It was sometime before he fully realized what he had done. Although he knew that the window was barely five feet from the ground, and though he was fully convinced that it had been absolutely necessary to fling her from the window, he felt troubled and uneasy about it, especially because the Signora had made it clear to him that she was pregnant. He scarcely had the courage to ask about her, and he was not a little surprised when about eight months later he received a tender letter from his beloved wife which contained no mention of what had happened at the country house, but rather informed him that she had given birth to a lovely little girl and concluded with the heartfelt request that the *marito amato e padre felicissimo* come to Venice at once. Krespel did not go; instead he requested a close friend to supply him with details as to what was really going on. And he learned that the Signora had landed that day on the grass as gently as a bird and that the only consequence of her fall had been emotional. As a result of Krespel's heroic deed, she seemed transformed; no longer was there evidence of her former capriciousness or willfulness or of her old teasing habits; and the *maestro* who had composed the music for the next carnival was the happiest man under the sun, for the Signora was willing to sing his arias without a thousand changes to which he would otherwise have had to consent. All in all, there was every reason for keeping secret the method by which Angela had been cured; otherwise primadonnas would come flying through windows every day.

The Councillor grew very excited, ordered horses, and was seated in the carriage when he suddenly cried, "Stop!" He murmured to himself, "Why, isn't it certain that the evil spirit will again take possession of Angela the moment she sees me again? Since I have already thrown her out of the window, what will I do if the same situation were to occur again? What would there be left for me to do?"

He got out of the carriage and wrote his wife an affectionate letter, in which he gracefully alluded to her kindness in expressly detailing the fact that his little daughter had a little mole behind her ear, just as he did, and—remained in Germany. A very spirited exchange of letters ensued. Assurances of love—invitations—regrets over the absence of the loved one—disappointment—hopes—and so on—flew back and forth between Venice and H—— and H—— to Venice. Finally Angela came to Germany, and as is well known, sang triumphantly as primadonna at the great theater in F——. Despite the fact that she was no longer young, she swept all before her with the irresistible charm of her marvelous singing. Her voice at that time had not deteriorated in the slightest degree. Meanwhile Antonia had grown up, and her mother never could write enough to her father about the potential she saw in her daughter, who was blossoming into a first-rate singer. Krespel's friends in F—— confirmed this information and urged him to come to F— to marvel at the rare experience of hearing two such absolutely sublime singers together. They did not suspect the intimate relationship which existed between Krespel and the ladies. He would have loved seeing his daughter, whom he adored from the depths of his heart, and who often appeared to him in his dreams; but as soon as he thought about his wife he felt very uneasy, and he remained at home among his dismembered violins.

You will have heard of the promising young composer B—— of F—— who suddenly disappeared, no one knows how. (Did you perhaps know him?) He fell desperately in love with Antonia and, Antonia returning his love, he begged her mother to consent to a union which would be sanctified by their art. Angela had no objection to this, and the Councillor gave his consent all the more readily because the young composer's music pleased his critical judgment. Krespel expected to receive news that the wedding had taken place, when instead he received an envelope, sealed in black, addressed in an unfamiliar hand. Dr. R—— informed the Councillor that Angela had fallen seriously ill as a result of a chill which she had caught at the theater the evening preceding what was to have been Antonia's wedding day, and had died. Angela had revealed to the doctor that she was Krespel's wife and that Antonia was his daughter. He was therefore to hasten there to assume responsibility for the orphan. Despite the fact that the Councillor was deeply disturbed by this news of Angela's death, he nevertheless soon felt that a disturbing influence had left his life and that now he could breathe freely for the first time.

That very same day he started out for F——. You cannot imagine how dramatically the Councillor described the moment when he first saw Antonia. Even in the very bizarre nature of his language there was a wonderful power of description which I am completely incapable of conveying. Antonia had all of her mother's amiability and charm, but she had none of the meanness which was the reverse side of her mother's character. There was no ambiguous cloven hoof to peep out from time to time. The young bridegroom arrived; and Antonia, who was able through her own affectionate nature intuitively to understand her remarkable father, sang one of the old Padre Martini motets, which she knew Angela had had to sing repeatedly to Krespel when their courtship had been in full bloom. Tears flooded the Councillor's cheeks; he had never heard Angela sing so beautifully. The timbre of Antonia's voice was quite individual and rare, sometimes like the sound of an Aeolian harp, sometimes like the warbling of a nightingale. It was as if there were no room for such notes within the human breast. Antonia, glowing with love and joy, sang all of her most lovely songs, and B—— in the intervals played as only enraptured inspiration can play. Krespel was at first transported by delight, but then he grew thoughtful—quiet—introspective. Finally he leaped to his feet, pressed Antonia to his breast, and begged her softly and sadly: "If you love me, sing no more—my heart is bursting—the anguish! The anguish! Sing no more."

"No," the Councillor said the next day to Dr. R——. "When she sang, the color gathered into two dark red spots on her pale cheeks, and I knew that it could not be accounted for by any silly family resemblance; it was what I had dreaded."

The doctor, whose face had shown deep concern from the beginning of the conversation, replied, "Whether it results from her having overexerted herself in singing when she was too young, or whether it results from congenital weakness, Antonia suffers from an organic deficiency in her chest from which her voice derives its wonderful power and its strange, I might say, divine timbre and by which it transcends the capabilities of human song. But it will cause her early death; for if she continues to sing, she will live six months at the most."

The Councillor's heart felt as if it were pierced by a hundred daggers. It was as though a lovely tree and its superb blossoms had, for the first time, cast its shadow over him, and now it was to be cut down to the roots so that it could no longer grow green and blossom. His decision was made. He told Antonia everything and presented her with a choice—she could either follow her fiancé and surrender to his and the world's allurements with the certainty of dying young, or give to her father in his old age a happiness and a peace which he had never known, and thereby live for many years. Antonia collapsed sobbing into her father's arms, and he, aware of the agony the next few minutes might bring, asked for nothing explicit. He spoke with her fiancé, but despite his assurance that no note would ever cross Antonia's lips, the Councillor was fully aware that B—— himself would never be able to resist the temptation to hear her sing—at least the arias he was composing. The musical world, even though it knew of Antonia's suffering, would surely never surrender its claim to her, for people like this can be selfish and cruel when their own enjoyment is at issue.

The Councillor disappeared from F—— with Antonia and arrived at H——. B—— was in despair when he learned of their departure. He followed their tracks, overtook the Councillor, and arrived at H—— simultaneously.

"Let me see him only once and then die," Antonia entreated.

"Die? Die?" the Councillor cried in wild anger, an icy shudder running through him. His daughter, the only being in the wide world who could kindle in him a bliss he had never known, the one who had reconciled him to life, tore herself violently from his embrace; and he wanted this dreadful event to happen!

B—— went to the piano, Antonia sang, Krespel played the violin merrily until the red spots appeared on Antonia's cheeks. Then he ordered a halt; and when B——said goodbye to Antonia, she suddenly collapsed with a loud cry.

"I thought," Krespel told me, "I thought that she was really dead, as I had foreseen; but as I had prepared myself to the fullest degree, I remained very calm and controlled. I seized B——, who was staring stupidly like a sheep, by the shoulders and said" (and the Councillor now returned to his singsong voice): " 'Now, my dear and estimable piano master, now that you have, as you wished and desired, succeeded in murdering your beloved bride, you will quietly leave, unless you would be good enough to wait around until I run my bright little dagger through your heart, so that my daughter, who you see, has grown rather pale, could use some of your precious blood to restore her color. Get out of here quickly, or I may throw this nimble little knife at you!'

"I must have looked rather terrifying as I said this, for with a cry of the deepest horror, B—— tore himself from my grasp, rushed through the door and down the steps."

As soon as he was gone, Krespel went to lift Antonia, who lay unconscious on the floor, and she opened her eyes with a deep sigh, but soon closed them again as if she were dead. Krespel broke into loud and inconsolable grief. The doctor, who had been fetched meanwhile by the housekeeper, announced that Antonia was suffering from a serious but by no means fatal attack; and she did, in fact, recover more quickly than the Councillor had dared to hope. She now clung to Krespel with a most devoted and daughterly affection and shared with him all of his favorite hobbies, his peculiar schemes and whims. She helped him take old violins apart and put new ones together. "I will not sing anymore, but I will live just for you," she often said to her father, smiling softly, after someone had asked for a song and she had refused. The Councillor tried as hard as possible to spare her from such situations, and therefore, he was unwilling to take her out into society and scrupulously shunned all music. He was well aware of how painful it must be for Antonia to forgo completely the art in which she had attained such perfection.

When the Councillor bought the wonderful violin that he later buried with Antonia and was about to take it apart, Antonia looked at him very sadly and, in a gentle, imploring voice, asked, "This one, too?" The Councillor himself couldn't understand what unknown power had impelled him to spare his violin and to play it.

He had barely drawn the first few notes when Antonia cried aloud with joy, "Why that is me—I am singing again!" In truth, there was something about the silvery bell-like tones of the violin that was very striking; they seemed to come from a human soul. Krespel was so deeply moved that he played more magnificently than ever before, and when he ran up and down the scale with consumate power and expression, Antonia clapped her hands and cried with delight, "I sang that well! I sang that very well!" From this time on a great serenity and happiness came into her life. She often said to Krespel, "I would like to sing something, Father." Then Krespel would take his violin from the wall and play her most beautiful songs, and she was surpassingly happy.

One night, shortly before I arrived in H——, it seemed to Krespel that he heard someone playing the piano in the next room, and soon he distinctly recognized that it was B——, who was improvising in his usual style. He was about to rise, but it was as if there were a heavy weight upon him; he could not so much as stir. Then he heard Antonia's voice singing softly and delicately until it slowly grew into a shattering fortissimo. The wonderful sounds became the moving song which B—— had once composed for her in the devotional style of the old masters. Krespel said that the state in which he found himself was incomprehensible, for an appalling fear was combined with a rapture he had never before experienced.

Suddenly he was overwhelmed by a dazzling lucidity, and he saw B—— and Antonia embracing and gazing at each other rapturously. The notes of the song and the accompaniment of the piano continued, although Antonia was not visibly singing nor B—— playing. The Councillor fell into a profound unconsciousness in which the vision and the music vanished. When he awoke, the terrible anxiety of his dream still possessed him. He rushed into Antonia's room. She lay on the sofa with her eyes shut, her hands devoutly folded, as if she were asleep and dreaming of heavenly bliss and joy. But she was dead.

Franz Grillparzer is Austria's Shakespeare, her greatest dramatist. From his mother he inherited musical sympathies, and numbered Beethoven among his acquaintances. Vienna's Grinzinger Strasse 64 is referred to as the "Beethoven-Grillparzer-Haus" because both men lived there in 1808. At a time of high romanticism in German literature, Grillparzer seems often intensely non-romantic. Indeed, "The Poor Fiddler" presents a character remarkably like a contemporary anti-hero. The story, written between the years 1831 and 1841, was published in 1847.

The Poor Fiddler

by Franz Grillparzer
Translated by E. B. Ashton

In Vienna the Sunday after the full moon in July of each year, along with the following day, is a people's holiday if ever a festival deserved the name. The people themselves give and visit it; and if patricians attend they can do so only in their quality as members of the people. Segregation is impossible—at least, a few years ago it was.

On this day the Brigittenau, linked with the Augarten, Leopoldstadt and the Prater in an unbroken chain of pleasure, celebrates its Kirchweih. From Brigid's Church Day to Brigid's Church Day the laboring population counts its good times. Eventually the long-expected Saturnalian fête arrives, and an upheaval starts in the benignly quiet city. A billowing throng fills the streets, with the sound of footsteps and murmurs of talk ignited here and there by a loud exclamation. Class distinction has vanished. Emotions are shared by citizen and soldier. The pressure grows near the gates of the city; the way out has to be fought for, won, lost and regained in the end. But the Danube Bridge presents new difficulties. Victorious here again, two rivers, the Old Danube and the more heavily swollen tide of the people, finally flow across, above and beneath one another, the Danube in its old bed while the human river, freed from the confinement of the bridge, pours out as a broad, roaring, all-inundating lake. A novice would find the signs disquieting. But it is the tumult of joy, the unshackling of pleasure.

Even before the bridge, wicker-wagons have lined up for the real hierophants of this consecration, the children of labor and service. Though overcrowded, they fly at a gallop through the human wall which opens just before them and closes behind them, unworried and unhurt. For in Vienna there is a tacit understanding between vehicles and people: not to run over even at full speed, and not to be run over even though careless.

The interval from vehicle to vehicle decreases by the second. Already, single patrician carriages mingle with the oft-interrupted parade. The wagons fly no more. Until at last, five to six hours before nightfall, the individual horse-and-carriage atoms have congealed into a solid line which, braking itself and braked by others joining from every side street, plainly refutes the old proverb, "A bad ride is better than a walk." Inspected, pitied, ridiculed, the bedizened ladies sit in coaches seeming to stand still. Unaccustomed to the ceaseless halts, a black Holstein stallion blocked by the preceding wicker-wagon rears as if to go over and above it—which the screaming women and children populating the plebeian vehicle also seem clearly afraid of. The speedy fiaker, for the first time false to his nature, grimly calculates the loss involved in having to spend three hours on a trip requiring five minutes. Squabbles, shouts, mutual disparagement of drivers, now and then the crack of a whip.

Eventually, as in this world every stoppage, however obstinate, is but an unnoticed advance, a ray of hope appears in this *status quo*. The first trees of the Augarten and Brigittenau come in sight. Land! Land! Land! All suffering is forgotten. Those come by car alight and mingle with the pedestrians. Sounds of distant dance music float across, answered by the jubilation of the new arrivals. And so on and so forth, until at last the broad harbor of pleasure opens and forest and meadow, music and dance, feast and wine, shadow-play and tightrope-walker, illumination and fireworks combine into a *pays de cocagne,* an Eldorado, a real Pleasure Land which unfortunately—or fortunately, as you take it—lasts but one day and the next, and then disappears as the dream of a summer night, remaining only in memory and perhaps in hope.

I do not lightly miss this celebration. As one who so passionately loves people, notably the people, that even as a dramatic poet I have always found the unbridled outburst of an overcrowded theater ten times more interesting, even instructive, than the concocted judgment of a literary matador crippled in body and soul and bloated spider-like with blood sucked out of authors—as one who loves people, I say, especially in masses when they temporarily forget their individual ends and feel parts of the whole, the ultimate seat of divinity, even deity—as such a one I regard every people's holiday as a true holiday of the soul, a pilgrimage, a devotion. As in an immense Plutarch, unrolled and escaped from its bookish frame, I read the biographies of the uncelebrated in their gay or secretly sad faces, their lively or depressed gait, the mutual behavior of family members, the sundry, half-involuntary remarks; and indeed, one cannot understand the celebrated without having felt out the obscure. From the exchanges of wine-heated cart-pushers an invisible but unbroken thread leads to the feud of the godlings, and the young wench who half-willingly follows her urgent lover aside from the bustle of the dance contains the embryo of every Juliet, Dido and Medea.

Two years ago, as usual, I had joined the pleasure-hungry Kirchweih guests as a pedestrian. The main difficulties of the journey were surmounted and I found myself at the end of the Augarten, with the longed-for Brigittenau right in front of me. Another battle, though the last, remains to be fought there. A narrow causeway between impenetrable enclosures is the only link of the two pleasure grounds, whose common boundary is marked by a wooden gate in the middle. On ordinary days and for ordinary strollers this connecting pathway offers ample room; but on Kirchweih day its fourfold width would still be too narrow for the endless multitude which, violently pushing and crossed in the opposite direction by the homeward bound, has only the universal good nature to thank for passably arriving in the end.

I had surrendered to the human tide and was halfway across the causeway, on classical ground already, only regrettably forced again and again to stand still, step aside and wait. There was time enough, then, to observe the features of the roadside. For, lest the fun-loving throng lack a foretaste of impending bliss, the left-hand slope of the elevated causeway had been occupied by individual musicians who, probably fearing heavier competition, sought here at the propylaea to reap the first-fruits of unspent munificence. A female harpist with repulsively staring eyes. A one-legged old invalid who on a horrible, evidently self-made instrument, half hurdy-gurdy and half carving-board, sought to make the pains of his injury analogously sensible to general sympathy. A lame, hunchbacked boy indistinguishably tangled with his violin, playing endlessly continuing waltzes with all the hectic violence of his deformed breast. Finally—and he attracted my whole attention—an old, easily seventy-year-old man in a shabby but not untidy Molton overcoat, with smiling, self-applauding features. His bald head bared, he stood in the manner of these people with his hat before him on the ground as a collection box, and thus he belabored an old, badly cracked violin, marking time not only by raising and lowering his foot but simultaneously by corresponding motions of his whole bent body. But all this effort to bring harmony into his work was wasted, for what he played seemed to be a disjointed sequence of tones without rhythm or melody. At that, he was fully immersed in his work: his lips quavered, his eyes were rigidly fixed ahead, on the music sheet—yes indeed, music sheet! For while all the other musicians, incomparably more appreciated, were depending on their memories, the old man had amidst the tumult put up a small, easily movable stand before him, with dirty, much-handled sheet music in which all that he presented out of context might be contained in the most beautiful order. This odd equipment was just what had drawn my attention, as it evoked the mirth of the passing throng which laughed at him and left the old man's hat empty, while the remaining orchestra pocketed whole copper mines. I had stepped on the side slope of the causeway, to regard the eccentric at leisure. He continued to play for awhile. At last he paused, as if awakening from a long absence, looked at the sky which began to show traces of the approaching evening, then downward into his hat; finding it empty, he put it on his head with unclouded cheer and pushed the bow of his violin between the strings: *"Sunt certi denique fines,"* he said, seized his music stand and laboriously made his way through the crowds flocking to the fête but in the opposite direction, as one who was homeward bound.

Everything about the old man was as if made to excite my anthropological curiosity. His needy, yet noble figure, his invincible cheer, and such artistic zeal paired with such clumsiness; his going home precisely at a time when others of his kind found their proper harvest beginning; finally the few Latin words uttered with the most perfect pronunciation, with complete fluency. So the man had received a better education, had acquired knowledge, and now—a musical beggar! I trembled with eagerness to know the connection.

But already a tight human wall lay between us. Short as he was, and molesting everybody with the music-stand in his hand, he was pushed from one to the other and through the exit gate while I was still in the middle of the causeway struggling with the human tide that engulfed me. Thus he disappeared from my view, and when at last I myself reached the calm open space, no fiddler was to be seen far and wide in any direction.

The abortive adventure had killed my interest in the people's holiday. I roamed all over the Augarten and finally decided to return home.

Come as far as the little gate which opens from the Augarten on Taborstrasse, I suddenly heard the familiar sound of the old violin. I quickened my steps, and behold! the object of my curiosity stood playing for dear life in a circle of boys who impatiently demanded a waltz of him. "Play a waltz!" they cried; "a waltz, don't you hear?" The oldster kept fiddling, apparently without heeding them, until his little audience left, mocking and jeering, and gathered round an organgrinder who had set up his hurdy-gurdy not far away.

"They don't want to dance," the old man said as if saddened, gathering up his musical implements.

I had come very close to him. "The children don't know any dance but the waltz," I said.

"I was playing a waltz," he replied, indicating with his violin bow how the piece he had just played was designated on the music sheet. "One has to carry that sort of thing, too, for the crowd. But the children have no ear," he said, shaking his head pensively.

"At least let me make up for their ingratitude," I said, taking a silver piece out of my pocket and offering it to him.

"Please! please!" cried the old man, making anxiously repelling gestures with his hands, "in the hat! in the hat!" I placed the money in the hat before him, from which the oldster immediately removed and contently pocketed it. "That's going home once with rich profit," he chuckled.

"That just reminds me," I said, "of a circumstance which made me curious before. Your receipts today seem not to have been the best, and yet you retire at a moment when the real harvest is only beginning. The celebration, as you may know, lasts throughout the night, and there you easily might earn more than on eight ordinary days. How am I to explain that?"

"How are you to explain that?" replied the oldster. "Pardon me,

I don't know who you are; but you must be a charitable gentleman and a friend of music." With that he took the silver piece out of his pocket again and pressed it between hands lifted to his breast. "So I'll tell you the reasons, although they have brought me much ridicule. Firstly, I was never a nightly reveler and don't think it's right to incite others to such repulsive doings, by play and song; secondly, man must in all things fix a certain order for himself, or else he'll turn wild and unbridled. Thirdly and lastly—sir, I play all day for the noisy people and scarcely earn my scant bread; but the evening belongs to me and to my poor art. In the evening I stay at home, and then"—his voice fell lower and lower, a blush covered his face and his eyes sought the ground—"then I play from imagination, just for myself, without notes. Improvising, I believe, is what they call it in the music books."

Both of us had fallen—he from shame at the betrayal of his inner secret, I from amazement, to hear a man speak of the highest stages of art who was incapable of rendering the easiest waltz comprehensibly. Meanwhile, he was preparing to leave.

"Where do you live?" I asked. "I should like once to attend your lonely exercises."

"Oh," he replied almost imploringly, "you know that prayer belongs into the private chamber."

"Then I'll visit you in the daytime," I said.

"In the daytime," he replied, "I try to make my living among the people."

"Well, in the morning then."

"It almost seems," the old man said with a smile, "as if you, dear sir, were the recipient and I the benefactor, if I am permitted to say so—you so friendly, and I so disagreeably retiring. Your noble visit will always honor my abode; only, I beg you generously to set the day of your arrival in advance, so you will neither be detained by incivility nor will I be forced into undue interruption of possibly started business. For my morning also serves a purpose. At least, I deem it my duty to offer my protectors and benefactors an exchange not quite unworthy of their gifts. I do not wish to be a beggar, dear sir. I well know that other public musicians are content to play a few ditties they've learned by heart, German waltzes or even melodies of indecent songs, on and on and always the same, so that one gives them money to get rid of them or because their playing revives memories of dances or other disorderly pleasures one has enjoyed. That's why they play from memory and at times, frequently even, out of key. Far be it from me to cheat, though. Therefore, partly because my memory is none the best, partly because it should be difficult for anyone to keep involved compositions by respected musical authors in mind note by note, I myself have written out these copybooks."

He pointed to his music, turning pages on which, in a careful but repugnantly stiff handwriting, I was shocked to perceive enormously difficult compositions of famous old masters, black with passages and arpeggios. And such things the old man played with his clumsy fingers!

"In playing these pieces," he went on, "I show my reverence to the duly esteemed, long departed masters and authors, satisfy myself, and live in the pleasant hope that the gift kindly handed to me will bear a return by ennobling the tastes and hearts of an audience disturbed and misguided from so many sides. As this sort of thing, however, to stick to my subject"—and with that a smile of self-gratification spread over his features—"as this sort of thing needs to be rehearsed, however, my morning hours are exclusively devoted to this exercise. The three first hours of the day for practice, the middle to earn a living, and the evening for myself and the dear Lord—that's not dishonestly shared," he said and his eyes gleamed as if moistly; but he was smiling.

"Well, then," I said, "so I'll surprise you some day in the morning. Where do you live?" He named the Gärtnergasse. "House number?"

"Number 34, on the second floor."

"Indeed," I said, "on the upper class floor?"

"The house," he said, "has really only a ground floor; but above, besides the attic, there is another small room which I inhabit together with two journeymen carpenters."

"One room for three?"

"It's divided," he said, "and I have my own bed."

"It's getting late," I said, "and you want to go home. *Auf Wiedersehen!*" and I reached into my pocket, meaning at least to double the previously handed, overly small gratuity.

But he, with the music-stand in one hand and his violin in the other, hastily exclaimed, "Which I must humbly decline! For my playing I have been fully remunerated, and I am not aware at present of having earned more." And with a variant of aristocratic elegance he scraped a rather awkward bow and withdrew as fast as his old legs would carry him.

As said before, I had lost interest in the fête for that day and headed homeward. Taking the way through the Leopoldstadt and exhausted by the dust and the heat, I entered one of the many garden taverns there which usually are overcrowded but today had lost all their customers to Brigittenau. The calm of the place felt good after the noisy throng; I yielded to various thoughts, in which the old fiddler had no mean share, and it was late at night when I finally thought of going home, laid the amount of my bill on the table and walked toward the city.

Gärtnergasse was where the old man had said that he was living. "Is there a Gärtnergasse near here?" I asked a little boy who scurried across the street.

"There, sir," he said, pointing to a side street which ran away from the suburban mass of houses toward the open fields. I followed the direction. The street consisted of single houses scattered among large vegetable gardens which made the business of the residents as evident as the origin of the name Gärtnerstrasse. In which of these wretched shacks might my eccentric live? I had already forgotten the house number; besides, in the darkness recognition of any marking was hardly conceivable. Then a man walked toward me and past, heavily laden with vegetables. "Is the old boy scraping again," he muttered, "and robbing decent folk of their night's rest?" Just then, as I walked on, the soft, long-sustained tone of a violin caught my ear. It seemed to come from the open attic window of a poor house not far away, low and single-storied as the others but distinguished from them by this very gabled window in the roof. I stood still. A softly but firmly held tone swelled up to violence, diminished, faded, only to rise again immediately to the loudest yell—always the same tone, reiterated with a sort of relishing insistence. At last there came an interval. It was the fourth. If the player had reveled first in the sound of the single tone, the all but voluptuous savoring of the harmonious relationship now was even more noticeable. Jerkily struck, simultaneously stroked, connected bumpily by the intervening notes of the scale, the third indicated and repeated, the fifth joined to it, tremblingly once like quiet sobbing, sustained, fading, then interminably repeated at whirling speed, always the same intervals, the same tones—and this was what the old man called improvising! Although at bottom it certainly was improvising—for him, that is, if not for the listener.

I do not know how long this may have lasted and how bad it had become, when suddenly the door of the house opened and a man clad only in a shirt and loosely buttoned trousers stepped from the threshold into the middle of the street and shouted up at the gabled window: "Won't that have any end tonight?" His tone of voice was cross but not harsh or insulting. The violin stopped before he had finished speaking. The man went back into the house, the gabled window was closed, and soon dead silence reigned about me. I set out for home, finding my way with difficulty and through the unknown alleys, improvising too, but by myself, in my head, without disturbing anyone.

For me the morning hours always have had their own value. It is as though I felt a need to sanctify the rest of my day, as it were, by taking up something inspiring, important in its first hours. I thus have difficulty making up my mind to leave my room early in the morning, and if once I force myself to it without a valid reason the remaining day will leave me but a choice of thoughtless distraction or self-tormenting gloom. So it happened that for some days I put off my visit to the old man, which we had agreed was to take place in the morning. At last impatience gained the upper hand and I went. The Gärtnergasse was easily found, as was the house. The sound of the violin was heard again, though muffled to the point of indistinction by the closed window. I entered the house. A gardener's wife, half speechless with amazement, showed me the stairs to the attic. I faced a low and badly closing door, knocked, received no answer, finally turned the knob and entered. I stood in a fairly spacious but otherwise extremely miserable chamber, with the walls on all sides following the outline of the sharply gabled roof. Next to the door, a dirty, repulsively rumpled bed was surrounded by all the attributes of slovenliness; opposite me, beside the window, a second sleeping-place was shabby but clean, very carefully made and covered. By the window, a little table bore music paper and writing materials. The window itself held some flower pots. The room was divided by a line drawn on the floor with chalk, from wall to wall; and it is hard to think of a more glaring contrast of dirt and cleanliness than prevailed on the two sides of that line, that Equator of a world in miniature.

Right by the Equator the old man had put up his music-stand; he stood before it, fully and carefully dressed, and—exercised. So much has already been said here of the disharmonies wrought by this favorite of mine and, I almost fear, mine only that I shall spare the reader a description of that hellish concert. With the exercise consisting in the main of passages, there was no question of recognizing the pieces played, which otherwise might not have been so easy, either. Listening awhile, I finally made out the guiding thread in this maze, the method in the madness, as it were. The oldster enjoyed while playing; and so, since his only distinction was between consonance and dissonance—of which the first pleased, even delighted him, while the latter, however well founded harmoniously, was shunned as much as possible—he never interpreted a piece of music according to its sense and rhythm but simply accented and prolonged the notes and intervals pleasing to the ear. He did not even shrink from repeating them arbitrarily, with his face often bearing a virtually entranced expression. As at the same time he dismissed the dissonances as curtly as possible—besides playing passages too difficult for him, of which conscientiously he never dropped a note, at much too slow a tempo in relation to the whole—one easily may conceive the ensuing confusion. In the end it became too much even for me. Having fruitlessly tried several means to bring him out of his absence, I intentionally dropped my hat.

The old man gave a start, his knees shook, he could hardly hold the lowered violin. I went over to him. "Oh, it's you, sir!" he said, as if slowly coming to. "I hadn't counted on the fulfillment of your noble promise." He obliged me to sit down, tidied up, put things away, cast a few embarrassed glances about the room, suddenly seized a plate from the table by the door and walked out with it. I heard him talk to the gardener's wife outside; but when he came back he seemed still embarrassed, hid the plate behind his back and secretly put it away. He evidently had asked for some fruit to offer me but failed to obtain it.

"You live quite nicely here," I tried to put him at ease. "The disorder is forgiven. It is retreating through the door even if it has not yet quite crossed the threshold."

"My home extends only as far as the line," said the oldster, pointing to the chalk mark dividing the room. "Over there live two journeymen carpenters."

"And do they honor your marking?"

"They don't, but I do," he said. "Only the door is common property."

"Don't your neighbors disturb you?"

"Hardly," he said. "They come home late at night, when I am in bed, and even if they startle me a little, the pleasure of going to sleep again is so much greater. But in the morning I wake them when I clean my room, and they swear a little and go."

By then I had looked him over. He was very neatly dressed, the figure well enough preserved for his years, only the legs somewhat short and hands and feet strikingly delicate. "You are looking at me," he said, "and thinking what?"

"That I'd like to hear your story," I replied.

"Story?" he repeated after me. "I have no story. Today is like yesterday, and tomorrow is like today. The next day, of course, and beyond —who can tell? But God will provide. He knows."

"Your present life may be monotonous enough," I continued; "but your previous experiences. How it came—"

"That I joined the musicians?" he broke into the pause I made involuntarily. I now told about his striking me at first sight, and of the impression of the Latin words he had uttered. "Latin," he said, "Latin? To be sure, I learned that, too, at one time—or rather, I should and could have learned it. *Loqueris latine?*" he turned to me, "but I couldn't go on. It's been too long. So that's what you call my story? How it came? Well, yes, there was a good deal that happened, of course; nothing special, but still, a good deal. I'd like to tell it to myself once again. Just to see whether I have not forgotten. It's still early morning," he contined, reaching into his watch-pocket. There was no watch in it. I drew mine; it was barely 9 o'clock. He said, "We have time, and I almost feel tempted to chat."

He was now feeling visibly more at ease. His figure had straightened. Without too much circumstance he released his hat and put it on the bed, seated himself, crossed his legs and generally assumed the position of a comfortable narrator.

"You have," he began, "doubtlessly heard of Privy Councillor—" and he named a statesman who about the middle of the past century under the modest title of a Bureau Chief had exerted an enormous, almost ministerial influence. I said I had heard of the man. "He was my father," he continued.—His father? The old fiddler's? The beggar's? The influential, powerful man—his father?

The oldster did not seem to notice my astonishment. Visibly cheered, he followed the thread of his story. "I was the second of three sons. My brothers rose fairly high in the government service but are long dead now; I alone am still alive," he said, looking down and plucking on his shabby trousers to remove some tiny feathers. "My father was ambitious and temperamental. My brothers satisfied him. I was called slow-witted; and indeed I was slow. If I remember correctly," he said, turning sideways as if to look far into the distance and propping up his head with his left hand, "if I remember correctly I might have learned all sorts of things if only I had been allowed the time and order. My brothers would leap like the mountain-goats from peak to peak in the subjects of instruction; but I could leave nothing behind and had to start all over if a single word was missing. So I was always under pressure. The new was to take places not yet vacated by the old, and I began to get reniten

For instance, music, now the joy and at the same time the support of my life, they managed then to make actually hateful to me. If I took up the violin in the twilight of the evening, to amuse myself without notes, after my fashion, they took the instrument away and said that I was ruining my application and torturing their ears, and instead limited me to the musical instruction hour when my own torture began. In all my life I've loathed nothing and no one as much as in those days I loathed the violin.

"My father, extremely dissatisfied, frequently scolded me and threatened to apprentice me to an artisan. I did not dare say how happy I should have been—I'd have loved to be a wood-carver or printer—but my father's pride would have prevented it, anyway. To assuage him one persuaded him to attend a public examination at my school; it proved the final straw. A dishonest teacher told me in advance what he would ask me; and so everything went splendidly until the end, when I had to recite some verses of Horace by heart and could not think of one word. My teacher, who had sat nodding his head and smiling at my father, tried to help and whispered it to me. But I, seeking the word in myself and in connection with the rest, did not hear. He repeated it several times; in vain. At last my father lost patience. *'Cachinnum!'* (this was the word) he thundered at me. I was done for. Though I knew the one word now I had forgotten all others. Every effort to put me back on the right track was wasted; I had to rise in shame, and when I went to kiss my father's hand, as usual, he thrust me back, rose, curtly bowed to the gathering and left. *Ce gueux,* he branded me—which I wasn't then but am now. Parents prophesy when they speak! Besides, my father was a good man. Only temperamental and ambitious.

"From that day on he never spoke with me. His orders reached me through the others in the house. Thus, on the very next day, I was informed that my studies were at an end. I was frightened, knowing how bitterly this must have hurt my father. I cried all day, and in between recited those Latin verses which I now knew to a *T,* along with those that came before and after. I promised, if permitted further to attend the school, to make up by hard work for my lack of talent. But my father never revoked a decision.

"For awhile then I remained idle in my paternal home. At last I was given a trial with an accounting office; but I never had excelled at figures. As for the proposal of a military career, I rejected that with horror. Even now I can see no uniform without shuddering inwardly. To defend one's own, at the risk of his life if need be, may be good and comprehensible; but bloodshed and mutilation as a profession, as a class—no! no! no!" And he drew both hands over both arms, as though feeling his own and other men's piercing wounds.

"I then came into the chancellery as a copyist. There I was right in my place. I had always liked to write; even now I know of no more pleasing entertainment than with good ink, on good paper, to combine thin and thick pen strokes to words or even mere letters, and musical notes are quite exceedingly beautiful. But I was not yet thinking of music, then.

"I was zealous but over-anxious. A wrong punctuation mark, a word illegible or missing in the draft, though it might be filled in from the meaning, would trouble me for hours. Doubts, whether strictly to follow the original or to add of my own, let the time pass anxiously, and I acquired a reputation for negligence while working harder than anyone else in the service. Thus I spent several years—without salary, for when I came up for promotion my father, in the Council, cast his vote for another, and the rest respectfully agreed with him.

"About this time—why," he interrupted himself, "it does make a kind of a story! Let's tell the story. About this time two events occurred: the saddest and the happiest of my life. My removal from the paternal home was one, and the other was my return to the fair art of music, to my violin which has been faithful to me to this day.

"In my father's house I lived unheeded by the others, in a little back room opening upon a neighbor's yard. In the beginning I ate at the family table where no one talked to me. But when my brothers were promoted to posts out of town and my father was dining out almost daily—my mother had long been dead—it was found inconvenient to keep the kitchen going just for me. The servants received a food allowance and so did I—only mine was not paid to me, but monthly to a restaurant. So I spent little time in my room—except in the evening, for my father insisted on my being home no later than a half hour after office closing time. Then I would sit in the dusk without a light, because of my eyes which even then were strained, and I'd be thinking about this and that and be neither sad nor happy.

"One day, sitting like this, I heard a song rise from the neighbor's yard—or several songs, rather, of which I especially liked one, however. It was so simple, so moving, and with the accent so in the right place that there was no need at all to hear the words. I think the words only spoil the music, anyway." He now opened his mouth and brought forth some hoarse, rough sounds. "Nature has denied me a voice," he said and reached for the violin. He played, and this time with the right expression, the tune of a cozy, otherwise quite undistinguished song, while his fingers trembled on the strings and tears ran down his cheeks.

"That was the song," he said and put down the violin. "It delighted me time and again. But however clearly I recalled it, I never managed to hit even two tones of it correctly with my voice. It almost made me impatient to listen. Then my eye fell on the violin which hung on the wall like an old piece of armor, unused since my boyhood. I took it down, and—the servant might have been using it in my absence—it turned out to be well-tuned. And as I now drew the bow over the strings, sir, it was as if God's finger had touched me. The sound went into my innermost being and out again. The air about me was as if pregnant with drunkenness. The song in the yard and the sound rising from my fingers to my ear, fellow-dwellers in my solitude—I fell on my knees and prayed aloud and could not grasp how in my childhood I could have neglected, even loathed God's lovely creature, and I kissed the violin and pressed it to my heart and kept playing on and on.

"The song in the yard—it was a woman who sang—rang ceaselessly meanwhile; but playing it proved not so easy.

"I did not have the song in notes, you see. Too, I found that I had pretty much forgotten what little of the fiddling art I had known. I could not play this or that; I could just play. Although, with the sole exception of that song, I have always been and remained fairly indifferent to the temporary What of music. They play Wolfgang Amadeus Mozart and Sebastian Bach, but no one plays the dear Lord. The eternal bounty and grace of tone and sound; its miraculous concord with the thirsty, yearning ear; that"—he lowered his voice and blushed—"the third tone goes together with the first, and so does the fifth, and the *nota sensibilis* rises like a hope fulfilled, while the dissonance is bent low like knowing malice or presumptuous arrogance; and the wonders of phrasing and reversal, whereby even the second is admitted to grace in the lap of euphony—all this, though much later, was explained to me by a musician. And the things I know nothing about: the *fuga* and the *punctum contra punctum* and the *canon a duo, a tre* and so forth—a whole celestial structure, one fitting into the other, bound without mortar and held by the hand of God—of this none but a few want to know anything. They rather spoil this inhaling and exhaling of souls; adding words which may also be spoken, as the children of God united with the daughters of man—to make it feel nice and suit a horny soul. Sir," he closed, half exhausted, "speech is as necessary to man as food, but one should also purify the drink which comes from God."

I hardly knew my man, he had become so lively. He paused a little. "Where did I leave my story?" he finally said. "Oh, yes, at the song and my attempts to play it. It was impossible. I went to the window, to hear better, just as the singer came across the yard. I only saw her from the rear, and yet she seemed familiar. She carried a basket with what seemed to me still unbaked pieces of cake, and entered a little door in the corner of the yard. It probably led to a baking oven, for with her singing I now heard scraping of wooden tools and the voice rang now dull, now brightly, as when a person stoops to sing into a hollow and then straightens up again and stands erect. After awhile she returned, and only now I saw why she had seemed familiar. I really had known her for some time. From the chancellery.

"It was like this. Our office hours began early and lasted past noon. Toward eleven o'clock some of the younger officials, either from hunger or so as to pass a half hour, used to consume a trifle. The tradespeople, knowing how to turn everything to their advantage, saved the gluttons the way and brought their merchandise into the building, where they posted themselves in the corridor and on the stairs. A baker sold rolls; the fruiterer's wife sold cherries. Favored above all else, however, were certain cakes which a neighboring grocer's daughter baked and marketed still warm. Her customers came out to her on the corridor; only rarely, if called for, would she enter the office, where the somewhat crusty supervisor, if he saw her, would as rarely fail to order her out again—a command she would heed only with resentment and muttering angrily.

"The girl was not deemed beautiful by my colleagues. They found her too short and did not know how to describe the color of her hair. Some denied that she had cat's eyes, but all admitted pock marks. Her sturdy build alone found general approval; but they called her rude, and one had much to tell of a box on the ears that he had felt for a week.

"I was not one of her customers. Partly I lacked the money; partly, while always constrained—often too much so—to admit the necessity of food and drink, I've never looked for any pleasure and delight therein. So we paid no attention to each other. Only once, to josh me, my colleagues made her believe that I had asked for her victuals. She came to my desk and held out her basket to me.

" 'I don't buy, dear Mistress,' I said.

" 'Then why do you ask for people?' she said irately. I apologized and, at once perceiving the roguish trick, explained it to her as best I could.

" 'Well, at least give me some paper to wrap my cakes in,' she said.

"I pointed out that this was chancellery paper and not mine to give, but said I had some of my own at home which I should bring her.

" 'At home I've got plenty,' she mocked me and gave a little laugh in walking away.

"That had only been a few days since, and I promptly thought of using this acquaintance for my desire. So on the next morning I buttoned a whole pad of paper, of which we were never short at home, under my coat and took it to the office—where, lest I betray myself, I wore this armor at great inconvenience until, toward noon, the going and coming of my colleagues and the noise of chewing jaws told me that the cake vendor had come and the customers' main pressure seemed to be past. Then I went out, produced my paper, gathered my courage and walked up to the girl who stood with the basket before her on the ground, her right foot on a stool that she used to sit on, humming softly and beating time with the foot on the stool. She looked me over from head to foot, increasing my embarrassment. 'Dear Mistress,' I finally began, 'you asked me for paper the other day, when I had none on hand that was mine. I have now brought some from home, and—' I held out the paper to her.

" 'I told you already,' she replied, 'that I've got paper at home. However, one can use everything.' She took my gift with a slight nod of her head and placed it into her basket. 'You don't want any cake?' she asked, rummaging in her merchandise; 'but the best of it is gone, anyway.'

"I thanked her, adding that I had another request.

" 'Well?' she said. Pushing one arm through the basket handle, she stood up straight and looked at me with flashing eyes.

"I quickly said I was a music lover, though of recent date, and had heard her singing such lovely songs—one in particular.

" 'You? Me? Songs?' she flared up. 'And where?'

"I went on to tell her that I lived in her neighborhood and had listened to her while she worked in the yard. I liked one of her songs especially, so much so that I had even tried to play it on the violin. 'Then maybe you're the one,' she cried, 'who scrapes so on the fiddle?'

"I was then a mere beginner, as I said. It was only later that with a great deal of effort I trained these fingers to the necessary skill," the old man interrupted himself, fingering the air with his left hand in the manner of a violinist. "I had become quite hot in the face," he continued his narrative, "and I saw that she also regretted the harsh words. 'Dear Mistress,' I said, 'the scraping is due to the fact that I lack the music of the song, which is why I'd like politely to request a copy.'

" 'A copy?' she said. 'The song's been printed and they sell it on the street corners.'

" 'The song?' I replied. 'Those are probably only the words.'

" 'Well, yes, the words of the song.'

" 'But the tune that you sing it in.'

" 'Are they writing that up, too?' she asked.

" 'Indeed!' was my answer. 'That's just the main point. How else did you learn it, dear Mistress?'

" 'I heard someone sing it; so I sang it, too.'

"I marveled at this natural ingenuity; as in general the unstudied people often have the most talent. But still, it isn't the right thing, the real art. I now was desperate again. 'Which song is it, anyway?' she asked. 'I know so many.'

" 'All without music sheets?'

" 'Why, of course. So which was it?'

" 'It's so very lovely,' I explained myself. 'Rises up right at the beginning, then returns within itself and ends quite softly. You sing it most frequently, too.'

" 'Oh, then it's probably this one,' she said, put the basket down, and her foot back on the stool and sang the song, in a voice very low and yet clear, ducking her head while she sang so beautifully, so sweetly that even before she had finished I reached for the hand which hung by her side. 'Oh, ho,' she said and withdrew her arm which she may have thought I wished to touch unbecomingly—but no, I wished to kiss her hand, although she was only a poor girl. Well, today I'm a poor man.

"When I now tore my hair with eagerness to have the song, she comforted me and said that the organist of St. Peter's Church often came to her father's shop for nutmeg; she would ask him to write down the music. I might call for it in a few days. Then she took up her basket and left, accompanied by me as far as the stairs. On the top step, during my final bow, I was surprised by the supervisor who ordered me back to my work and railed at the girl, asserting that there was not a good hair on her head. Greatly enraged, I was just about to reply that with his permission I was convinced of the contrary when I noticed that he was back in his room already. So I controlled myself and also went back to my desk; yet from that time on he remained convinced that I was a dissolute official and a libertine.

"Indeed, on this and the following days I could do hardly any sensible work, so much was the song in my mind, and I felt lost. A few days passed; I did not know whether or not it was time to call for the music. The girl had said the organist came to the shop to buy nutmeg; he could only use that for beer. But the cool weather which had prevailed for some days made it seem probable that the musical artist would stick to wine and not need any nutmeg for awhile. Asking too soon seemed an uncivil importunity; waiting too long might be considered indifference. I did not dare speak to the girl in the corridor, as our first meeting had become known to my colleagues who burned with desire for a joke at my expense.

"In the meantime I had eagerly resumed the violin and was now thoroughly practicing the foundation, also permitting myself to play out of my head from time to time, but carefully closing the windows, because I knew that my interpretation displeased. But even by the open window I no longer heard my song. The neighbor's girl sang partly not at all, partly behind closed doors and in so low a voice that I could not make out two tones.

"Finally—after about three weeks had passed—I could not stand it any longer. For two evenings I had been sneaking out on the street—hatless, so as to make the servants believe that I was just looking for something in the house—but whenever I came near the grocer's shop I began to tremble so that I had to turn back whether I wanted to or not. But finally, as I said, I couldn't stand it any longer. I gathered my courage and one evening—hatless again—went out of my room, down the stairs, and with firm steps down the street to the grocer's shop, where I stood still for the moment and pondered what might be done. The shop was lighted, and I heard voices inside. After some hesitation I bent forward and peered in from the side. I saw the girl sit by the light, close to the counter, winnowing peas or beans in a wooden bowl. Before her, a coarse, robust man stood with his coat hung round his shoulders and a sort of club in his hand, somewhat like a butcher. The two were talking, evidently in a cheerful mood, for the girl laughed aloud a few times but without interrupting or even looking up from her work. Whether it was due to my forced, oblique position or something else, I started trembling again—when suddenly I felt myself roughly seized from behind and dragged forward. In a trice I was standing in the vault, and when I was released and looking about I saw that it was the owner himself who in coming home had surprised me on the lookout and detained me as suspect. 'What in thunder!' he shouted, 'now I know where the plums go and the handful of peas and rolled barley that always gets filched in the dark! Why, blast you in tarnation,' and he went for me as if really to blast me.

"I was as though annihilated. But soon the thought of my honesty being doubted brought me back to myself. I bowed quite curtly and told the boor that neither his plums nor his rolled barley but his daughter was the object of my visit. At that, the butcher who stood in the center of the shop laughed loudly and turned to go, having whispered something to the girl who by way of reply, laughing also, resoundingly smacked his back with her flat hand. The grocer saw the departing guest to the door, and I, with all of my courage gone again, stood facing the girl who indifferently culled her peas and beans, as if none of this concerned her. Then the father came rumbling back through the door.

"What in tarnation, sir," he said, 'what's that about my daughter?' I tried to explain the connection, and the reason for my visit. 'What song?' he said, 'I'll sing you something,' and he suspiciously moved his right arm up and down.

" 'There it is,' said the girl, leaning sideways in her chair and pointing at the counter without releasing her vegetable bowl.

"I hurried over and saw a sheet of music. It was the song. But the old man got there before me and grabbed the beautiful paper with his hand, crumpling it. 'I'm asking what this means,' he said. 'Who's this fellow?'

" 'He's a gentleman from the chancellery,' she replied, throwing a worm-eaten pea somewhat farther away than the rest.

" 'A gentleman from the chancellery?' he cried. 'In the dark and without a hat?'

"I explained the lack of a hat by the circumstance of my living nearby, and described the house.

" 'I know that house,' he cried. 'There's no one living in there except the Privy Councillor'—and he mentioned my father's name— 'and I know all the servants.'

" 'I'm the Councillor's son,' I said in a low voice, as though it were a lie.

"I've seen many changes in my life, but none so abrupt as the grocer's. The mouth which he had opened to abuse me remained open; the eyes were still threatening; but round the lower part of the face a sort of smile spread, wider and wider. The girl retained her stooped, indifferent position, merely patting her loosened hair back behind the ears as she worked on.

" 'The son of the Privy Councillor?' finally screamed the old man, his face now completely brightened. 'Won't your Grace make themselves comfortable? Barbara, a chair!'

"The girl unwillingly shifted on her own. 'Well, just you wait, lazybones!' he said, lifting a basket himself and wiping the dust off the chair beneath it with a rag. 'I'm honored,' he said. 'So the esteemed Privy Councillor—I mean, the esteemed son practices music, too? Singing, perhaps, like my daughter, or rather differently, of course, with notes, according to the art?' I explained to him that nature had denied me a voice. 'Or tickling the pianoforte, as the better people do?' I said I was playing the violin. 'Been scraping the fiddle myself in my youth, he cried. At the word scraping I looked involuntarily at the girl and saw a mocking smile which greatly displeased me.

" 'Ought to do something for the girl—in music, I mean,' he continued. 'Sings a good voice; has other qualities too, but the refinement, dear Lord, where should that come from?' and he repeatedly moved the thumb and forefinger of his right hand across each other.

"I was quite ashamed, to be undeservedly credited with such important musical knowledge, and just about to clarify the true state of affairs, when a passer-by called into the shop from outside, 'Good evening everybody!' I was frightened, for the voice was that of one of our servants. The grocer had recognized it too. Pushing out the tip of his tongue and raising his shoulders, he whispered, 'Was one of the esteemed servants of the gracious papa. Couldn't have known you, though, standing with your back to the door like this.' As to the last, he was correct. Still the feeling of something secretive and wrong overcame me painfully. I merely stammered a few words of farewell and left. I should have forgotten even my song if the old man had not carried it after me into the street and there thrust it into my hand.

"Thus I got home and to my room and waited for things to happen. Nor did I have long to wait. The servant had recognized me, after all. A few days later, my father's secretary came to my room and informed me that I had to leave my father's house. No protest availed. A small room in a distant suburb had been rented for me, and so I was banished completely from the vicinity of my relations. I no longer saw my singer, either. Her cake business at the chancellery had been stopped, and I could not bring myself to enter her father's shop, knowing that it would displease mine. When I met the old grocer by chance in the street, he turned away with a grim face and I was thunderstruck. Alone for half of my days, I took out my violin and played and practiced.

"Things would get even worse, though. The fortunes of our house declined. My youngest brother, headstrong and reckless, an officer in the Dragoons, swam the Danube on a bet with horse and armor, still hot from a long ride—it was far down in Hungary—and paid with his life for his rashness. The oldest, the favorite, served on a provincial council; in continuous opposition to his immediate superiors and, as they said, secretly encouraged by my father, he allowed himself to make false statements against his adversaries. There was an investigation and my brother secretly fled the country. My father's many enemies used the occasion to discredit him. Attacked from all sides, and resenting his diminishing influence, he daily made the most aggressive speeches in the Council. In the middle of one of these he suffered a stroke and was carried home, speechless. I myself did not hear of it. On the next day, at the office, I did notice secret whispers and fingers pointing at me; but by then I was accustomed to that and suspected nothing. It had happened on a Wednesday— on Friday a black suit with a mourning veil was suddenly delivered to my room. I wondered, and asked, and heard. My body is otherwise strong and resistant, but at that time I was overcome. I dropped to the floor in a faint. They carried me to my bed, where I lay feverish and delirious all day and throughout the night. On the next morning nature had gained the upper hand, but my father was dead and buried.

"I had been unable to talk to him; unable to beg his forgiveness for all the grief I had caused him; unable to thank him for the undeserved mercies—yes, mercies! For he meant well, and at some time I hope to find him again in a place where we are judged by our intentions and not by our works.

"For several days I remained in my room and hardly took any food; when I did go out again I would return right after dinner. Only in the evenings I roamed the dark streets like Cain, the fratricide. In those days my father's home was a frightening specter which I carefully avoided. Once, however, thoughtlessly staring in front of me, I suddenly found myself near the dreaded house. My knees shook so that I had to steady myself. Reaching for the wall behind me, I recognized the door of the grocer's shop and Barbara sitting inside, a letter in her hand, the light on the counter beside her and on the other side, standing erect, her father who seemed to be exhorting her. If my life had been at stake I could not have helped entering. To have no one to tell your grief to, no one to sympathize! The old man, as I well knew, was angry with me, but the girl would give me a kind word.

"It turned out quite differently. Barbara rose as I entered, gave me a haughty look and walked into the back room, locking the door. But the old man took my hand, asked me to be seated, comforted me and said I was now a rich man and no longer obliged to care for anybody. He asked how much I had inherited. I did not know. He made me promise to inquire from the courts; at the chancelleries, he said, nothing was to be done. I should invest my inheritance in a business; spices and fruits yielded ample profits; a partner who knew his way about could turn pennies into guilders. He himself had done a lot there once. In between he repeatedly called for the girl; but no sign of life came from her, although now and then I seemed to hear something rustle behind the door. As she never came, however, and the old man talked only of money, I finally took my leave. He regretted that he could not escort me, being alone in the store. I was saddened by the failure of my hope, and yet wonderfully comforted. Standing in the street and looking over to my father's house, I suddenly heard a muffled and resentful voice behind me: 'Don't be so quick to trust people. Not everybody means well.'

Fast as I turned, I could see no one. Only the rattle of a window, on the ground floor which belonged to the grocer's home, told me that Barbara had been the secret warner. So she had heard, after all, what had been said in the store. Did she mean to warn me of her father? Or had she heard that since my father's death I had been flooded with requests for assistance and help in need— partly by colleagues from the chancellery, partly by other, completely unknown people—and that, moreover, I had promised to do everything once I should be in the money. My pledges had to be kept; but in future I decided to be more cautious. I applied for my inheritance. Less than expected, it was still very much: close to eleven thousand guilders. All day my room was full of petitioners and aid-seekers. I had become almost hard, however, and only gave where the need was greatest. Barbara's father came, too. He chided me for not having called for three days, to which I truthfully replied that I feared to annoy his daughter. He told me never to mind, he had already fixed that; and he laughed maliciously enough to startle me. Reminded of Barbara's warning, when the conversation got around to my inheritance, I did not disclose the amount and also skillfully evaded his business proposals.

"In fact, I already had other prospects in mind. In the chancellery, where I had been tolerated only for my father's sake, my place was now occupied by another; as the job carried no salary, this did not bother me much. My father's secretary, also deprived of his job by the recent events, told me of a plan to start an investigating, copying and translating agency. I was to advance the cost of initial equipment, while he was prepared to take over the direction. At my insistence music was to be included in the copying activities, and now I was happy. I put up the necessary money—but, having grown cautious, not without having a note signed for the amount. I also advanced the bond for the agency; although considerable, it hardly seemed worth mentioning, since it had to be deposited with the Commercial Court and there remained as much mine as if I'd kept it in my closet.

"The matter was settled and I felt relieved, elated, independent for the first time in my life, a man. I hardly thought of my father any more. I moved to a better apartment, made some changes in my clothing, and in the evening walked through well-known streets to the grocer's shop, shaking my legs and humming my song between my teeth, although not quite correctly. With my voice I never could hit the B in the second half. I arrived glad and cheerful, but an ice-cold glance of Barbara's promptly hurled me back into my earlier timidity. Her father gave me a most cordial reception; but she acted as if there were no one around, continued to fold paper bags and did not join with a word in our conversation. Only when my inheritance was mentioned, she half-started and almost threateningly said, 'Father!' whereupon the old man promptly changed the subject. Otherwise she said nothing all evening and did not give me a second glance, and when I finally left her 'Good night' rang almost like 'Thank God.'

"But I kept coming, and gradually she yielded. Not that I could do a thing to please her. She never ceased chiding and reproving me. Everything was clumsy; God had made me with two left hands; my coat hung as on a scarecrow; I walked like a duck, with a slight touch of the rooster. Especially repugnant to her was my politeness toward the customers. For as I was unoccupied until the opening of the copying agency, and mindful of the fact that there I would be dealing with the public, I practiced by engaging actively in the retail grocery business, often half through the day. I weighed off spices, counted out nuts and dried plums to the boys and made change—the last not without frequent errors, at every one of which Barbara sailed in, violently took things out of my hands and mocked and ridiculed me in front of the customers. If I bowed to one of the purchasers or commended myself to them, she would say gruffly, 'The merchandise recommends!' and turn her back on me even before the people had reached the door. At times, though, she was all kindness. She listened to my stories of what was going on in the city, of my childhood years, of the officials in the chancellery where we had first met. But she always let me talk alone, and only by a word now and then expressed her approval or, more frequently, her disapproval.

"We never talked of music or song. Firstly, she held that one had to sing or shut up; it was nothing to talk about. And to sing was not feasible; it was not fitting in the store, and the back room where she lived together with her father was closed to me. Once, however, I came in unnoticed and found her standing on tiptoe with her back to me and her upraised hands feeling on one of the upper shelves in search of something. And she softly sang to herself.—It was the song, my song!—She twittered like a little bird washing its throat by the brook's edge, throwing its head and ruffling and smoothing the feathers with its bill. I sneaked closer and closer, so close that the song no longer seemed to come from outside but from within myself, a song of our souls. And I, no longer able to control myself, grabbed with both hands at the body which was straining forward in the middle, with the shoulders inclined toward me. But then it happened. She whirled like a top. Her face red with anger, she stood before me; her hand twitched and before I could apologize—

"At the office, as I said before, they had often told how Barbara as a cake vendor had boxed the ears of a pest. Their remarks about the strength of the rather short girl and the vigor of her hand had seemed greatly, jocosely exaggerated. But it was all true and approached the gigantic. I stood as though struck by lightning. Lights danced before my eyes—but they were heavenly lights like the sun, the moon and the stars; like angels playing hide-and-seek and singing. I had visions; I was entranced. And she, as upset as I was, drew her hand soothingly over the injured spot: 'Maybe it was too strong,' she said, and suddenly—like a second stroke of lightning—I felt her warm breath on my cheek and her two lips, and she kissed me; just lightly, lightly, but it was a kiss on this, my cheek—here!"

The old man slapped his cheek, and tears welled up in his eyes. "What further happened, I don't know," he went on. "Only that I rushed at her, and she ran into the living room and slammed the glass door while I pushed after her from the other side. And now, with her glued to the window as it were, doubled up and resisting with all force, I took my heart in my hands, dear sir, and vehemently returned her kiss, through the glass.

" 'Well, having a right merry time,' I heard someone say behind me. It was the grocer, who was just coming home. 'Well, he who jests,' he said. 'Why don't you come out, Barbara, and stop being silly?'

"She did not come, however. As for me, I left after a few words, stammered as though unconscious, and took the grocer's hat until he laughingly exchanged it in my hand, for my own. This was, as I called it before, the happy day of my life. I almost should have said the only one—which would be untrue, though, for God grants many mercies.

"I was not quite sure how I stood with the girl. Should I imagine her more angry or more placated? My next call required stern resolution. But she was kind. Humble and quiet, not flaring up as usual, she sat over her work. She inclined her head toward a footstool beside her, indicating that I should sit down and help her. We sat and worked. The old man got up to leave. 'Why don't you stay, father,' she said; 'what you want done is already settled.'

"He stamped his foot hard on the floor and stayed. Walking to and fro, he talked of this and that. I did not dare to join in the conversation. Suddenly the girl gave a little scream. She had scratched her finger, and although usually not soft at all, she shook her hand up and down. I wanted to look, but she motioned to me to continue. 'Balderdash and no end!' muttered the old man and, stepping before the girl, said in a strong voice, 'What's to be done isn't half settled!' and resoundingly strode out the door.

"I wanted to start apologizing for yesterday; but she interrupted me and said, 'Never mind, and now let's talk of more sensible things.'

"She lifted her head, examined me from top to toe, and in a quiet tone of voice continued, 'I hardly know any more how we became acquainted, but for some time now you've been coming more and more often and we've become used to you. No one will deny that you're an honest soul, but you're weak, always thinking of trifles, so you'd hardly be able to manage your own affairs. That makes it then the plain duty of friends and acquaintances to look after you, so you won't suffer. You sit in the store here for days counting and weighing, measuring and marketing; but nothing can come of that. What do you mean to do in future, to have your security?'

"I mentioned my father's inheritance.

" 'That may be pretty big,' she said.

"I told her the amount.

" 'That's both little and much,' she replied. 'Much to start with; little to eat up. My father's had a proposal for you, but I advised you against it because, to begin with, he's already lost his own money in such things, and then,' she added in a low voice, 'he's so used to profiting from strangers that he might not give a friend a better deal. You must have someone by your side who's honest.'

"I pointed at her.

" 'Yes, I'm honest,' she said. She put her hand on her heart, and her eyes, grayish at other times, gleamed bright blue, blue as the sky. 'But I'm peculiar. Our business doesn't yield much, and my father is thinking of opening a tavern. There'd be no room for me, then. The only thing left would be needlework, because I won't go into service.' And she looked like a queen as she said that. 'I've had another proposal, of course,' she continued, drawing a letter from beneath her apron and throwing it on the counter half in disgust. 'But for that I'd have to go away from here.'

" 'Far away?' I asked.

" 'Why? What do you care?'

"I explained that I'd like to move to the same place.

" 'You're a child! she said. 'That wouldn't be fitting and would be something quite different. But if you trust me and like to be near me, get hold of the millinery shop that's for sale here, next door. I know the work, and you needn't worry over a fair profit on your money. Besides, the writing and figuring would make a proper occupation for yourself. What else might come of it we won't discuss now. But you'd have to change! I despise womanish men.'

"I had jumped up and was reaching for my hat.

" 'What's the matter?' she asked. 'Where are you going?'

" 'Cancel everything,' I said breathlessly.

" 'Cancel what?'

"I told her of my plan to start a writing and investigating agency.

" 'There isn't much in that,' she said. 'Everyone can do his own investigating, and everyone has learned to write in school.'

"I remarked that music was to be copied, too, which wasn't a matter for everyone.

"She flared up. 'That foolishness again? Forget the music and think about necessities! Besides, you wouldn't be capable of run-

56

ning a business.'

"I explained that I had found a partner.

" 'A partner?' she exclaimed. 'He'll surely want to cheat you. I hope you've given him no money yet?'

"I trembled, without knowing why.

" 'Did you give him money?' she asked once more.

"I confessed the three thousand guilders for the initial equipment.

" 'Three thousand guilders?' she cried. 'So much money!'

" 'The rest,' I went on, 'is deposited with the court and therefore safe in any case.'

" 'So it's still more!' she screamed.

"I told her the amount of the bond.

" 'And you yourself have deposited that with the court?'

"It had been done by my partner.

" 'And you have a receipt about it?'

"I had no receipt.

" 'And what's the name of your fine partner?'

"It relieved me somewhat to be able to name her my father's secretary.

" 'Almighty God!' she cried, leaping up and wringing her hands. 'Father! Father!'

"The old man came in.

" 'What did you read from the paper today?'

" 'About the secretary?' he asked.

" 'Yes! Yes!'

" 'Well, he's run away, left debts upon debts and cheated people. They've got warrants out for him.'

" 'Father,' she cried, 'he's cheated this one, too! He trusted him with his money. He's ruined.'

" 'Blockheads and no end!' shouted the old man. 'Didn't I say so always? And what excuses! Now she was laughing at him, and then again he was an honest soul. But I'll put a stop to that! I'll see who's master in this house. Barbara, get to your room! And you, sir, get out of this house and spare us your visits in future. Alms aren't given out here.'

" 'Father,' said the girl, 'don't be hard on him. He's wretched enough.'

" 'Just for that,' cried the old man, 'I don't want to be the same. That, sir,' he continued, pointing to the letter Barbara had thrown on the table, 'that's a man! Has brains in his head and money in his pocket. Doesn't cheat people but won't be cheated, either; and that's the main point about honesty.'

"I stammered that the loss of the bond was not yet certain.

" 'Sure,' he cried, 'maybe the secretary was a fool! He's a rogue, but smart. Just hurry up now, maybe you can still catch him!'

"With that he put his hand flat on my shoulder and pushed me to the door. I slipped away sideways and turned to the girl who stood leaning on the counter, her eyes on the floor, her bosom heaving violently. I wanted to go to her but she angrily stamped her foot on the floor, and when I held out my hand she half-jerked with her own, as if to hit me again. So I left, and the old man locked the door behind me.

"I staggered through the streets, out of the gate, into the fields. Sometimes despair attacked me, then hope returned. I remembered having accompanied the secretary to the Commercial Court when he deposited the bond. I had waited in the gateway and he had gone up alone; when he came down again, he had told me that everything was in order and the receipt would be sent to me at home. That had not happened, of course, but there still remained the possibility. At dawn I was back in the city. My first call was at the secretary's address. But the people there laughed and asked me if I hadn't read the papers. The Commercial Court was only a few houses distant. I had the books searched, but neither his name nor mine was found. There was no trace of a bond payment. So my misfortune was assured. In fact, it almost got worse: with a partnership contract existing, some of his creditors would have turned to me for satisfaction if the courts had not forbidden it—praise and thanks to them! Though in the end it would have made no difference.

"All these troubles, I'll admit, had pushed the grocer and his daughter quite into the background. Now that things calmed down and I was beginning to ponder what to do, the memory of the last evening vividly returned. The old man, selfish as he was, I could well understand, but the girl! Sometimes it seemed to me that if I had kept my own together, and could have offered to provide for her, she even might have—but she wouldn't have liked me." His hands dropped apart; he looked at his whole scant figure. "Besides, my politeness toward everybody always repelled her.

"So I spent whole days musing and pondering. One evening at dusk—it was the time I usually had spent in the shop—I was sitting again and in my thoughts transporting myself to the accustomed place I heard them talk and abuse me; they even seemed to be laughing about me. Suddenly there was a rustle at my door.

It opened and a woman came in. It was Barbara.

"I sat as if nailed to my chair, as if seeing a ghost. She was pale and carried a bundle under her arm. In the center of the room she stopped, looked around her at the bare walls, then down at the poor furnishings and sighed deeply. Then she went to the chest on the side wall, unwrapped her package which contained a few shirts and towels—she had lately cared for my laundry—pulled out the drawer, clapped her hands as she saw the meager contents, but immediately began to arrange the laundry and sort the things she had brought. Then she took a few steps back from the chest and, looking at me and pointing her finger at the open drawer, said, 'Five shirts and three towels. That's what I had; that's what I'm bringing back.' Then she slowly closed the drawer, leaned her hand on the chest and began to cry aloud.

"She seemed almost ill, sitting on a chair beside the chest and hiding her face in her shawl. Her jerky breathing told me that she continued to cry. I had gently come close to her and took her hand, which she willingly yielded. But when I slid along the hanging arm as far as the elbow, to attract her eyes, she quickly got up, freed her hand and said in a composed voice, 'What's the use of all that? What's done is done. You wanted it that way; you've made yourself and us unhappy—yourself most of all, of course. You really don't deserve pity'—she became more and more violent—'if you're too weak to keep your affairs in order and so gullible as to trust everybody, no matter whether he's a rogue or an honest man. And yet I'm sorry for you. I've come to say good-bye. Yes, now you're frightened. It's your work. Now I must do what I've so long fought against and go out among the crude people. But it can't be helped. I've given you my hand already, and so farewell—forever.'

"I saw the tears rise in her eyes again, but she angrily shook her head and turned to go. My limbs felt like lead. At the door she turned back once more and said, 'The laundry is in order now. See that nothing gets lost. There'll be hard times coming.' And now she raised her hand, moved it as though to make the sign of the cross in the air, and cried, 'God be with you, Jacob!—In all eternity, Amen,' she added more gently, and left.

"Only now I regained the use of my limbs. I hurried after her, and standing on the landing called after her, 'Barbara!' I heard her stop on the stairs. But as I took the first step down she called up from below, 'Stay!' and went down the rest of the stairs and out the door.

"I have experienced hard days, since then, but none like that; even the following one was less so. For I still did not quite know what was underfoot, and therefore sneaked about the grocer's shop in the morning, to see what I might learn. Since nothing appeared, I finally peered sideways into the store and saw a strange woman weighing out and making change. I ventured inside and asked whether she had bought the store. 'Not just yet,' she said.

" 'And where are the owners?'

" 'They've gone on a trip this morning, to Langenlebarn.'

" 'The daughter, too?' I stammered.

" 'Why, sure,' she said, 'when she's getting married there.'

"The woman may have told me all that I later heard from others: the butcher of the place she mentioned—the same whom I had met at the time of my first visit to the store—had long been pursuing the girl with proposals which she kept rejecting, until in the last few days, pressed by her father and despairing of everything else, she finally had consented. On that morning father and daughter had left, and at that moment Barbara was the butcher's wife.

"The saleswoman, as I said, may have told me all that. But I did not hear and stood motionless until new customers pushed me aside and the woman gruffly asked whether I wanted anything else, whereupon I withdrew.

"You may believe, dear sir," he went on, "that now I felt like the unhappiest of men. And so I was, at first. But when I came out of the store and, turning back, saw the small windows where Barbara surely had often stood and looked out, a feeling of bliss overcame me. That she would now be rid of all sorrow, the mistress of her own house and not obliged to bear grief and distress as in linking her fate with a man without hearth and home—that knowledge fell upon my breast like soothing balm, and I blessed her and her paths.

"Then, as I sank lower and lower, I decided to turn to music for a living; and while the rest of my money lasted, I studied and practiced the works of great masters, especially the old ones, which I copied. And when the last penny had been spent I set out to put my knowledge to use. I began in private company; a party given in the house of my landlady provided the first occasion. But when the compositions I played were not appreciated there, I posted myself in the back yards of houses—since among so many residents there might be some who valued serious music—and finally on public walks, where indeed I had the satisfaction that some would stop, make inquiries, and go on not without sympathy. Their throwing money down for me did not make me ashamed. For in the first place this was my very purpose; and then I also saw that celebrated virtuosi whom I could not flatter myself with having equaled would permit themselves to be remunerated for their efforts, very amply at times. So I've made an honest, if poor, living until this day.

"After some years fortune smiled on me once more. Barbara returned. Her husband had made money and acquired· a butcher shop in one of the suburbs. She was the mother of two children, of whom the oldest is named Jacob like myself. My professional activities and the memory of old times did not allow me to obtrude, but in the end I was invited to the house myself, to give the oldest boy violin lessons. He has not much talent, to be sure, and can only play on Sundays as his father uses him in the business throughout the week; but Barbara's song, which I taught him, already goes very nicely and sometimes when we practice and manipulate like that his mother will fall in and sing with us. Although she has greatly changed in these many years, has grown stout and no longer cares much for music, it still sounds as pretty now as it did then."

And the oldster reached for his violin and started playing the song, and played on and on without taking further notice of me. Eventually I had enough, got up, laid a few pieces of silver on the table and left, with the oldster zealously fiddling on and on.

Soon after this I took a trip, from which I did not return until the beginning of winter. New images replaced the old, and my fiddler had been pretty much forgotten. It was not until the terrible flood which in the next spring inundated the low-lying suburbs that I remembered him. The vicinity of the Gärtnergasse had become a lake. There seemed to be no reason to fear for the life of the old man who lived high up in the roof, while death—only too frequently—had chosen its victims among the ground-floor residents. But how greatly in want might he be, denuded from all aid! There was nothing to be done while the flood lasted; besides, the authorities had done everything possible to bring food and assistance by ship to those who were cut off. But when the waters had receded and the streets were passable again, I decided to take my share of the collection which had been started, and risen to incredible sums, in person to the address which most concerned me.

The view of the Leopoldstadt was horrible. Broken ships and utensils in the streets; the ground floors still partly filled with water and swimming property. When I leaned against an unlocked yard gate to avoid the crowd, it gave and in the gateway revealed a stack of corpses obviously collected and placed there for the purposes of official inspection; and in the interior of the rooms one could still see here and there, standing upright, clutching the window frames, unfortunate dwellers who—there simply were not enough time and officials for the judicial determination of so many fatalities.

I walked on and on, surrounded on all sides by sounds of weeping and church bells, by searching mothers and erring children. Finally I reached the Gärtnergasse. There, too, the black-clad escorts of a funeral procession had posted themselves, but seemingly far from the house for which I was looking. As I came closer, however, I could not fail to notice a connection of preparations and people walking to and fro between the funeral train and the gardener's house. Standing by the gate was an honest-looking, elderly but sturdy man. With his high boots, yellow leather trousers and long frock-coat he resembled a country butcher. He gave orders, but in between talked indifferently with the spectators.

I walked past him into the yard. The old gardener's wife came toward me, recognized me at once and welcomed me tearfully. "Are you too giving us the honor?" she said. "Yes, our poor oldster. He's making music now with the dear angels, who can't be much better, either, than he was down here. The honest soul was sitting safely in his room up there. But when the water came and he heard the children scream, he came running down and rescued and dragged and carried and brought to safety till he was breathing like a blacksmith's furnace. Yes—after all, one can't have his eyes everywhere—when it turned out at the very end that my husband had forgotten his tax books and the few guilders of paper money in the closet, the old man took a hatchet, went right into the water that came up to his chest already, broke the closet open and faithfully brought everything. That was probably where he caught cold, and when there was no help to be had in the first moment he became delirious and got worse and worse, even though we stood by him as much as possible and suffered more than he did himself. For he was making music all the time, with his voice, that is, and beating time and giving lessons. When the water had gone down a little and we could call the barber and the priest, he suddenly sat straight up in the bed, turned his head and ears sideways as if hearing something very beautiful in the distance, smiled, dropped back and was dead. Just go upstairs; he's talked of you often. The madam is up there, too. We wanted to pay for his burial, but she wouldn't let us."

She pushed me up the steep stairs to the little room in the attic which stood open and was quite empty except for the coffin in the middle, which was already closed and waiting only for the bearers. By the top end sat a rather stout woman, past middle age, in a colored printed cotton pelerine but with a black shawl and a black ribbon on her bonnet. It seemed scarcely possible that she had ever been beautiful. Before her stood two fairly grown-up children, a boy and a girl, to whom she evidently was teaching funeral manners. Just as I entered she knocked down the boy's arm, which he had leaned rather clumsily on the coffin, and carefully smoothed the visible edges of the shroud. The gardener's wife led me forward; but then the trumpets sounded below, and at the same time the butcher's voice rang up from the street: "Barbara, it's time!" The bearers appeared, and I withdrew to make room for them.

The coffin was lifted up and carried down, and the procession began to move. In the van the school children with cross and flag, and the priest with the sexton. Directly behind the coffin the two children of the butcher, followed by the couple. The man kept moving his lips as though in prayer, but was looking right and left the while. The woman eagerly read in her prayer book; but the two children kept her busy pushing them forward or holding them back—as her heart in general seemed to hang on the order of the procession. But she always kept returning to her book. Thus the procession reached the churchyard. The grave was open. The children threw down the first handful of earth. The man, standing, did likewise. The woman knelt and held her book close to her eyes. The gravediggers finished their job, and the procession, half-dissolved, returned. At the door there was still a little exchange, with the woman seeming to protest the demands of the undertaker. The escorts scattered in all directions. The old fiddler lay buried.

A few days later—it was on a Sunday—my psychological curiosity drove me to the butcher's home, on the pretext of wishing to possess the old man's violin as a keepsake. I found the family together; there was no trace of a deep or lasting impression. But the violin hung on the wall in a certain symmetry, beside the mirror and opposite the crucifix. When I explained my desire and offered a comparatively high price, the man did not seem loath to make a profitable deal. The woman, however, started from her chair and said, "Why should we! The fiddle belongs to our Jacob, and a few guilders more or less don't matter to us."

She took the instrument down from the wall, looked at it from all sides, blew the dust away, and laid it into a drawer which, as though fearing a robbery, she violently closed and locked. Her face was averted from me, so I could not see what might be showing in it. Since at the same time the maid entered with the soup, and the butcher, without letting my visit disturb him, loudly began to say Grace and the children as loudly chimed in, I wished a blessed mealtime to all and went out the door. My last glimpse was of the woman. She had turned, and tears were streaming down her cheeks.

"The Kreutzer Sonata" (1889), Leo Tolstoy's unusual and passionate novella, is named for Beethoven's most famous composition for violin and piano. But Tolstoy's earlier story "Albert" (1857) contains a violinist more a central focus than the fiddler of Sonata No. 9. Apparently the character Albert was based loosely on the writer's childhood music teacher—a German named Rudolf who was something of a drunkard. As we can see from this story, Tolstoy was much interested in society's inability to recognize art or accommodate artistic genius.

Albert

by Leo Tolstoy
Translated by Nathan Haskell Dole

Five rich young men went at three o'clock in the morning to a ball in Petersburg to have a good time.

Much champagne was drunk; a majority of the gentlemen were very young; the girls were pretty; a pianist and a fiddler played indefatigably one polka after another; there was no cease to the noise of conversation and dancing. But there was a sense of awkwardness and constraint; every one felt somehow or other—and this is not unusual—that all was not as it should be.

There were several attempts made to make things more lively, but simulated liveliness is much worse than melancholy.

One of the five young men, who was more discontented than any one else, both with himself and with the others, and who had been feeling all the evening a sense of disgust, took his hat, and went out noiselessly on purpose, intending to go home.

There was no one in the ante-room, but in the next room at the door he heard two voices disputing. The young man paused, and listened.

"It is impossible, there are guests in there," said a woman's voice.

"Come, let me in, please. I will not do any harm," urged a man in a gentle voice.

"Indeed I will not without madame's permission," said the woman. "Where are you going? Oh, what a man you are!"

The door was flung open, and on the threshold appeared the figure of a stranger. Seeing a guest, the maid ceased to detain the man; and the stranger, timidly bowing, came into the room with a somewhat unsteady gait.

He was a man of medium stature, with a lank, crooked back, and long dishevelled hair. He wore a short paletot, and tight ragged pantaloons over coarse dirty boots. His necktie, twisted into a string, exposed his long white neck. His shirt was filthy, and the sleeves came down over his lean hands.

But, notwithstanding his thoroughly emaciated body, his face was attractive and fair; and a fresh color even mantled his cheeks under his thin dark beard and side-whiskers. His dishevelled locks, thrown back, exposed a low and remarkably pure forehead. His dark, languid eyes looked unswervingly forward with an expression of serenity, submission, and sweetness, which made a fascinating combination with the expression of his fresh, curved lips, visible under his thin moustache.

Advancing a few steps, he paused, turned to the young man, and smiled. He found it apparently rather hard to smile. But his face was so lighted up by it, that the young man, without knowing why, smiled in return.

"Who is that man?" he asked of the maid in a whisper, as the stranger walked toward the room where the dancing was going on.

"A crazy musician from the theatre," replied the maid. "He sometimes comes to call upon madame."

"Where are you going, Delesof?" some one at this moment called from the drawing-room.

The young man who was called Delesof returned to the drawing-room. The musician was now standing at the door; and, as his eyes fell on the dancers, he showed by his smile and by the beating of his foot how much pleasure this spectacle afforded him.

"Won't you come, and have a dance too?" said one of the

guests to him. The musician bowed, and looked at the hostess inquiringly.

"Come, come. Why not, since the gentlemen have invited you?" said the hostess. The musician's thin, weak face suddenly assumed an expression of decision; and smiling and winking, and shuffling his feet, he awkwardly, clumsily went to join the dancers in the drawing-room.

In the midst of a quadrille a jolly officer, who was dancing very beautifully and with great liveliness, accidentally hit the musician in the back. His weak, weary legs lost their equilibrium; and the musician, making ineffectual struggles to keep his balance, measured his length on the floor.

Notwithstanding the sharp, hard sound made by his fall, almost everybody at the first moment laughed.

But the musician did not rise. The guests grew silent, even the piano ceased to sound. Delesof and the hostess were the first to reach the prostrate musician. He was lying on his elbow, and gloomily looking at the ground. When he had been lifted to his feet, and set in a chair, he threw back his hair from his forehead with a quick motion of his bony hand, and began to smile without replying to the questions that were put.

"Mr. Albert! Mr. Albert!" exclaimed the hostess. "Were you hurt? Where? Now, I told you that you had better not try to dance. . . . He is so weak," she added, addressing her guests. "It takes all his strength."

"Who is he?" some one asked the hostess.

"A poor man, an artist. A very nice young fellow; but he's a sad case, as you can see."

She said this without paying the least heed to the musician's presence. He suddenly opened his eyes as though frightened at something, collected himself, and remarked to those who were standing about him, "It's nothing at all," said he suddenly, arising from the chair with evident effort.

And in order to show that he had suffered no injury, he went into the middle of the room, and was going to dance; but he tottered, and would have fallen again, had he not been supported.

Everybody felt constrained. All looked at him, and no one spoke. The musician's glance again lost its vivacity; and, apparently forgetting that any one was looking, he put his hand to his knee. Suddenly he raised his head, advanced one faltering foot, and, with the same awkward gesture as before, tossed back his hair, and went to a violin-case, and took out the instrument.

"It was nothing at all," said he again, waving the violin. "Gentlemen, we will have a little music."

"What a strange face!" said the guests among themselves.

"Maybe there is great talent lurking in that unhappy creature," said one of them.

"Yes: it's a sad case,—a sad case," said another.

"What a lovely face! . . . There is something extraordinary about it," said Delesof. "Let us have a look at him." . . .

Albert by this time, not paying attention to any one, had raised his violin to his shoulder, and was slowly crossing over to the piano, and tuning his instrument. His lips were drawn into an expression of indifference, his eyes were almost shut; but his lank, bony back, his long white neck, his crooked legs, and disorderly black hair presented a strange but somehow not entirely ridiculous appearance. After he had tuned his violin, he struck a quick chord, and, throwing back his head, turned to the pianist who was waiting to accompany him. *"Melancholie, G sharp,"* he said, turning to the pianist with a peremptory gesture. And immediately after, as though in apology for his peremptory gesture, he smiled sweetly, and with the same smile turned to his audience again.

Tossing back his hair with the hand that held the bow, Albert stood at one side of the piano, and, with a flowing motion of the bow, touched the strings. Through the room there swept a pure, harmonious sound, which instantly brought absolute silence.

At first, it was as though a ray of unexpectedly brilliant light had flashed across the inner world of each hearer's consciousness; and the notes of the theme immediately followed, pouring forth abundant and beautiful.

Not one discordant or imperfect note distracted the attention of the listeners. All the tones were clear, beautiful, and full of meaning. All silently, with trembling expectation, followed the development of the theme. From a state of tedium, of noisy gayety, or of deep drowsiness, into which these people had fallen, they were suddenly transported to a world whose existence they had forgotten.

In one instant there arose in their souls, now a sentiment as though they were contemplating the past, now of passionate remembrance of some happiness, now the boundless longing for power and glory, now the feelings of humility, of unsatisfied love, and of melancholy.

Now bitter-sweet, now vehemently despairing, the notes, freely intermingling, poured forth and poured forth, so sweetly, so power-fully, and so spontaneously, that it was not so much that sounds were heard, as that some sort of beautiful stream of poetry, long known, but now for the first time expressed, gushed through the soul.

At each note that he played, Albert grew taller and taller. At a little distance, he had no appearance of being either crippled or peculiar. Pressing the violin to his chin, and with an expression of listening with passionate attention to the tones that he produced, he convulsively moved his feet. Now he straightened himself up to his full height, now thoughtfully leaned forward.

His left hand, curving over spasmodically on the strings, seemed as though it had swooned in its position, while it was only the bony fingers that changed about spasmodically; the right hand moved smoothly, gracefully, without effort.

His face shone with complete, enthusiastic delight; his eyes gleamed with a radiant, steely light; his nostrils quivered, his red lips were parted in rapture.

Sometimes his head bent down closer to his violin, his eyes almost closed, and his face, half shaded by his long locks, lighted up with a smile of genuine blissfulness. Sometimes he quickly straightened himself up, changed from one leg to the other, and his pure fore-head, and the radiant look which he threw around the room, were alive with pride, greatness, and the consciousness of power. Once the pianist made a mistake, and struck a false chord. Physical pain was apparent in the whole form and face of the musician. He paused for a second, and with an expression of childish anger stamped his foot, and cried, *"Moll, ce moll!"* The pianist corrected his mistake; Albert closed his eyes, smiled, and, again forgetting himself and everybody else, gave himself up with beatitude to his work. Everybody who was in the room while Albert was playing preserved an attentive silence, and seemed to live and breathe only in the music.

The gay officer sat motionless in a chair by the window, with his eyes fixed upon the floor, and drawing long heavy sighs. The girls, awed by the universal silence, sat along by the walls, only occasion-ally exchanging glances expressive of satisfaction or perplexity.

The fat smiling face of the hostess was radiant with happiness. The pianist kept his eyes fixed on Albert's face, and while his whole figure from head to foot showed his solicitude lest he should make some mistake, he did his best to follow him. One of the guests, who had been drinking more heavily than the rest, lay at full length on the sofa, and tried not to move lest he should betray his emotion. Delesof experienced an unusual sensation. It seemed as though an icy band, now contracting, now expanding, were pressed upon his head. The roots of his hair seemed endued with consciousness; the cold shivers ran down his back, something rose higher and higher in his throat, his nose and palate were full of little needles, and the tears stole down his cheeks.

He shook himself, tried to swallow them back and wipe them away without attracting attention, but fresh tears followed and streamed down his face. By some sort of strange association of impressions, the first tones of Albert's violin carried Delesof back to his early youth.

Old before his time, weary of life, a broken man, he suddenly felt as though he were a boy of seventeen again, self-satisfied and handsome, blissfully dull, unconsciously happy. He remembered his first love for his cousin who wore a pink dress, he remembered his first confession of it in the linden alley; he remembered the warmth and the inexpressible charm of the fortuitous kiss; he remembered the immensity and enigmatical mystery of Nature as it surrounded them then.

In his imagination as it went back in its flight, *she* gleamed in a mist of indefinite hopes, of incomprehensible desires, and the indubitable faith in the possibility of impossible happiness. All the priceless moments of that time, one after the other, arose before him, not like unmeaning instants of the fleeting present, but like the immutable, full-formed, reproachful images of the past.

He contemplated them with rapture, and wept,—wept not because the time had passed and he might have spent it more profitably (if that time had been given to him again he would not have spent it any more profitably), but he wept because it had passed and would never return. His recollections evolved themselves without effort, and Albert's violin was their mouthpiece. It said, "They have passed, forever passed, the days of thy strength, of love, and of happiness; passed forever, and never will return. Weep for them, shed all thy tears, let thy life pass in tears for these days; this is the only and best happiness that remains to thee."

At the end of the next variation, Albert's face grew serene, his eyes flushed, great clear drops of sweat poured down his cheeks. The veins swelled on his forehead; his whole body swayed more and more; his pale lips were parted, and his whole figure expressed an enthusiastic craving for enjoyment. Despairingly swaying with his whole body, and throwing back his hair, he laid down his violin, and with a smile of proud satisfaction and happiness gazed at the bystanders. Then his back assumed its ordinary curve, his head sank, his lips grew set, his eyes lost their fire; and as though he were ashamed of himself, timidly glancing round, and stumbling, he went into the next room.

Something strange came over all the audience, and something strange was noticeable in the dead silence that succeeded Albert's playing. It was as though each desired, and yet dared not, to acknowledge the meaning of it all.

What did it mean,—this brightly lighted, warm room, these brilliant women, the dawn just appearing at the windows, these hurrying pulses, and the pure impressions made by the fleeting tones of music? But no one ventured to acknowledge the meaning of it all; on the contrary, almost all, feeling incapable of throwing themselves completely under the influence of what the new impression concealed from them, rebelled against it.

"Well, now, he plays mighty well," said the officer.

"Wonderfully," replied Delesof, stealthily wiping his cheek with his sleeve.

"One thing sure, it's time to be going, gentlemen," said the gentleman who had been lying on the sofa, straightening himself up a little. "We'll have to give him something, gentlemen. Let us make a collection."

At this time, Albert was sitting alone in the next room, on the sofa. As he supported himself with his elbows on his bony knees, he smoothed his face with his dirty, sweaty hand, tossed back his hair, and smiled at his own happy thoughts.

A large collection was taken up, and Delesof was chosen to present it. Aside from this, Delesof, who had been so keenly and unwontedly affected by the music, had conceived the thought of conferring some benefit upon this man.

It came into his head to take him home with him, to feed him, to establish him somewhere,—in other words, to lift him from his vile position.

"Well, are you tired?" asked Delesof, approaching him. Albert replied with a smile. "You have creative talent; you ought seriously to devote yourself to music, to play in public."

"I should like to have something to drink," exclaimed Albert, as though suddenly waking up.

Delesof brought him some wine, and the musician greedily drained two glasses.

"What splendid wine!" he exclaimed.

"What a lovely thing that *Melancholie* is!" said Delesof.

"Oh, yes, yes," replied Albert with a smile. "But pardon me, I do not know with whom I have the honor to be talking; maybe you are a count or a prince. Couldn't you let me have a little money?" He paused for a moment. "I have nothing—I am a poor man: I couldn't pay it back to you."

Delesof flushed, grew embarrassed, and hastened to hand the musician the money that had been collected for him.

"Very much obliged to you," said Albert, seizing the money. "Now let us have some more music; I will play for you as much as you wish. Only let me have something to drink, something to drink," he repeated, as he started to his feet.

Delesof gave him some more wine, and asked him to sit down by him.

"Pardon me if I am frank with you," said Delesof. "Your talent has interested me so much. It seems to me that you are in a wretched position."

Albert glanced now at Delesof, now at the hostess, who just then came into the room.

"Permit me to help you," continued Delesof. "If you need any thing, then I should be very glad if you would come and stay with me for a while. I live alone, and maybe I could be of some service to you."

Albert smiled, and made no reply.

"Why don't you thank him?" said the hostess. "It seems to me that this would be a capital thing for you.—Only I would not advise you," she continued, turning to Delesof, and shaking her head warningly.

"Very much obliged to you," said Albert, seizing Delesof's hand with both his moist ones. "Only now let us have some music, please."

But the rest of the guests were already making their preparations to depart; and as Albert did not address them, they came out into the ante-room.

Albert bade the hostess farewell; and having taken his worn hat with wide brim, and a last summer's *alma viva,* which composed his only protection against the winter, he went with Delesof down the steps.

As soon as Delesof took his seat in his carriage with his new friend, and became conscious of that unpleasant odor of intoxication and filthiness exhaled by the musician, he began to repent of

the step that he had taken, and to curse himself for his childish softness of heart and lack of reason. Moreover, all that Albert said was so foolish and in such bad taste, and he seemed so near a sudden state of beastly intoxication, that Delesof was disgusted. "What shall I do with him?" he asked himself.

After they had been driving for a quarter of an hour, Albert relapsed into silence, took off his hat, and laid it on his knee, then threw himself into a corner of the carriage, and began to snore. . . . The wheels crunched monotonously over the frozen snow, the feeble light of dawn scarcely made its way through the frosty windows.

Delesof glanced at his companion. His long body, wrapped in his mantle, lay almost lifeless near him. It seemed to him that a long head with large black nose was swaying on his trunk; but on examining more closely he perceived that what he took to be nose and face was the man's hair, and that his actual face was lower down.

He bent over, and studied the features of Albert's face. Then the beauty of his brow and of his peacefully closed mouth once more charmed him. Under the influence of nervous excitement caused by the sleepless hours of the long night and the music, Delesof, as he looked at that face, was once more carried back to the blessed world of which he had caught a glimpse once before that night; again he remembered the happy and magnanimous time of his youth, and he ceased to repent of his rashness. At that moment he loved Albert truly and warmly, and firmly resolved to be a benefactor to him.

The next morning when Delesof was awakened to go to his office, he saw, with an unpleasant feeling of surprise, his old screen, his old servant, and his clock on the table.

"What did I expect to see if not the usual objects that surround me?" he asked himself.

Then he recollected the musician's black eyes and happy smile; the motive of the *Melancholie* and all the strange experiences of the night came back into his consciousness. It was never his way, however, to reconsider whether he had done wisely or foolishly in taking the musician home with him. After he had dressed, he carefully laid out his plans for the day: he took some paper, wrote out some necessary directions for the house, and hastily put on his cloak and galoshes.

As he went by the dining-room he glanced in at the door. Albert, with his face buried in the pillow and lying at full length in his dirty, tattered shirt, was buried in the profoundest slumber on the saffron sofa, where in absolute unconsciousness he had been laid the night before.

Delesof felt that something was not right: it disturbed him. "Please go for me to Boriuzovsky, and borrow his violin for a day or two," said he to his man; "and when he wakes up, bring him some coffee, and get him some clean linen and some old suit or other of mine. Fix him up as well as you can, please."

When he returned home in the afternoon, Delesof, to his surprise, found that Albert was not there.

"Where is he?" he asked of his man.

"He went out immediately after dinner," replied the servant. "He took the violin, and went out, saying that he would be back again in an hour; but since that time we have not seen him."

"Ta, ta! how provoking!" said Delesof. "Why did you let him go, Zakhár?"

Zakhár was a Petersburg lackey, who had been in Delesof's service for eight years. Delesof, as a single young bachelor, could not help intrusting him with his plans; and he liked to get his judgment in regard to each of his undertakings.

"How should I have ventured to detain him?" replied Zakhár, playing with his watch-charms. "If you had intimated, Dmitri Ivánovitch, that you wished me to keep him here, I might have kept him at home. But you only spoke of his wardrobe."

"Ta! how vexatious! Well, what has he been doing while I was out?"

Zakhár smiled.

"Indeed, he's a real artist, as you may say, Dmitri Ivánovitch. As soon as he woke up he asked for some madeira: then he began to keep the cook and me pretty busy. Such an absurd . . . However, he's a very interesting character. I brought him some tea, got some dinner ready for him; but he would not eat alone, so he asked me to sit down with him. But when he began to play on the fiddle, then I knew that you would not find many such artists at Izler. One might well keep such a man. When he played 'Down the Little Mother Volga' for us, why, it was enough to make a man weep. It was too good for any thing! The people from all the floors came down into our entry to listen."

"Well, did you give him some clothes?" asked the bárin.

"Certainly I did: I gave him your dress-shirt, and I put on him an overcoat of mine. You want to help such a man as that, he's a fine fellow." Zakhár smiled. "He asked me what rank you were, and if you had had important acquaintances, and how many *souls* of peasantry you had."

"Very good: but now we must send and find him; and henceforth don't give him any thing to drink, otherwise you'll do him more harm than good."

"That is true," said Zakhár in assent. "He doesn't seem in very robust health: we used to have an overseer who, like him" . . .

Delesof, who had already long ago heard the story of the drunken overseer, did not give Zakhár time to finish, but bade him make every thing ready for the night, and then go out and bring the musician back.

He threw himself down on his bed, and put out the candle; but it was long before he fell asleep, for thinking about Albert.

"This may seem strange to some of my friends," said Delesof to himself, "but how seldom it is that I can do any thing for any one beside myself! and I ought to thank God for a chance when one presents itself. I will not send him away. I will do every thing, at least every thing that I can, to help him. Maybe he is not absolutely crazy, but only inclined to get drunk. It certainly will not cost me very much. Where one is, there is always enough to satisfy two. Let him live with me awhile, and then we will find him a place, or get him up a concert; we'll help him off the shoals, and then there will be time enough to see what will come of it." An agreeable sense of self-satisfaction came over him after making this resolution.

"Certainly I am not a bad man: I might say I am far from being a bad man," he thought. "I might go so far as to say that I am a good man, when I compare myself with others."

He was just dropping off to sleep when the sound of opening doors, and steps in the ante-room, roused him again. "Well, shall I treat him rather severely?" he asked himself; "I suppose that is best, and I ought to do it."

He rang.

"Well, did you find him?" he asked of Zakhár, who answered his call.

"He's a poor wretched fellow, Dmitri Ivánovitch," said Zakhár, shaking his head significantly, and closing his eyes.

"What! is he drunk?"

"Very weak."

"Had he the violin with him?"

"I brought it: the lady gave it to me."

"All right. Now please don't bring him to me to-night: let him sleep it off; and to-morrow don't under any circumstances let him out of the house."

But before Zakhár had time to leave the room, Albert came in.

"You don't mean to say that you've gone to bed at this time," said Albert with a smile. "I was there again, at Anna Ivánovna's. I spent a very pleasant evening. We had music, told stories; there was a very pleasant company there. Please let me have a glass of something to drink," he added, seizing a carafe of water that stood on the table, "only not water."

Albert was just as he had been the night before,—the same lovely smiling eyes and lips, the same fresh inspired brow, and weak features. Zakhár's overcoat fitted him as though it had been made for him, and the clean, tall, stiffly-starched collar of the dress-shirt picturesquely fitted around his delicate white neck, giving him a peculiarly childlike and innocent appearance.

He sat down on Delesof's bed, smiling with pleasure and grati-tude, and looked at him without speaking. Delesof gazed into Albert's eyes, and suddenly felt himself again under the sway of that smile. All desire for sleep vanished from him, he forgot his resolu-tion to be stern: on the contrary, he felt like having a gay time, to hear some music, and to talk confidentially with Albert till morning. Delesof bade Zakhár bring a bottle of wine, cigarettes, and the violin.

"This is excellent," said Albert. "It's early yet, we'll have a little music. I will play whatever you like."

Zakhár, with evident satisfaction, brought a bottle of Lafitte, two glasses, some mild cigarettes such as Albert smoked, and the violin. But, instead of going off to bed as his bárin bade him, he lighted a cigar, and sat down in the next room.

"Let us talk instead," said Delesof to the musician, who was beginning to tune the violin.

Albert sat down submissively on the bed, and smiled pleasantly.

"Oh, yes!" said he, suddenly striking his forehead with his hand, and putting on an expression of anxious curiosity. The expression of his face always foretold what he was going to say. "I wanted to ask you,"—he hesitated a little,—"that gentleman who was there with you last evening. . . . You called him N. Was he the son of the celebrated N.?"

"His own son," replied Delesof, not understanding at all what Albert could find of interest in him.

"Indeed!" he exclaimed, smiling with satisfaction. "I instantly noticed that there was something peculiarly aristocratic in his manners. I love aristocrats. There is something splendid and elegant about an aristocrat. And that officer who danced so beautifully," he went on to ask. "He also pleased me very much, he was so gay and noble looking. It seems he is called Adjutant N. N."

"Who?" asked Delesof.

"The one who ran into me when we were dancing. He must be a splendid man."

"No, he is a silly fellow," replied Delesof.

"Oh, no! it can't be," rejoined Albert hotly. "There's something very, very pleasant about him. And he's a fine musician," added Albert. "He played something from an opera. It's a long time since I have seen any one who pleased me so much."

"Yes, he plays very well; but I don't like his playing," said Delesof, anxious to bring his companion to talk about music. "He does not understand classic music, but only Donizetti and Bellini; and that's no music, you know. You agree with me, don't you?"

"Oh, no, no! Pardon me," replied Albert with a gentle expression of vindication. "The old music is music; but modern music is music too. And in the modern music there are extraordinarily beautiful things. Now, 'Somnambula,' and the *finale* of 'Lucia,' and Chopin, and 'Robert'! I often think,"—he hesitated, apparently collecting his thoughts,—"that if Beethoven were alive, he would weep tears of joy to hear **'Somnambula'** It's so beautiful all through. I heard **'Somnambula'** first when Viardot and Rubini were here. That was something worth while," he said, with shining eyes, and making a gesture with both hands, as though he were casting something from his breast. "I'd give a good deal, but it would be impossible, to bring it back."

"Well, but how do you like the opera nowadays?" asked Delesof.

"Bosio is good, very good," was his reply, "exquisite beyond words; but she does not touch me here," he said, pointing to his sunken chest. "A singer must have passion, and she hasn't any. She is enjoyable, but she doesn't torture you."

"Well, how about Lablache?"

"I heard him in Paris, in 'The Barber of Seville.' Then he was the only one, but now he is old. He can't be an artist, he is old."

"Well, supposing he is old, still he is fine in *morceaux d'ensemble*," said Delesof, still speaking of Lablache.

"Who said that he was old?" said Albert severely. "He can't be old. The artist can never be old. Much is needed in an artist, but fire most of all," he declared with glistening eyes, and raising both hands in the air. And, indeed, a terrible inner fire seemed to glow throughout his whole frame. "Ah, my God!" he exclaimed suddenly. "You don't know Petrof, do you,—Petrof, the artist?"

"No, I don't know him," replied Delesof with a smile.

"How I wish that you and he might become acquainted! You would enjoy talking with him. How he does understand art! He and I often used to meet at Anna Ivánovna's, but now she is vexed with him for some reason or other. But I really wish that you might make his acquaintance. He has great, great talent."

"Oh! Does he paint pictures?" asked Delesof.

"I don't know. No, I think not; but he was an artist of the Academy. What thoughts he had! Whenever he talks, it is wonderful. Oh, Petrof has great talent, only he leads a very gay life! . . . It's too bad," said Albert with a smile. The next moment he got up from the bed, took the violin, and began to play.

"Have you been at the opera lately?" asked Delesof.

Albert looked round, and sighed.

"Ah, I have not been able to!" he said, clutching his head. Again he sat down by Delesof. "I will tell you," he went on to say, almost in a whisper. "I can't go: I can't play there. I have nothing, nothing at all,—no clothes, no home, no violin. It's a wretched life,—a wretched life!" he repeated the phrase. "Yes, and why have I got into such a state? Why, indeed? It ought not to have been," said he, smiling. "*Akh! Don Juan.*"

And he struck his head.

"Now let us have something to eat," said Delesof.

Albert, without replying, sprang up, seized the violin, and began to play the *finale* of the first act of "Don Juan," accompanying it with a description of the scene in the opera.

Delesof felt the hair stand up on his head, when he played the voice of the dying commander.

"No, I cannot play to-night," said Albert, laying down the instrument. "I have been drinking too much." But immediately after he went to the table, poured out a brimming glass of wine, drank it at one gulp, and again sat down on the bed near Delesof.

Delesof looked steadily at Albert. The latter occasionally smiled, and Delesof returned his smile. Neither of them spoke, but the glance and smile brought them close together into a reciprocity of affection. Delesof felt that he was growing constantly fonder and fonder of this man, and he experienced an inexpressible pleasure.

"Were you ever in love?" he asked suddenly. Albert remained

sunk in thought for a few seconds, then his face lighted up with a melancholy smile. He bent over toward Delesof, and gazed straight into his eyes.

"Why did you ask me that question?" he whispered. "But I will tell you all about it. I like you," he added, after a few moments of thought, and glancing around. "I will not deceive you, I will tell you all, just as it was, from the beginning." He paused, and his eyes took on a strange wild appearance. "You know that I am weak in judgment," he said suddenly. "Yes, yes," he continued. "Anna Ivánovna has told you about it. She tells everybody that I am crazy. It isn't true, she says it for a joke; she is a good woman, but I really have not been quite well for some time." Albert paused again, and stood up, gazing with wide-opened eyes at the dark door. "You asked me if I had ever been in love. Yes, I have been in love," he whispered, raising his brows. "That happened long ago; it was at a time when I still had a place at the theatre. I went to play second violin at the opera, and she came into a parquet box at the left."

Albert stood up, and bent over to Delesof's ear. "But no," said he, "why should I mention her name? You probably know her, everybody knows her. I said nothing, but simply looked at her: I knew that I was a poor artist, and she an aristocratic lady. I knew that very well. I only looked at her, and had no thoughts."

Albert paused for a moment, as though making sure of his recollections.

"How it happened I know not, but I was invited once to accompany her on my violin. . . . Now I was only a poor artist!" he repeated, shaking his head and smiling. "But no, I cannot tell you, I cannot!" he exclaimed, again clutching his head. "How happy I was!"

"What? did you go to her house often?" asked Delesof.

"Once, only once. . . . But it was my own fault; I wasn't in my right mind. I was a poor artist, and she an aristocratic lady. I ought not to have spoken to her. But I lost my senses, I committed a folly. Petrof told me the truth: 'It would have been better only to have seen her at the theatre.'"

"What did you do?" asked Delesof.

"Ah! wait, wait, I cannot tell you that."

And, hiding his face in his hands, he said nothing for some time.

"I was late at the orchestra. Petrof and I had been drinking that evening, and I was excited. She was sitting in her box, and talking with some general. I don't know who that general was. She was sitting at the very edge of the box, with her arm resting on the rim. She wore a white dress, with pearls on her neck. She was talking with him, but she looked at me. Twice she looked at me. She had arranged her hair in such a becoming way! I stopped playing, and stood near the bass, and gazed at her. Then, for the first time, something strange took place in me. She smiled on the general, but she looked at me. I felt certain that she was talking about me; and suddenly I seemed to be not in my place in the orchestra, but was standing in her box, and seizing her hand in that place. What was the meaning of that?" asked Albert, after a moment's silence.

"A powerful imagination," said Delesof.

"No, no, . . . I cannot tell," said Albert frowning. "Even then I was poor. I hadn't any room; and when I went to the theatre, I sometimes used to sleep there."

"What, in the theatre?" asked Delesof.

"Ah! I am not afraid of these stupid things. Ah! just wait a moment. As soon as everybody was gone, I went to that box where she had been sitting, and slept there. That was my only pleasure. How many nights I spent there! Only once again did I have that experience. At night many things seemed to come to me. But I cannot tell you much about them." Albert contracted his brows, and looked at Delesof. "What did it mean?" he asked.

"It was strange," replied the other.

"No, wait, wait!" he bent over to his ear, and said in a whisper,—

"I kissed her hand, wept there before her, and said many things to her. I heard the fragrance of her sighs, I heard her voice. She said many things to me that one night. Then I took my violin, and began to play softly. And I played beautifully. But it became terrible to me. I am not afraid of such stupid things, and I don't believe in them, but my head felt terribly," he said, smiling sweetly, and moving his hand over his forehead. "It seemed terrible to me on account of my poor mind; something happened in my head. Maybe it was nothing; what do you think?"

Neither spoke for several minutes.

"*Und wenn die Wolken sie verhüllen,*
Die Sonne bleibt doch ewig klar.

hummed Albert, smiling gently. "That is true, isn't it?" he asked.

"*Ich auch habe gelebt und genossen.*"

"Ah, old man Petrof! how this would have made things clear

to you!"

Delesof, in silence and with dismay, looked at his companion's excited and colorless face.

"Do you know the Juristen waltzes?" suddenly asked Albert in a loud voice, and without waiting for an answer, jumped up, seized the violin, and began to play the waltz. In absolute self-forgetfulness, and evidently imagining that a whole orchestra was playing for him, Albert smiled, began to dance, to shuffle his feet, and to play admirably.

"Hey, we will have a good time!" he exclaimed, as he ended, and waved his violin. "I am going," said he, after sitting down in silence for a little. "Won't you come along too?"

"Where?" asked Delesof in surprise.

"Let us go to Anna Ivánovna's again. It's gay there,—bustle, people, music."

Delesof for a moment was almost persuaded. However, coming to his senses, he promised Albert that he would go with him the next day.

"I should like to go this minute."

"Indeed, I wouldn't go."

Albert sighed, and laid down the violin.

"Shall I stay, then?" He looked over at the table, but the wine was gone; and so, wishing him a goodnight, he left the room.

Delesof rang. "Look here," said he to Zakhár, "don't let Mr. Albert go anywhere without asking me about it first."

The next day was a holiday. Delesof, on waking, sat in his parlor, drinking his coffee and reading a book. Albert, who was in the next room, had not yet moved. Zakhár discreetly opened the door, and looked into the dining-room.

"Would you believe it, Dmitri Ivánovitch, there he lies asleep on the bare sofa. I would not send him away for any thing, God knows. He's like a little child. Indeed, he's an artist!"

At twelve o'clock, there was a sound of yawning and coughing on the other side of the door.

Zakhár again crept into the dining-room; and the bárin heard his wheedling voice, and Albert's gentle, beseeching voice.

"Well, how is he?" asked Delesof, when Zakhár came out.

"He feels blue, Dmitri Ivánovitch. He doesn't want to get dressed. He's so cross. All he asks for is something to drink."

"Now, if we are to get hold of him, we must strengthen his character," said Delesof to himself. And, forbidding Zakhár to give him any wine, he again devoted himself to his book; in spite of himself, however, listening all the time for developments in the dining-room.

But there was no movement there, only occasionally were heard a heavy chest cough and spitting. Two hours passed. Delesof, after dressing to go out, resolved to look in upon his guest. Albert was sitting motionless at the window, leaning his head on his hands.

He looked round. His face was sallow, morose, and not only melancholy but deeply unhappy. He tried to welcome his host with a smile, but his face assumed a still more woe-begone expression. It seemed as though he were on the point of tears.

With effort he stood up and bowed. "If I might have just a little glass of simple vodka," he exclaimed with a supplicating expression. "I am so weak. If you please!"

"Coffee will be more strengthening, I would advise you."

Albert's face lost its childish expression; he gazed coldly, sadly, out of the window, and fell back into the chair.

"Wouldn't you like some breakfast?"

"No, thank you, I haven't any appetite."

"If you want to play on the violin, you will not disturb me," said Delesof, laying the instrument on the table. Albert looked at the violin with a contemptuous smile.

"No, I am too weak, I cannot play," he said, and pushed the instrument from him.

After that, in reply to all Delesof's propositions to go to walk, to go to the theatre in the evening, or any thing else, he only shook his head mournfully, and refused to speak.

Delesof went out, made a few calls, dined out, and before the theatre hour, he returned to his rooms to change his attire and find out how the musician was getting along.

Albert was sitting in the dark ante-room, and, with his head resting on his hand, was gazing at the heated stove. He was neatly dressed, washed and combed; but his eyes were sad and vacant, and his whole form expressed even more weakness and debility than in the morning.

"Well, have you had dinner, Mr. Albert?" asked Delesof.

Albert nodded his head, and, after looking with a terrified expression at Delesof, dropped his eyes. It made Delesof feel uncomfortable.

"I have been talking to-day with a manager," said he, also dropping his eyes. "He would be very glad to make terms with you, if you would like to accept an engagement."

"I thank you, but I cannot play," said Albert, almost in a whisper;

and he went into his room, and closed the door as softly as possible. After a few minutes, lifting the latch as softly as possible, he came out of the room, bringing the violin. Casting a sharp, angry look at Delesof, he laid the instrument on the table, and again disappeared.

Delesof shrugged his shoulders, and smiled.

"What am I to do now? Wherein am I to blame?" he asked himself.

"Well, how is the musician?" was his first question when he returned home late that evening.

"Bad," was Zakhár's short and ringing reply. "He sighs all the time, and coughs, and says nothing at all, only he has asked for vodka four or five times, and once I gave him some. How can we avoid killing him this way, Dmitri Ivánovitch? That was the way the overseer" . . .

"Well, hasn't he played on the fiddle?"

"Didn't even touch it. I took it to him, twice—Well, he took it up slowly, and carried it out," said Zakhár with a smile. "Do you still bid me to refuse him something to drink?"

"Don't give him anything to-day; we'll see what'll come of it. What is he doing now?"

"He has shut himself in the parlor."

Delesof went into his library, took down a few French books, and the Testament in German. "Put these books tomorrow in his room; and look out, don't let him get away," said he to Zakhár.

The next morning Zakhár informed his bárin that the musician had not slept a wink all night. "He kept walking up and down his rooms, and going to the sideboard to try to open the cupboard and door; but every thing, in spite of his efforts, remained locked."

Zakhár told how, while he was going to sleep, he heard Albert muttering to himself in the darkness and gesticulating.

* * * * *

Each day Albert grew more gloomy and taciturn. It seemed as though he were afraid of Delesof, and his face expressed painful terror whenever their eyes met. He did not touch either book or violin, and made no replies to the questions put to him.

On the third day after the musician came to stay with him, Delesof returned home late in the evening, tired and worried. He had been on the go all day, attending to his duties. Though they had seemed very simple and easy, yet, as is often the case, he had not made any progress at all, in spite of his strenuous endeavors. Afterwards he had stopped at the club, and lost at whist. He was out of spirits.

"Well, God be with him," he replied to Zakhár, who had been telling him of Albert's pitiable state. "To-morrow I shall be really worried about him. Is he willing or not to stay with me, and follow my advice? No? Then it's idle. I have done the best that I could."

"That's what comes of trying to be a benefactor to people," said he to himself. "I am putting myself to inconvenience for him. I have taken this filthy creature into my rooms, which keeps me from receiving strangers in the morning; I work and trot; and yet he looks upon me as some enemy who, against his will, would keep him in pound. But the worst is, that he is not willing to take a step in his own behalf. That's the way with them all."

That word *all* referred to people in general, and especially to those with whom he had been associated in business that day. "But what is to be done for him now? What is he contemplating? Why is he melancholy? Is he melancholy on account of the debauch from which I rescued him? on account of the degradation in which he has been? the humiliation from which I saved him? Can it be that he has fallen so low that it is a burden for him to look on a pure life? . . .

"No, this was a childish action," reasoned Delesof. "Why should I undertake to direct others, when it is as much as I can do to manage my own affairs?"

The impulse came over him to let him go immediately, but after a little deliberation he postponed it till the morning.

During the night Delesof was aroused by the noise of a falling table in the ante-room, and the sound of voices and stamping feet.

"Just wait a little, I will tell Dmitri Ivánovitch," said Zakhár's voice; Albert's voice replied passionately and incoherently.

Delesof leaped up, and went with a candle into the ante-room. Zakhár in his nightdress was standing against the door; Albert in cap and *alma viva* was trying to pull him away, and was screaming at him in a pathetic voice.

"You have no right to detain me; I have a passport; I have not stolen any thing from you. You must let me go. I will go to the police."

"I beg of you, Dmitri Ivánovitch," said Zakhár, turning to his bárin, and continuing to stand guard at the door. "He got up in the night, found the key in my overcoat-pocket, and he has drunk up the whole decanter of sweet vodka. Was that good? And now he wants to go. You didn't give me orders, and so I could not let him out."

Albert, seeing Delesof, began to pull still more violently on Zakhár. "No one has the right to detain me! He cannot do it," he screamed, raising his voice more and more.

"Let him go, Zakhár," said Delesof. "I do not wish to detain you, and I have no right to, but I advise you to stay till to-morrow," he added, addressing Albert.

"No one has the right to detain me. I am going to the police," screamed Albert more and more furiously, addressing only Zakhár, and not heeding Delesof. "Guard!" he suddenly shouted at the top of his voice.

"Now, what are you screaming like that for? You see you are free to go," said Zakhár, opening the door.

Albert ceased screaming. "How did they dare? They were going to murder me! No!" he muttered to himself as he put on his galoshes. Not offering to say good-by, and still muttering something unintelligible, he went out of the door. Zakhár accompanied him to the gate, and came back.

"Thank the Lord, Dmitri Ivánovitch! Any longer would have been a sin," said he to his bárin. "And now we must count the silver."

Delesof only shook his head, and made no reply. There came over him a lively recollection of the first two evenings which he and the musician had spent together; he remembered the last wretched days which Albert had spent there; and above all he remembered the sweet but absurd sentiment of wonder, of love, and of sympathy, which had been aroused in him by the very first sight of this strange man; and he began to pity him.

"What will become of him now?" he asked himself. "Without money, without warm clothing, alone at midnight!" He thought of sending Zakhár after him, but now it was too late.

"Is it cold out doors?" he asked.

" A healthy frost, Dmitri Ivánovitch," replied the man. "I forgot to tell you that you will have to buy some more firewood to last till spring."

"But what did you mean by saying that it would last?"

Out of doors it was really cold; but Albert did not feel it, he was so excited by the wine that he had taken and by the quarrel.

As he entered the street, he looked around him, and rubbed his hands with pleasure. The street was empty, but the long lines of lights were still brilliantly gleaming; the sky was clear and beautiful. "What!" he cried, addressing the lighted window in Delesof's apartments; and then thrusting his hands in his trousers pockets under his coat, and looking straight ahead, he walked with heavy and uncertain steps straight up the street.

He felt an absolute weight in his legs and abdomen, something hummed in his head, some invisible power seemed to hurl him from side to side; but he still plunged ahead in the direction of where Anna Ivánovna lived.

Strange, disconnected thoughts rushed through his head. Now he remembered his quarrel with Zakhár, now something recalled the sea and his first voyage in the steamboat to Russia; now the merry night that he had spent with some friend in the wine-shop by which he was passing; then suddenly there came to him a familiar air singing itself in his recollections, and he seemed to see the object of his passion and the terrible night in the theatre.

But notwithstanding their incoherence, all these recollections presented themselves before his imaginations with such distinctness that when he closed his eyes he could not tell which was nearer to the reality: what he was doing, or what he was thinking. He did not realize and he did not feel how his legs moved, how he staggered and hit against a wall, how he looked around him, and how he made his way from street to street.

As he went along the Little Morskaya, Albert tripped and fell. Collecting himself in a moment, he saw before him some huge and magnificent edifice, and he went toward it.

In the sky not a star was to be seen, nor sign of dawn, nor moon, neither were there any street-lights there; but all objects were perfectly distinguishable. The windows of the edifice, which loomed up at the corner of the street, were brilliantly lighted, but the lights wavered like reflections. The building kept coming nearer and nearer, clearer and clearer, to Albert.

But the lights vanished the moment that Albert entered the wide portals. Inside it was dark. He took a few steps under the vaulted ceiling, and something like shades glided by and fled at his approach.

"Why did I come here?" wondered Albert; but some irresistible power dragged him forward into the depths of the immense hall.

There stood some lofty platform, and around it in silence stood what seemed like little men. "Who is going to speak?" asked Albert. No one answered, but some one pointed to the platform. There stood now on the platform a tall, thin man, with bushy hair and dressed in a variegated gown. Albert immediately recognized his friend Petrof.

"How strange! what is he doing here?" said Albert to himself.

"No, brethren," said Petrof, pointing to something, "you did not appreciate the man while he was living among you; you did not appreciate him! He was not a cheap artist, not a merely mechanical performer, not a crazy, ruined man. He was a genius, a great musical genius, who perished among you unknown and unvalued."

Albert immediately understood of whom his friend was speaking; but not wishing to interrupt him, he hung his head modestly. "He, like a sheaf of straw, was wholly consumed by the sacred fire which we all serve," continued the voice. "But he has completely fulfilled all that God gave him; therefore he ought to be considered a great man. You may despise him, torture him, humiliate him," continued the voice, more and more energetically, "but he has been, is, and will be immeasurably higher than you all. He is happy, he is good. He loved you all alike, or cared for you, it is all the same; but he has served only that with which he was so highly endowed. He loved one thing,—beauty, the only infinite good in the world. Oh, yes, what a man he is! Fall all of you before him. On your knees!" cried Petrof in a thundering voice.

But another voice mildly answered from another corner of the hall. "I do not wish to bow my knee before him," said the voice.

Albert instantly recognized Delesof.

"Why is he great? And why should we bow before him? Has he conducted himself in an honorable and righteous manner? Has he brought society any advantage? Do we not know how he borrowed money, and never returned it; how he carried off a violin that belonged to a brother artist, and pawned it?"

"My God! how did he know all that?" said Albert to himself, drooping his head still lower.

"Do we not know," the voice went on, "how he pandered to the lowest of the low, pandered to them for money? Do we not know how he was driven out of the theatre? How Anna Ivánovna threatened to hand him over to the police?"

"My God! that is all true, but protect me," cried Albert. "You are the only one who knows why I did so."

"Stop, for shame!" cried Petrof's voice again. "What right have you to accuse him? Have you lived his life? Have you experienced his enthusiasms?"

"Right! right!" whispered Albert.

"Art is the highest manifestation of power in man. It is given only to the favored few, and it lifts the chosen to such an eminence that the head swims, and it is hard to preserve its integrity. In art, as in every struggle, there are heroes who bring all under subjection to them, and perish if they do not attain their ends."

Petrof ceased speaking; and Albert lifted his head, and tried to shout in a loud voice, "Right! right!" but his voice died without a sound.

"That is not the case with you. This does not concern you," sternly said the artist Petrof, addressing Delesof. "Yes, humble him, despise him," he continued, "for he is better and happier than all the rest of you."

Albert, with rapture in his heart at hearing these words, could not contain himself, but went up to his friend, and was about to kiss him.

"Get thee gone, I do not know you," replied Petrof. "Go your own way, you cannot come here."

"Here, you drunken fellow, you cannot come here," cried a policeman at the crossing.

Albert hesitated, then collected all his forces, and, endeavoring not to stumble, crossed over to the next street.

It was only a few steps to Anna Ivánovna's. From the hall of her house a stream of light fell on the snowy *dvor,* and at the gate stood sledges and carriages.

Clinging with both hands to the balustrade, he made his way up the steps, and rang the bell.

The maid's sleepy face appeared at the open door, and looked angrily at Albert.

"It is impossible," she cried; "I have been forbidden to let you in," and she slammed the door. The sounds of music and women's voices floated down to him.

Albert sat down on the ground, and leaned his head against the wall, and shut his eyes. At that very instant a throng of indistinct but correlated visions took possession of him with fresh force, mastered him, and carried him off into the beautiful and free domain of fancy.

"Yes! he is better and happier," involuntarily the voice repeated in his imagination.

From the door were heard the sounds of a polka. These sounds also told him that he was better and happier. In a neighboring church was heard the sound of a prayer-bell; and the prayer-bell also told him that he was better and happier.

"Now I will go back to that hall again," said Albert to himself. "Petrof must have many things still to tell me."

There seemed to be no one now in the hall; and in the place of the artist Petrof, Albert himself stood on the platform, and was playing on his violin all that the voice had said before.

But his violin was of strange make: it was composed of nothing but glass, and he had to hold it with both hands, and slowly rub it on his breast to make it give out sounds. The sounds were so sweet and delicious, that Albert felt he had never before heard any thing like them. The more tightly he pressed the violin to his breast, the more sweet and consoling they became. The louder the sounds, the more swiftly the shadows vanished, and the more brilliantly the walls of the hall were illuminated. But it was necessary to play very cautiously on the violin, lest it should break.

Albert played on the instrument of glass cautiously and well. He played things the like of which he felt no one would ever hear again.

He was growing tired, when a heavy distant sound began to annoy him. It was the sound of a bell, but this sound seemed to have a language.

"Yes," said the bell, with its notes coming from somewhere far off and high up, "yes, he seems to you wretched; you despise him, but he is better and happier than you. No one ever will play more on that instrument!"

These words which he understood seemed suddenly so wise, so novel, and so true to Albert, that he stopped playing, and, while trying not to move, lifted his eyes and his arms toward heaven. He felt that he was beautiful and happy. Although no one was in the hall, Albert expanded his chest, and proudly lifted his head, and stood on the platform so that all might see him.

Suddenly someone's hand was gently laid on his shoulder; he turned around, and in the half light saw a woman. She looked pityingly at him, and shook her head. He immediately became conscious that what he was doing was wrong, and a sense of shame came over him.

"Where shall I go?" he asked her. Once more she gazed long and fixedly at him, and bent her head pityingly. She was the one, the very one whom he loved, and her dress was the same; on her round white neck was the pearl necklace, and her lovely arms were bare above the elbows.

She took him in her arms, and bore him away through the hall. At the entrance of the hall, Albert saw the moon and water. But the water was not below as is usually the case, and the moon was not above; there was a white circle in one place as sometimes happens. The moon and the water were together,— everywhere, above and below, and on all sides and around them both. Albert and his love darted off toward the moon and the water, and he now realized that she whom he loved more than all in the world was in his arms: he embraced her, and felt inexpressible felicity.

"Is not this a dream?" he asked himself. But no, it was the reality, it was more than reality: it was reality and recollection combined.

Then he felt that the indescribable pleasure which he had felt during the last moment was gone, and would never be renewed.

"Why am I weeping?" he asked of her. She looked at him in silence, with pitying eyes. Albert understood what she desired to say in reply. "Just as when I was alive," he went on to say. She, without replying, looked straight forward.

"This is terrible! How can I explain to her that I *am* alive?" he asked himself in horror. "My God, I am alive! Do understand me," he whispered.

"He is better and happier," said a voice.

But something kept oppressing Albert ever more powerfully. Whether it was the moon or the water, or her embrace or his tears, he could not tell, but he was conscious that he could not say all that it was his duty to say, and that all would be quickly over.

* * * * *

Two guests coming out from Anna Ivánovna's rooms stumbled against Albert lying on the threshold. One of them went back to Anna Ivánovna, and called her. "That was heartless," he said. "You might let a man freeze to death that way."

"*Akh!* why, that is my Albert. See where he was lying!" exclaimed the hostess. "Annushka, have him brought into the room; find a place for him somewhere," she added, addressing the maid.

"Oh! I am alive, why do you bury me?" muttered Albert, as they brought him unconscious into the room.

Thomas Hardy was himself a fiddler. So too was his father, a tall, dark, and handsome stone mason by trade, who loved to dance and was a favorite with the ladies. The older Hardy died a year before "The Fiddler of the Reels" appeared (1893), so the story would seem to be a memorial tribute. But the flattery is at best ambiguous—Wat Ollamoor, the fiddler of the reels, does not engage the reader's affections. One commentator has called "The Fiddler of the Reels" "perhaps the best story Hardy ever wrote." It was first published in *Scribner's Magazine* to mark the Chicago World's Fair.

The Fiddler of the Reels

by Thomas Hardy

"Talking of Exhibitions, World's Fairs, and what not," said the old gentleman, "I would not go round the corner to see a dozen of them nowadays. The only exhibition that ever made, or ever will make, any impression upon my imagination was the first of the series, the parent of them all, and now a thing of old times—the Great Exhibition of 1851, in Hyde Park, London. None of the younger generation can realize the sense of novelty it produced in us who were then in our prime. A noun substantive went so far as to become an adjective in honor of the occasion. It was 'exhibition' hat, 'exhibition' razor-strop, 'exhibition' watch; nay, even 'exhibition' weather, 'exhibition' spirits, sweethearts, babies, wives—for the time.

"For South Wessex, the year formed in many ways an extraordinary chronological frontier or transit-line, at which there occurred what one might call a precipice in Time. As in a geological 'fault,' we had presented to us a sudden bringing of ancient and modern into absolute contact, such as probably in no other single year since the Conquest was ever witnessed in this part of the country."

These observations led us onward to talk of the different personages, gentle and simple, who lived and moved within our narrow and peaceful horizon at that time; and of three people in particular, whose queer little history was oddly touched at points by the Exhibition, more concerned with it than that of anybody else who dwelt in those outlying shades of the world, Stickleford, Mellstock, and Egdon. First in prominence among these three came Wat Ollamoor —if that were his real name.

He was a woman's man—supremely so—and externally very little else. To men he was not attractive; perhaps a little repulsive at times. Musician, dandy, and company-man in practice; veterinary surgeon in theory, he lodged awhile in Mellstock village, coming from nobody knew where; though some said his first appearance in this neighborhood had been as fiddle-player in a show at Greenhill Fair.

Many a worthy villager envied him his power over unsophisticated maidenhood—a power which seemed sometimes to have a touch of the weird and wizardly in it. Personally he was not ill-favored, though rather un-English, his complexion being a rich olive, his rank hair dark and rather clammy—made still clammier by secret ointments, which, when he came fresh to a party, caused him to smell like "boys'-love" (southernwood) steeped in lamp-oil. On occasion he wore curls—a double row—running almost horizontally around his head. But as these were sometimes noticeably absent, it was concluded that they were not altogether of Nature's making. By girls whose love for him had turned to hatred he had been nicknamed "Mop," from this abundance of hair, which was long enough to rest upon his shoulders; as time passed, the name more and more prevailed.

His fiddling, possibly, had the most to do with the fascination he exercised, for, to speak fairly, it could claim for itself a most peculiar and personal quality, like that in a moving preacher. There were tones in it which bred the immediate conviction that indolence and averseness to systematic application were all that lay between "Mop" and the career of a second Paganini.

While playing he invariably closed his eyes; using no notes, and, as it were, allowing the violin to wander on at will into the most plaintive passages ever heard by rustic man. There was a certain lingual character in the supplicatory expressions he produced, which would wellnigh have drawn an ache from the heart of a gate-post. He could make any child in the parish, who was at all sensitive to music, burst into tears in a few minutes by simply fiddling one of the old dance-tunes he almost entirely affected—country jigs, reels, and "Favorite Quick-Steps" of the last century—some mutilated remains of which even now reappear as nameless phantoms in new quadrilles and gallops, where they are recognized only by the curious, or by such old-fashioned and far-between people as have been thrown with men like Wat Ollamoor in their early life.

His date was a little later than that of the old Mellstock choir-band, which comprised the Dewys, Mail, and the rest—in fact, he did not rise above the horizon thereabout till those well-known musicians were disbanded as ecclesiastical functionaries. In their honest love of thoroughness they despised the new man's style. Theophilus Dewy (Reuben the tranter's younger brother) used to say there was no "plumness" in it—no bowing, no solidity—it was all fantastical. And probably this was true. Anyhow, Mop had, very obviously, never bowed a note of church-music from his birth; he never once sat in the gallery of Mellstock church, where the others had tuned their venerable psalmody so many hundreds of times; had never, in all likelihood, entered a church at all. All were devil's tunes in his repertory. "He could no more play the 'Wold Hundredth' to his true time than he could play the brazen serpent," the tranter would say. (The brazen serpent was supposed in Mellstock to be a musical instrument particularly hard to blow.)

Occasionally Mop could produce the aforesaid moving effect upon the souls of grown-up persons, especially young women of fragile and responsive organization. Such a one was Car'line Aspent. Though she was already engaged to be married before she met him, Car'line, of them all, was the most influenced by Mop Ollamoor's heart-stealing melodies, to her discomfort, nay, positive pain and ultimate injury. She was a pretty, invocating, weak-mouthed girl, whose chief defect as a companion with her sex was a tendency to peevishness now and then. At this time she was not a resident in Mellstock parish, where Mop lodged, but lived some miles off at Stickleford, farther down the river.

How and where she first made acquaintance with him and his fiddling is not truly known, but the story was that it either began or was developed on one spring evening, when, in passing through Lower Mellstock, she chanced to pause on the bridge near his house to rest herself, and languidly leaned over the parapet. Mop was standing on his door-step, as was his custom, spinning the insidious thread of semi- and demi-semi-quavers from the E string of his fiddle for the benefit of passers-by, and laughing as the tears rolled down the cheeks of the little children hanging around him. Car'line pretended to be engrossed with the rippling of the stream under the arches, but in reality she was listening, as he knew. Presently the aching of the heart seized her simultaneously with a wild desire to glide airily in the mazes of an infinite dance. To shake off the fascination she resolved to go on, although it would be necessary to pass him as he played. On stealthily glancing ahead at the performer, she found to her relief that his eyes were closed in abandonment to instrumentation, and she strode on boldly. But when closer her step grew timid, her tread convulsed itself more and more accordantly with the time of the melody, till she very nearly danced along. Gaining another glance at him when immediately opposite, she saw that *one* of his eyes was open, quizzing her as he smiled at her emotional state. Her gait could not divest itself of its compelled capers till she had gone a long way past the house; and Car'line was unable to shake off the strange infatuation for hours.

After that day, whenever there was to be in the neighborhood a dance to which she could get an invitation, and where Mop Ollamoor was to be the musician, Car'line contrived to be present, though it sometimes involved a walk of several miles; for he did not play so often in Stickleford as elsewhere.

The next evidences of his influence over her were singular enough, and it would require a neurologist to fully explain them. She would be sitting quietly, any evening after dark, in the house of her father, the parish-clerk, which stood in the middle of Stickleford village street, this being the high-road between Lower Mellstock and Moreford, six miles eastward. Here, without a moment's warning, and in the midst of a general conversation between her father, sister, and the young man before alluded to, who devotedly wooed her in ignorance of her infatuation, she would start from her seat in the chimney-corner as if she had received a galvanic shock, and spring convulsively towards the ceiling; then she would burst into tears, and it was not till some half-hour had passed that she grew calm as usual. Her father, knowing her hysterical tendencies, was always excessively anxious about this trait in his youngest girl, and feared the attack to be a species of epileptic fit. Not so her sister Julia.

Julia had found out what was the cause. At the moment before the jumping, only an exceptionally sensitive ear situated in the chimney-nook could have caught from down the flue the beat of a man's footstep along the highway without. But it was in that foot-fall, for which she had been waiting, that the origin of Car'line's involuntary springing lay. The pedestrian was Mop Ollamoor, as the girl well knew; but his business that way was not to visit her; he sought another woman, whom he spoke of as his Intended, and who lived at Moreford, two miles farther on. On one, and only one, occasion did it happen that Car'line could not control her utterance; it was when her sister alone chanced to be present. "Oh—oh—oh—!" she cried. "He's going to *her,* and not coming to *me!*"

To do the fiddler justice, he had not at first thought greatly of, or spoken much to, this girl of impressionable mould. But he had soon found out her secret, and could not resist a little by-play with her too easily hurt heart, as an interlude between his more serious performances at Moreford. The two became well acquainted, though only by stealth, hardly a soul in Stickleford except her sister, and her lover Ned Hipcroft, being aware of the attachment. Her father disapproved of her coldness to Ned; her sister, too, hoped she might get over this nervous passion for a man of whom so little was known. The ultimate result was that Car'line's manly and simple wooer Edward found his suit becoming practically hopeless. He was a respectable mechanic, in a far sounder position than Mop the nominal horse-doctor; but when, before leaving her, Ned put his flat and final question, would she marry him, then and there, now or never, it was with little expectation of obtaining more than the negative she gave him. Though her father supported him and her sister supported him, he could not play the fiddle so as to draw your soul out of your body like a spider's thread, as Mop did, till you felt as limp as withy-wind and yearned for something to cling to. Indeed, Hipcroft had not the slightest ear for music; could not sing two notes in tune, much less play them.

The No he had expected and got from her, in spite of a preliminary encouragement, gave Ned a new start in life. It had been uttered in such a tone of sad entreaty that he resolved to persecute her no more; she should not even be distressed by a sight of his form in the distant perspective of the street and lane. He left the place, and his natural course was to London.

The railway to South Wessex was in process of construction, but it was not as yet opened for traffic; and Hipcroft reached the capital by a six days' trudge on foot, as many a better man had done before him. He was one of the last of the artisan class who used that now extinct method of travel to the great centres of labor, so customary then from time immemorial.

In London he lived and worked regularly at his trade. More fortunate than many, his disinterested willingness recommended him from the first. During the ensuing four years he was never out of employment. He neither advanced nor receded in the modern sense; he improved as a workman, but he did not shift one jot in social position. About his love for Car'line he maintained a rigid silence. No doubt he often thought of her; but being always occupied, and having no relations at Stickleford, he held no communication with that part of the country, and showed no desire to return. In his quiet lodging in Lambeth he moved about after working-hours with the facility of a woman, doing his own cooking, attending to his stocking-heels, and shaping himself by degrees to a life-long bachelorhood. For this conduct one is bound to advance the canonical reason that time could not efface from his heart the image of little Car'line Aspent—and it may be in part true; but there was also the inference that his was a nature not greatly dependent upon the ministrations of the other sex for its comforts.

The fourth year of his residence as a mechanic in London was the year of the Hyde-Park Exhibition already mentioned, and at the construction of this huge glass-house, then unexampled in the world's history, he worked daily. It was an era of great hope and activity among the nations and industries. Though Hipcroft was, in his small way, a central man in the movement, he plodded on with his usual outward placidity. Yet for him, too, the year was destined to have its surprises, for when the bustle of getting the building ready for the opening day was past, the ceremonies had been witnessed, and people were flocking thither from all parts of the globe, he received a letter from Car'line. Till that day the silence of four years between himself and Stickleford had never been broken.

She informed her old lover, in an uncertain penmanship which suggested a trembling hand, of the trouble she had been put to in ascertaining his address, and then broached the subject which had prompted her to write. Four years ago, she said, with the greatest delicacy of which she was capable, she had been so foolish as to refuse him. Her willful wrongheadedness had since been a grief to her many times, and of late particularly. As for Mr. Ollamoor, he had been absent almost as long as Ned—she did not know where. She would gladly marry Ned now if he were to ask her again, and be a tender little wife to him till her life's end.

A tide of warm feeling must have surged through Ned Hipcroft's frame on receipt of this news, if we may judge by the issue. Unquestionably he loved her still, even if not to the exclusion of every other happiness. This from his Car'line, she who had been dead to him these many years, alive to him again as of old, was in itself a pleasant, gratifying thing. Ned had grown so resigned to, or satisfied with, his lonely lot, that he probably would not have shown much jubilation at anything. Still, a certain ardor of preoccupation, after his first surprise, revealed how deeply her confession of faith in him had stirred him. Measured and methodical in his ways, he did not answer the letter that day, nor the next, nor the next. He was having "a good think." When he did answer it, there was a great deal of sound reasoning mixed in with the unmistakable tenderness of his reply; but the tenderness itself was sufficient to reveal that he was pleased with her straightforward frankness; that the anchorage she had once obtained in his heart was renewable, if it had not been continuously firm.

He told her—and as he wrote his lips twitched humorously over the few gentle words of raillery he indited among the rest of his sentences—that it was all very well for her to come round at this time of day. Why wouldn't she have him when he wanted her? She had no doubt learned that he was not married, but suppose his affections had since been fixed on another? She ought to beg his pardon. Still, he was not the man to forget her. But, considering how he had been used, and what he had suffered, she could not quite expect him to go down to Stickleford and fetch her. But if she would come to him, and say she was sorry, as was only fair; why, yes, he would marry her, knowing what a good little woman she was to the core. He added that the request for her to come to him was a less one to make than it would have been when he first left Stickleford, or even a few months ago; for the new railway into South Wessex was now open, and there had just begun to be run wonderfully contrived special trains, called excursion-trains, on account of the Great Exhibition; so that she could come up easily alone.

She said in her reply how good it was of him to treat her so generously, after her hot-and-cold treatment of him; that though she felt frightened at the magnitude of the journey, and was never as yet in a railway-train, having only seen one pass at a distance, she embraced his offer with all her heart; and would, indeed, own to him how sorry she was, and beg his pardon, and try to be a good wife always, and make up for lost time.

The remaining details of when and where were soon settled, Car'line informing him, for her ready identification in the crowd, that she would be wearing "my new sprigged-laylock cotton gown," and Ned gayly responding that, having married her the morning after her arrival, he would make a day of it by taking her to the Exhibition. One early summer afternoon, accordingly, he came from his place of work, and hastened toward Waterloo Station to meet her. It was as wet and chilly as an English June day can occasionally be, but as he waited on the platform in the drizzle he glowed inwardly, and seemed to have something to live for again.

The "excursion-train"—an absolutely new departure in the history of travel—was still a novelty on the Wessex line, and probably everywhere. Crowds of people had flocked to all the stations on the way up to witness the unwonted sight of so long a train's passage, even where they did not take advantage of the opportunity it offered. The seats for the humbler class of travellers in these early experiments in steam-locomotion were open trucks, without any protection whatever from the wind and rain; and damp weather having set in with the afternoon, the unfortunate occupants of these vehicles were, on the train drawing up at the London terminus, found to be in a pitiable condition from their long journey; blue-faced, stiff-necked, sneezing, rain-beaten, chilled to the marrow, many of the men being hatless; in fact, they resembled people who had been out all night in an open boat on a rough sea, rather than inland excursionists for pleasure. The women had in some degree protected themselves by turning up the skirts of their gowns over their heads, but as by this arrangement they were additionally exposed about the hips, they were all more or less in a sorry plight.

In the bustle and crush of alighting forms of both sexes which followed the entry of the huge concatenation into the station, Ned Hipcroft soon discerned the slim little figure his eye was in search of in the sprigged lilac, as described. She came up to him with a frightened smile—still pretty, though so damp, weather-beaten, and shivering from long exposure to the wind.

"Oh, Ned!" she sputtered, "I—I—" He clasped her in his arms and kissed her, whereupon she burst into a flood of tears.

"You are wet, my poor dear! I hope you'll not get cold," he said. And surveying her and her multifarious surrounding packages, he noticed that by the hand she led a toddling child—a little girl of three or so—whose hood was as clammy and tender face as blue as those of the other travellers.

"Who is this—somebody you know?" asked Ned, curiously.

"Yes, Ned. She's mine."

"Yours?"

"Yes—my own!"

"Your own child?"

"Yes!"

"Well—as God's in—"

"Ned, I didn't name it in my letter, because, you see, it would have been so hard to explain. I thought that when we met I could tell you how she happened to be born, so much better than in writing. I hope you'll excuse it this once, dear Ned, and not scold me, now I've come so many, many miles!"

"This means Mr. Mop Ollamoor, I reckon!" said Hipcroft, gazing palely at them from the distance of the yard or two to which he had withdrawn with a start.

Car'line gasped. "But he's been gone away for years!" she supplicated. "And I never had a young man before! And I was so unlucky to be catched the first time, though some of the girls down there go on like anything!"

Ned remained in silence, pondering.

"You'll forgive me, dear Ned?" she added, beginning to sob outright. "I haven't taken 'ee in after all, because you can pack us back again, if you want to; though 'tis hundreds o' miles, and so wet, and night a-coming on, and I with no money!"

"What the devil can I do?" Hipcroft groaned.

A more pitiable picture than the pair of helpless creatures presented was never seen on a rainy day, as they stood on the great, gaunt, puddled platform, a whiff of drizzle blowing under the roof upon them now and then; the pretty attire in which they had started from Stickleford in the early morning bemuddled and sodden, weariness on their faces, and fear of him in their eyes; for the child began to look as if she thought she too had done some wrong, remaining in an appalled silence till the tears rolled down her chubby cheeks.

"What's the matter, my little maid?" said Ned, mechanically.

"I do want to go home!" she let out, in tones that told of a bursting heart. "And my totties be cold, an' I sha'n't have no bread-an'-butter no more!"

"I don't know what to say to it all!" declared Ned, his own eye moist as he turned and walked a few steps with his head down; then regarded them again point-blank. From the child escaped troubled breaths and silently welling tears.

"Want some bread-and-butter, do 'ee?" he said, with factitious hardness.

"Ye-e-s!"

"Well, I dare say I can get 'ee a bit. Naturally, you must want some. And you, too, for that matter, Car'line."

"I do feel a little hungered. But I can keep it off," she murmured.

"Folk shouldn't do that," he said, gruffly. . . . "There, come along!" He caught up the child as he added, "You must bide here to-night, anyhow, I s'pose! What can you do otherwise? I'll get 'ee some tea and victuals; and as for this job, I'm sure I don't know what to say. This is the way out."

They pursued their way, without speaking, to Ned's lodgings, which were not far off. There he dried them and made them comfortable, and prepared tea; they thankfully sat down. The ready-made household of which he suddenly found himself the head imparted a cosy aspect to his room, and a paternal one to himself. Presently he turned to the child and kissed her now blooming cheeks; and, looking wistfully at Car'line, kissed her also.

"I don't see how I can send 'ee back all them miles," he growled, "now you've come all the way o' purpose to join me. But you must trust me, Car'line, and show you've real faith in me. Well, do you feel better now, my little woman?"

The child nodded, her mouth being otherwise occupied.

"I did trust you, Ned, in coming; and I shall always!"

Thus, without any definite agreement to forgive her, he tacitly acquiesced in the fate that Heaven had sent him; and on the day of their marriage (which was not quite so soon as he had expected it could be, on account of the time necessary for banns) he took her to the Exhibition when they came back from church, as he had promised. While standing near a large mirror in one of the courts devoted to furniture, Car'line started, for in the glass appeared the reflection of a form exactly resembling Mop Ollamoor's—so exactly that it seemed impossible to believe anybody but that artist in person to be the original. On passing round the objects which hemmed in Ned, her, and the child from a direct view, no Mop was to be seen. Whether he were really in London or not at that time was never known; and Car'line always stoutly denied that her readiness to go and meet Ned in town arose from any rumor that Mop had also gone thither; which denial there was no reasonable ground for doubting.

And then the year glided away, and the Exhibition folded itself up and became a thing of the past. The park trees that had been enclosed for six months were again exposed to the winds and storms, and the sod grew green anew. Ned found that Car'line resolved herself into a very good wife and companion, though she had made herself what is called cheap to him; but in that she was like another domestic article, a cheap teapot which often brews better tea than a dear one. One autumn Hipcroft found himself with but little work to do, and a prospect of less for the winter. Both being country born and bred, they fancied they would like to live again in their natural atmosphere. It was accordingly decided between them that they should leave the pent-up London lodging, and that Ned should seek out employment near his native place, his wife and her daughter staying with Car'line's father during the search for occupation and an abode of their own.

Tinglings of pleasure pervaded Car'line's spasmodic little frame as she journeyed down with Ned to the place she had left two or three years before in silence and under a cloud. To return to where she had once been despised, a smiling London wife with a distinct London accent, was a triumph which the world did not witness every day.

The train did not stop at the petty road-side station that lay nearest to Stickleford, and the trio went on to Casterbridge. Ned thought it a good opportunity to make a few preliminary inquiries for employment at workshops in the borough where he had been known; and feeling cold from her journey, and it being dry under-foot and only dusk as yet, with a moon on the point of rising, Car'line and her little girl walked on towards Stickleford, leaving Ned to follow at a quicker pace, and pick her up at a certain half-way house, widely known as an inn.

The woman and child pursued the well-remembered way comfortably enough, though they were both becoming wearied. In the course of three miles they had passed Heedless William's Pond, the familiar landmark by Bloom's End, and were drawing near the Quiet Woman Inn, a lone road-side hostel on the lower verge of the Egdon Heath, since and for many years abolished. In stepping up towards it Car'line heard more voices within than had formerly been customary at such an hour, and she learned that an auction of fat stock had been held near the spot that afternoon. The child would be the better for a rest as well as herself, she thought, and she entered.

The guests and customers overflowed into the passage, and Car'line had no sooner crossed the threshold than a man whom she remembered by sight came forward with a glass and mug in his hands towards a friend leaning against the wall; but, seeing her, very gallantly offered her a drink of the liquor, which was gin-and-beer hot, pouring her out a tumblerful and saying, in a moment or two: "Surely, 'tis little Car'line Aspent that was—down at Stickleford?"

She assented, and, though she did not exactly want this beverage, she drank it since it was offered, and her entertainer begged her to come in farther and sit down. Once within the room she found that all the persons present were seated close against the walls, and there being a chair vacant she did the same. An explanation of their position occurred the next moment. In the opposite corner stood Mop, rosining his bow and looking just the same as ever. The company had cleared the middle of the room for dancing, and they were about to dance again. As she wore a veil to keep off the wind she did not think he had recognized her, or could possibly guess the identity of the child; and to her satisfied surprise she found that she could confront him quite calmly—mistress of herself in the dignity her London life had given her. Before she had quite emptied her glass the dance was called, the dancers formed in two lines, the music sounded, and the figure began.

Then matters changed for Car'line. A tremor quickened itself to life in her, and her hand so shook that she could hardly set down her glass. It was not the dance nor the dancers, but the notes of that old violin which thrilled the London wife, these having still all the witchery that she had so well known of yore, and under which she had used to lose her power of independent will. How it all came back! There was the fiddling figure against the wall; the large, oily, mop-like head of him, and beneath the mop the face with closed eyes.

After the first moments of paralyzed reverie the familiar tune in the familiar rendering made her laugh and shed tears simultaneously. Then a man at the bottom of the dance, whose partner had dropped away, stretched out his hand and beckoned to her to take the place. She did not want to dance; she entreated by signs to be left where she was, but she was entreating of the tune and its player rather than of the dancing man. The saltatory tendency which the fiddler and his cunning instrument had ever been able to start in her was seizing Car'line just as it had done in earlier years, possibly assisted by the gin-and-beer hot. Tired as she was she grasped her little girl by the hand, and, plunging in at the bottom of the figure, whirled about with the rest. She found that her companions were mostly people of the neighboring hamlets and farms—Bloom's End, Mellstock, Lewgate, and elsewhere; and by degrees she was recognized as she convulsively danced on, wishing that Mop would cease and let her heart rest from the aching he caused, and her feet also.

After long and many minutes the dance ended, when she was urged to fortify herself with more gin-and-beer; which she did, feeling very weak and overpowered with hysteric emotion. She refrained from unveiling, to keep Mop in ignorance of her presence, if possible. Several of the guests having left, Car'line hastily wiped her lips and also turned to go; but, according to the account of some who remained, at that very moment a five-handed reel was proposed, in which two or three begged her to join.

She declined on the plea of being tired and having to walk to Stickleford, when Mop began aggressively tweedling "My Fancy Lad," in D major, as the air to which the reel was to be footed. He must have recognized her, though she did not know it, for it was the strain of all seductive strains which she was least able to resist— the one he had played when she was leaning over the bridge at the date of their first acquaintance. Car'line stepped despairingly into the middle of the room with the other four.

Reels were resorted to hereabouts at this time by the more robust spirits for the reduction of superfluous energy which the ordinary figure-dances were not powerful enough to exhaust. As everybody knows, or does not know, the five reelers stood in the form of a cross, the reel being performed by each line of three alternately, the persons who successively came to the middle place dancing in both directions. Car'line soon found herself in this place, the axis of the whole performance, and could not get out of it, the tune turning into the first part without giving her opportunity. And now she began to suspect that Mop did know her, and was doing this on purpose, though whenever she stole a glance at him his closed eyes betokened obliviousness to everything outside his own brain. She continued to wend her way through the figure of eight that was formed by her course, the fiddler introducing into his notes the wild and agonizing sweetness of a living voice in one too highly wrought; its pathos running high and running low in endless variation, projecting through her nerves excruciating spasms—a sort of blissful torture. The room swam, the tune was endless; and in about a quarter of an hour the only other woman in the figure dropped out exhausted, and sank panting on a bench.

The reel instantly resolved itself into a four-handed one. Car'line would have given anything to leave off; but she had, or fancied she had, no power, while Mop played such tunes; and thus another ten minutes slipped by, a haze of dust now clouding the candles, the floor being of stone, sanded. Then another dancer fell out—one of the men—and went into the passage, in a frantic search for liquor. To turn the figure into a three-handed reel was the work of a second, Mop modulating at the same time into "The Fairy Dance," as better suited to the contracted movement, and no less one of those foods of love which, as manufactured by his bow, had always intoxicated her.

In a reel for three there was no rest whatever, and four or five minutes were enough to make her remaining two partners, now thoroughly blown, stamp their last bar, and, like their predecessors, limp off into the next room to get something to drink. Car'line, half-stifled inside her veil, was left dancing alone, the apartment. now being empty of everybody save herself, Mop, and their little girl.

She flung up the veil, and cast her eyes upon him, as if imploring him to withdraw himself and his acoustic magnetism from the atmosphere. Mop opened one of his own orbs, as though for the first time, fixed it peeringly upon her, and smiling dreamily, threw into his strains the reserve of expression which he could not afford to waste on a big and noisy dance. Crowds of little chromatic subtleties, capable of drawing tears from a statue, proceeded straightway from the ancient fiddle, as if it were dying of the emotion which had been pent up within it ever since its banishment from some Italian city where it first took shape and sound. There was that in the look of Mop's one dark eye which said: "You cannot leave off, dear, whether you would or no," and it bred in her a paroxysm of desperation that defied him to tire her down.

She thus continued to dance alone, defiantly as she thought, but in truth slavishly and abjectly, subject to every wave of the melody, and probed by the gimlet-like gaze of her fascinator's open eye; keeping up at the same time a feeble smile in his face, as a feint to signify it was still her own pleasure which led her on. A terrified embarrassment as to what she could say to him if she were to leave off, had its unrecognized share in keeping her going. The child, who was beginning to bc distressed by the strange situation, came up and said: "Stop, mother, stop, and let's go home!" as she seized Car'line's hand.

Suddenly Car'line sank staggering to the floor; and rolling over on her face, prone she remained. Mop's fiddle thereupon emitted an elfin shriek of finality; stepping quickly down from the nine-gallon beer-cask which had formed his rostrum, he went to the little girl, who disconsolately bent over her mother.

The guests who had gone into the backroom for liquor and change of air, hearing something unusual, trooped back hitherward, where they endeavored to revive poor, weak Car'line by blowing her with the bellows and opening the window. Ned, her husband, who had been detained in Casterbridge, as aforesaid, came along the road at this juncture, and hearing excited voices through the open window, and, to his great surprise, the mention of his wife's name, he entered amid the rest upon the scene. Car'line was now in convulsions, weeping violently, and for a long time nothing could be done with her. While he was sending for a cart to take her onward to Stickleford, Hipcroft anxiously inquired how it had all happened; and then the assembly explained that a fiddler formerly known in the locality had lately revisited his old haunts, and had taken upon himself without invitation to play that evening at the inn.

Ned demanded the fiddler's name, and they said Ollamoor.

"Ah!" exclaimed Ned, looking round him. "Where is he, and where—where's my little girl?"

Ollamoor had disappeared, and so had the child. Hipcroft was in ordinary a quiet and tractable fellow, but a determination which was to be feared settled in his face now. "Blast him!" he cried. "I'll beat his skull in for'n, if I swing for it to-morrow!"

He had rushed to the poker which lay on the hearth, and hastened down the passage, the people following. Outside the house, on the other side of the highway, a mass of dark heath-land rose sullenly upward to its not easily accessible interior, a ravined plateau, whereon jutted into the sky, at the distance of a couple of miles, the fir-woods of Mistover backed by the Yalbury coppices— a place of Dantesque gloom at this hour, which would have afforded secure hiding for a battery of artillery, much less a man and a child.

Some other men plunged thitherward with him, and more went along the road. They were gone about twenty minutes altogether, returning without result to the inn. Ned sat down in the settle, and clasped his forehead with his hands.

"Well—what a fool the man is, and hev been all these years, if he thinks the child his, as a' do seem to!" they whispered. "And everybody else knowing otherwise!"

"No, I don't think 'tis mine!" cried Ned, hoarsely, as he looked up from his hands. "But she is mine, all the same! Ha'n't I nussed her? Ha'n't I fed her and teached her? Ha'n't I played wi' her? Oh, little Carry—gone with that rogue—gone!"

"You ha'n't lost your mis'ess, anyhow," they said to console him. "She's throwed up the sperrits, and she is feeling better, and she's more to 'ee than a child that isn't yours."

"She isn't! She's not so particular much to me, especially now she's lost the little maid! But Carry's everything!"

"Well, ver' like you'll find her to-morrow."

"Ah—but shall I? Yet he *can't* hurt her—surely he can't! Well—how's Car'line now? I am ready. Is the cart here?"

She was lifted into the vehicle, and they sadly lumbered on towards Stickleford. Next day she was calmer; but the fits were still upon her; and her will seemed shattered. For the child she appeared to show singularly little anxiety, though Ned was nearly distracted. It was nevertheless quite expected that the impish Mop would restore the lost one after a freak of a day or two; but time went on, and neither he nor she could be heard of, and Hipcroft murmured that perhaps he was exercising upon her some unholy musical charm, as he had done upon Car'line herself. Weeks passed, and still they could obtain no clew either to the fiddler's whereabouts or the girl's; and how he could have induced her to go with him remained a mystery.

Then Ned, who had obtained only temporary employment in the neighborhood, took a sudden hatred towards his native district, and a rumor reaching his ears through the police that a somewhat similar man and child had been seen at a fair near London, he playing a violin, she dancing on stilts, a new interest in the capital took possession of Hipcroft with an intensity which would scarcely allow him time to pack before returning thither. He did not, however, find the lost one, though he made it the entire business of his over-hours to stand about in by-streets in the hope of discovering her, and would start up in the night, saying, "That rascal's torturing her to maintain him!" To which his wife would answer, peevishly, "Don't 'ee raft yourself so, Ned! You prevent my getting a bit o' rest! He won't hurt her!" and fall asleep again.

That Carry and her father had emigrated to America was the general opinion; Mop, no doubt, finding the girl a highly desirable companion when he had trained her to keep him by her earnings as a dancer. There, for that matter, they may be performing in some capacity now, though he must be an old scamp verging on threescore-and-ten, and she a woman of four-and-forty.

Anton Chekhov's father, a Russian serf and petty shopkeeper, was passionately devoted to music. He directed the local church choir, and would often arouse his family to sing matins at 3 A.M.! Perhaps this early musical indoctrination contributed to the inspiration for "Rothschild's Fiddle" (1894). In any case, before Chekhov became an established playwright, he wrote stories to support his family and finance his education, and continued writing fiction throughout his life. Just as his plays, Chekhov's tales tend to be realistic "slices of life," examining social issues, human isolation, loneliness and, as in "Rothschild's Fiddle," loss.

Rothschild's Fiddle

by Anton Chekhov
Translated by Marian Fell

It was a tiny town, worse than a village, inhabited chiefly by old people who so seldom died that it was really vexatious. Very few coffins were needed for the hospital and the jail; in a word, business was bad. If Jacob Ivanoff had been a maker of coffins in the county town, he would probably have owned a house of his own by now, and would have been called Mr. Ivanoff, but here in this little place he was simply called Jacob, and for some reason his nickname was Bronze. He lived as poorly as any common peasant in a little old hut of one room, in which he and Martha, and the stove, and a double bed, and the coffins, and his joiner's bench, and all the necessities of housekeeping were stowed away.

The coffins made by Jacob were serviceable and strong. For the peasants and townsfolk he made them to fit himself and never went wrong, for although he was seventy years old, there was no man, not even in the prison, any taller or stouter than he was. For the gentry and for women he made them to measure, using an iron yardstick for the purpose. He was always very reluctant to take orders for children's coffins, and made them contemptuously without taking any measurements at all, always saying when he was paid for them:

"The fact is, I don't like to be bothered with trifles."

Beside what he received for his work as a joiner, he added a little to his income by playing the violin. There was a Jewish orchestra in the town that played for weddings, led by the tinsmith Moses Shakess, who took more than half of its earnings for himself. As Jacob played the fiddle extremely well, especially Russian songs, Shakess used sometimes to invite him to play in his orchestra for the sum of fifty copecks a day, not including the presents he might receive from the guests. Whenever Bronze took his seat in the orchestra, the first thing that happened to him was that his face grew red, and the perspiration streamed from it, for the air was always hot, and reeking of garlic to the point of suffocation. Then his fiddle would begin to moan, and a double bass would croak hoarsely into his right ear, and a flute would weep into his left. This flute was played by a gaunt, red-bearded Jew with a network of red and blue veins on his face, who bore the name of a famous rich man, Rothschild. This confounded Jew always contrived to play even the merriest tunes sadly. For no obvious reason Jacob little by little began to conceive a feeling of hatred and contempt for all Jews, and especially for Rothschild. He quarrelled with him and abused him in ugly language, and once even tried to beat him, but Rothschild took offence at this, and cried with a fierce look:

"If I had not always respected you for your music, I should have thrown you out of the window long ago!"

Then he burst into tears. So after that Bronze was not often invited to play in the orchestra, and was only called upon in cases of dire necessity, when one of the Jews was missing.

Jacob was never in a good humour, because he always had to endure the most terrible losses. For instance, it was a sin to work on a Sunday or a holiday, and Monday was always a bad day, so in that way there were about two hundred days a year on which he was compelled to sit with his hands folded in his lap. That was a great loss to him. If any one in town had a wedding without music, or if Shakess did not ask him to play, there was another loss. The police

112

inspector had lain ill with consumption for two years while Jacob impatiently waited for him to die, and then had gone to take a cure in the city and had died there, which of course had meant another loss of at least ten roubles, as the coffin would have been an expensive one lined with brocade.

The thought of his losses worried Jacob at night more than at any other time, so he used to lay his fiddle at his side on the bed, and when those worries came trooping into his brain he would touch the strings, and the fiddle would give out a sound in the darkness, and Jacob's heart would feel lighter.

Last year on the sixth of May, Martha suddenly fell ill. The old woman breathed with difficulty, staggered in her walk, and felt terribly thirsty. Nevertheless, she got up that morning, lit the stove, and even went for the water. When evening came she went to bed. Jacob played his fiddle all day. When it grew quite dark, because he had nothing better to do, he took the book in which he kept an account of his losses, and began adding up the total for the year. They amounted to more than a thousand roubles. He was so shaken by this discovery, that he threw the counting board on the floor and trampled it under foot. Then he picked it up again and rattled it once more for a long time, heaving as he did so sighs both deep and long. His face grew purple, and perspiration dripped from his brow. He was thinking that if those thousand roubles he had lost had been in the bank then, he would have had at least forty roubles interest by the end of the year. So those forty roubles were still another loss! In a word, wherever he turned he found losses and nothing but losses.

"Jacob!" cried Martha unexpectedly, "I am going to die!"

He looked round at his wife. Her face was flushed with fever and looked unusually joyful and bright. Bronze was troubled, for he had been accustomed to seeing her pale and timid and unhappy. It seemed to him that she was actually dead, and glad to have left this hut, and the coffins, and Jacob at last. She was staring at the ceiling, with her lips moving as if she saw her deliverer Death approaching and were whispering with him.

The dawn was just breaking and the eastern sky was glowing with a faint radiance. As he stared at the old woman it somehow seemed to Jacob that he had never once spoken a tender word to her or pitied her; that he had never thought of buying her a kerchief or of bringing her back some sweetmeats from a wedding. On the contrary, he had shouted at her and abused her for his losses, and had shaken his fist at her. It was true he had never beaten her, but he had frightened her no less, and she had been paralysed with fear every time he had scolded her. Yes, and he had not allowed her to drink tea because his losses were heavy enough as it was, so she had had to be content with hot water. Now he understood why her face looked so strangely happy, and horror overwhelmed him.

As soon as it was light he borrowed a horse from a neighbour and took Martha to the hospital. As there were not many patients, he had not to wait very long—only about three hours. To his great satisfaction it was not the doctor who was receiving the sick that day, but his assistant, Maksim Nicolaitch, an old man of whom it was said that although he quarrelled and drank, he knew more than the doctor did.

"Good morning, your Honour," said Jacob leading his old woman into the office. "Excuse us for intruding upon you with our trifling affairs. As you see, this subject has fallen ill. My life's friend, if you will allow me to use the expression——"

Knitting his grey eyebrows and stroking his whiskers, the doctor's assistant fixed his eyes on the old woman. She was sitting all in a heap on a low stool, and with her thin, long-nosed face and her open mouth, she looked like a thirsty bird.

"Well, well—yes—" said the doctor slowly, heaving a sigh. "This is a case of influenza and possibly fever; there is typhoid in town. What's to be done? The old woman has lived her span of years, thank God. How old is she?"

"She lacks one year of being seventy, your Honour."

"Well, well, she has lived long. There must come an end to everything."

"You are certainly right, your Honour," said Jacob, smiling out of politeness. "And we thank you sincerely for your kindness, but allow me to suggest to you that even an insect dislikes to die!"

"Never mind if it does!" answered the doctor, as if the life or death of the old woman lay in his hands. "I'll tell you what you must do, my good man. Put a cold bandage around her head, and give her two of these powders a day. Now then, good-by! Bonjour!"

Jacob saw by the expression on the doctor's face that it was too late now for powders. He realized clearly that Martha must die very soon, if not to-day, then to-morrow. He touched the doctor's elbow gently, blinked, and whispered:

"She ought to be cupped, doctor!"

"I haven't time, I haven't time, my good man. Take your old woman, and go in God's name. Good-by."

"Please, please, cup her, doctor!" begged Jacob. "You know

yourself that if she had a pain in her stomach, powders and drops would do her good, but she has a cold! The first thing to do when one catches cold is to let some blood, doctor!"

But the doctor had already sent for the next patient, and a woman leading a little boy came into the room.

"Go along, go along!" he cried to Jacob, frowning. "It's no use making a fuss!"

"Then at least put some leeches on her! Let me pray to God for you for the rest of my life!"

The doctor's temper flared up and he shouted:

"Don't say another word to me, blockhead!"

Jacob lost his temper, too, and flushed hotly, but he said nothing and, silently taking Martha's arm, led her out of the office. Only when they were once more seated in their wagon did he look fiercely and mockingly at the hospital and say:

"They're a pretty lot in there, they are! That doctor would have cupped a rich man, but he even begrudged a poor one a leech. The pig!"

When they returned to the hut, Martha stood for nearly ten minutes supporting herself by the stove. She felt that if she lay down Jacob would begin to talk to her about his losses, and would scold her for lying down and not wanting to work. Jacob contemplated her sadly, thinking that to-morrow was ·St. John the Baptist's day, and day after to-morrow was St. Nicholas the Wonder Worker's day, and that the following day would be Sunday, and the day after that would be Monday, a bad day for work. So he would not be able to work for four days, and as Martha would probably die on one of these days, the coffin would have to be made at once. He took his iron yardstick in hand, went up to the old woman, and measured her. Then she lay down, and he crossed himself and went to work on the coffin.

When the task was completed Bronze put on his spectacles and wrote in his book:

"To 1 coffin for Martha Ivanoff—2 roubles, 40 copecks."

He sighed. All day the old woman lay silent with closed eyes, but toward evening, when the daylight began to fade, she suddenly called the old man to her side.

"Do you remember, Jacob?" she asked. "Do you remember how fifty years ago God gave us a little baby with curly golden hair? Do you remember how you and I used to sit on the bank of the river and sing songs under the willow tree?" Then with a bitter smile she added: "The baby died."

Jacob racked his brains, but for the life of him he could not recall the child or the willow tree.

"You are dreaming," he said.

The priest came and administered the Sacrament and Extreme Unction. Then Martha began muttering unintelligibly, and toward morning she died.

The neighbouring old women washed her and dressed her, and laid her in her coffin. To avoid paying the deacon, Jacob read the psalms over her himself, and her grave cost him nothing, as the watchman of the cemetery was his cousin. Four peasants carried the coffin to the grave, not for money but for love. The old women, the beggars, and two village idiots followed the body, and the people whom they passed on the way cross themselves devoutly. Jacob was very glad that everything had passed off so nicely and decently and cheaply, without giving offence to any one. As he said farewell to Martha for the last time he touched the coffin with his hand and thought:

"That's a fine job!"

But walking homeward from the cemetery he was seized with great distress. He felt ill, his breath was burning hot, his legs grew weak, and he longed for a drink. Beside this, a thousand thoughts came crowding into his head. He remembered again that he had never once pitied Martha or said a tender word to her. The fifty years of their life together lay stretched far, far behind him, and somehow, during all that time, he had never once thought about her at all or noticed her more than if she had been a dog or a cat. And yet she had lit the stove every day, and had cooked and baked and fetched water and chopped wood, and when he had come home drunk from a wedding she had hung his fiddle reverently on a nail each time, and had silently put him to bed with a timid, anxious look on her face.

But here came Rothschild toward him, bowing and scraping and smiling.

"I have been looking for you, uncle!" he said. "Moses Shakess presents his compliments and wants you to go to him at once."

Jacob did not feel in a mood to do anything. He wanted to cry.

"Leave me alone!" he exclaimed, and walked on.

"Oh, how can you say that?" cried Rothschild, running beside him in alarm. "Moses will be very angry. He wants you to come at once!"

Jacob was disgusted by the panting of the Jew, by his blinking eyes, and by the quantities of reddish freckles on his face. He looked with aversion at his long green coat and at the whole of his frail, delicate figure.

"What do you mean by pestering me, garlic?" he shouted. "Get away!"

The Jew grew angry and shouted back:

"Don't yell at me like that or I'll send you flying over that fence!"

"Get out of my sight!" bellowed Jacob, shaking his fist at him. "There's no living in the same town with swine like you!"

Rothschild was petrified with terror. He sank to the ground and waved his hands over his head as if to protect himself from falling blows; then he jumped up and ran away as fast as his legs could carry him. As he ran he leaped and waved his arms, and his long, gaunt back could be seen quivering. The little boys were delighted at what had happened, and ran after him screaming: "Sheeny! Sheeny!" The dogs also joined barking in the chase. Somebody laughed and then whistled, at which the dogs barked louder and more vigorously than ever.

Then one of them must have bitten Rothschild, for a piteous, despairing scream rent the air.

Jacob walked across the common to the edge of the town without knowing where he was going, and the little boys shouted after him. "There goes old man Bronze! There goes old man Bronze!" He found himself by the river where the snipe were darting about with shrill cries, and the ducks were quacking and swimming to and fro. The sun was shining fiercely and the water was sparkling so brightly that it was painful to look at. Jacob struck into a path that led along the river bank. He came to a stout, red-cheeked woman just leaving a bath-house. "Aha, you otter, you!" he thought. Not far from the bath-house some little boys were fishing for crabs with pieces of meat. When they saw Jacob they shouted mischievously: "Old man Bronze! Old man Bronze!" But there before him stood an ancient, spreading willow tree with a massive trunk, and a crow's nest among its branches. Suddenly there flashed across Jacob's memory with all the vividness of life a little child with golden curls, and the willow of which Martha had spoken. Yes, this was the same tree, so green and peaceful and sad. How old it had grown, poor thing!

He sat down at its foot and thought of the past. On the opposite shore, where that meadow now was, there had stood in those days a wood of tall birch trees, and that bare hill on the horizon yonder had been covered with the blue bloom of an ancient pine forest. And sailboats had plied the river then, but now all lay smooth and still, and only one little birch tree was left on the opposite bank, a graceful young thing, like a girl, while on the river there swam only ducks and geese. It was hard to believe that boats had once sailed there. It even seemed to him that there were fewer geese now than there had been. Jacob shut his eyes, and one by one white geese came flying toward him, an endless flock.

He was puzzled to know why he had never once been down to the river during the last forty or fifty years of his life, or, if he had been there, why he had never paid any attention to it. The stream was fine and large; he might have fished in it and sold the fish to the merchants and the government officials and the restaurant keeper at the station, and put the money in the bank. He might have rowed in a boat from farm to farm and played on his fiddle. People of every rank would have paid him money to hear him. He might have tried to run a boat on the river, that would have been better than making coffins. Finally, he might have raised geese, and killed them, and sent them to Moscow in the winter. Why, the down alone would have brought him ten roubles a year! But he had missed all these chances and had done nothing. What losses were here! Ah, what terrible losses! And, oh, if he had only done all these things at the same time! If he had only fished, and played the fiddle, and sailed a boat, and raised geese, what capital he would have had by now! But he had not even dreamed of doing all this; his life had gone by without profit or pleasure. It had been lost for a song. Nothing was left ahead; behind lay only losses, and such terrible losses that he shuddered to think of them. But why shouldn't men live so as to avoid all this waste and these losses? Why, oh, why, should those birch and pine forests have been felled? Why should those meadows be lying so deserted? Why did people always do exactly what they ought not to do? Why had Jacob scolded and growled and clenched his fists and hurt his wife's feelings all his life? Why, oh why, had he frightened and insulted that Jew just now? Why did people in general always interfere with one another? What losses resulted from this? What terrible losses! If it were not for envy and anger they would get great profit from one another.

All that evening and night Jacob dreamed of the child, of the willow tree, of the fish and the geese, of Martha with her profile like a thirsty bird, and of Rothschild's pale, piteous mien. Queer faces seemed to be moving toward him from all sides, muttering to him about his losses. He tossed from side to side and got up five times during the night to play his fiddle.

He rose with difficulty next morning, and walked to the hospital. The same doctor's assistant ordered him to put cold bandages on his head, and gave him little powders to take; by his expression and the tone of his voice Jacob knew that the state of affairs was bad, and that no powders could save him now. As he walked home he reflected that one good thing would result from his death: he would no longer have to eat and drink and pay taxes, neither would he offend people any more, and, as a man lies in his grave for hundreds of thousands of years, the sum of his profits would be immense. So, life to a man was a loss—death, a gain. Of course this reasoning was correct, but it was also distressingly sad. Why should the world be so strangely arranged that a man's life which was only given to him once must pass without profit?

He was not sorry then that he was going to die, but when he reached home, and saw his fiddle, his heart ached, and he regretted it deeply. He would not be able to take his fiddle with him into the grave, and now it would be left an orphan, and its fate would be that of the birch grove and the pine forest. Everything in the world had been lost, and would always be lost for ever. Jacob went out and sat on the threshold of his hut, clasping his fiddle to his breast. And as he thought of his life so full of waste and losses he began playing without knowing how piteous and touching his music was, and the tears streamed down his cheeks. And the more he thought the more sorrowfully sang his violin.

The latch clicked and Rothschild came in through the garden-gate, and walked boldly half-way across the garden. Then he suddenly stopped, crouched down, and, probably from fear, began making signs with his hands as if he were trying to show on his fingers what time it was.

"Come on, don't be afraid!" said Jacob gently, beckoning him to advance. "Come on!"

With many mistrustful and fearful glances Rothschild went slowly up to Jacob, and stopped about two yards away.

"Please don't beat me!" he said with a ducking bow. "Moses Shakess has sent me to you again. 'Don't be afraid,' he said, 'go to Jacob,' says he, 'and say that we can't possibly manage without him.' There is a wedding next Thursday. Ye-es, sir. Mr. Shapovaloff is marrying his daughter to a very fine man. It will be an expensive wedding, ai, ai!" added the Jew with a wink.

"I can't go" said Jacob breathing hard. "I'm ill, brother."

And he began to play again, and the tears gushed out of his eyes over his fiddle. Rothschild listened intently with his head turned away and his arms folded on his breast. The startled, irresolute look on his face gradually gave way to one of suffering and grief. He cast up his eyes as if in an ecstasy of agony and murmured: "Ou—ouch!" And the tears began to trickle slowly down his cheeks, and to drip over his green coat.

All day Jacob lay and suffered. When the priest came in the evening to administer the Sacrament he asked him if he could not think of any particular sin.

Struggling with his fading memories, Jacob recalled once more Martha's sad face, and the despairing cry of the Jew when the dog had bitten him. He murmured almost inaudibly:

"Give my fiddle to Rothschild."

"It shall be done," answered the priest.

So it happened that every one in the little town began asking:

"Where did Rothschild get that good fiddle? Did he buy it or steal it or get it out of a pawnshop?"

Rothschild has long since abandoned his flute, and now only plays on the violin. The same mournful notes flow from under his bow that used to come from his flute, and when he tries to repeat what Jacob played as he sat on the threshold of his hut, the result is an air so plaintive and sad that every one who hears him weeps, and he himself at last raises his eyes and murmurs: "Ou—ouch!" And this new song has so delighted the town that the merchants and government officials vie with each other in getting Rothschild to come to their houses, and sometimes make him play it ten times in succession.

Sholom Aleichem, Hebrew for "Peace be with you," was the
pen name of Solomon Rabinowitz, the so-called Jewish Mark
Twain. Like Twain he was a regionalist writer—sketching in Yid-
dish the lives of poor and oppressed Russian peasants at the turn
of the century. Leaving his native Russia and residing for a time
in Europe, he finally settled in New York City just two years before
his death. The popular Broadway musical *Fiddler on the Roof* is
based upon a number of his stories.

The Fiddle

by Sholom Aleichem
Translated by Julius and Frances Butwin

Today I'll play you something on the fiddle.
I don't know how you feel, but as for me, there is nothing more
wonderful than to be able to play a fiddle. As far back as I can
remember my heart has gone out to the fiddle. In fact, I loved
everything about music. Whenever there was a wedding in our
town I was the first one on hand to greet the musicians. I would
steal up behind the bass violin, pluck a string—boom!—and run
off. Boom—and run off again. For doing this I once caught the
devil from Berel Bass. Berel Bass, a fierce-looking man with a flat
nose and a sharp eye, pretended not to see me as I stole up behind
his bass violin. But just as I was stretching my hand out to pull
at the string he caught me by the ear and led me to the door with
a great show of courtesy.

"Don't forget to kiss the *mazuza* on your way out," he said.

But that experience taught me nothing. I couldn't stay away from musicians. I was in love with every one of them, from Shaike Fiddele, with his fine black beard and slim white fingers to round-shouldered Getzie Peikler with the big bald spot that reached down to his ears. Many a time when they chased me away, I hid myself under a bench and listened to them playing. From under the bench I watched Shaike's nimble fingers dancing over the strings and listened to the sweet tones that he so skillfully drew out of his little fiddle.

After that I would go around for days in a trance with Shaike and his fiddle constantly before my eyes and moving through my dreams at night. Pretending that I was Shaike, I would crook my left arm, move my fingers, and draw the right arm across as though I held a bow. All this while I threw my head to one side and dreamily shut my eyes. Just like Shaike. Exactly like him.

When the rabbi caught me—this was in *cheder*—drumming my fingers in the air, throwing my head back and rolling my eyes, he gave me a loud smack. "You rascal, you are supposed to be learning something, and here you are—fooling around—catching flies!"

I vowed to myself, "Let the world come to an end, I must have a fiddle. No matter what it costs, I must have one." But how do you make a fiddle? Naturally, of cedarwood. It is easy to say—cedarwood. But where do you get this wood that is supposed to grow only in the Holy Land? So what does God do? He gives me this idea: we had an old sofa at our house, an inheritance from my grandfather, Reb Anshel, over which my two uncles and my father had quarreled for a long time. My uncle Ben argued that he was the oldest son, therefore the sofa was his. Uncle Sender argued that he was the youngest, therefore the sofa belonged to him. My father admitted that he, being only a son-in-law, had no claim to the sofa, but since his wife, my mother, was my grandfather's only daughter, the sofa rightfully belonged to her. All this time the sofa remained at our house. But my two aunts, Aunt Itke and Aunt Zlatke, entered the feud. They carried their bickerings back and forth between them. The sofa this, the sofa that. Your sofa, my sofa. The whole town rocked with it. Meanwhile, the sofa remained our sofa.

This sofa of which I speak had a wooden frame with a thin veneer which was loose and puffed out in several places. Now this veneer, which was loose in spots, was the real cedarwood that fiddles are made of. That was what I had heard in *cheder*. The sofa had one drawback which was really a virtue. When you sat down on it you couldn't get up, because it sloped—there was a bulge on one end and a depression in the middle. This meant that no one wanted to sit on it. So it was put away in a corner and was pensioned off.

But now I began to cast an eye at this sofa. I had already arranged for a bow a long time ago. I had a friend, Yudel the teamster's Shimeleh, and he promised me as many hairs as I would need from the tail of his father's horse. And a piece of resin, to rub the bow with, I had all my own. I hated to rely on miracles. I got it in a trade with another friend of mine—Maier, Lippe-Sarah's boy—for a small piece of steel from my mother's old crinoline that had been lying up in the attic. Later, out of this piece of steel, Maier made himself a knife sharpened at both ends, and I was even ready to trade back with him, but he wouldn't think of it. He shouted at me:

"You think you're smart! You and your father, too! Here I go and work for three nights, sharpening and sharpening, and cut all my fingers, and you come around and want it back again!"

Well, I had everything. There was only one thing to do—to pick off enough of the cedar veneer from the sofa. And for that I chose a very good time—when my mother was out shopping and my father lay down for his afternoon nap. I crept into the corner with a big nail and began clawing away with real energy. In his sleep my father heard someone burrowing, and apparently thought it was a mouse. He began to hiss: "Shhh, shhhhh." I didn't move, I didn't breathe.

My father turned over on his other side and when I heard that he was snoring again I went back to my work. Suddenly I looked up—there stood my father, watching me with a puzzled look. At first he didn't seem to know what was going on, but when he saw the gouged-out sofa he dragged me out by the ear and shook me till I rattled. I thought I was going to faint.

"God help you—what are you doing to the child?" my mother screamed from the threshold.

"Your pride and joy! He's driving me into my grave!" gasped my father, pale as the white-washed wall, as he clasped at his heart and went into a coughing spell.

"Why do you eat yourself up like that?" asked my mother.

"You're sick enough without that. Just take a look at yourself, just look!"

The desire to play the fiddle grew as I grew. The older I grew, the more anxious I was to be able to play, and as if in spite I had to listen to music every day. Just about halfway between home and *cheder* there was a small sod-covered shack, and whenever you passed that shack you heard all sorts of sounds, the strains of all kinds of instruments, and especially the sound of a fiddle. It was the home of a musician, Naftaltzi Bezborodka, a Jew with a shortened coat, with clipped earlocks and with a starched collar. His nose was large and looked almost as if it were pasted on, his lips were thick, his teeth black, his face was pockmarked and without the trace of a beard. And that was why they called him Bezborodka, the beardless one. His wife was a crone who was known as Mother Eve, and they had at least a dozen and half children—tattered, half-naked, barefoot, and every one of them, from the oldest to the youngest, played on some instrument—this one the fiddle, that one the cello, the other the bass, one the trumpet, another the flute, the bassoon, the harp, the cymbal, the balalaika, the drum. Some of them could whistle the most complicated melody with their lips, or through their teeth, on glass tumblers or pots, or on pieces of wood. They were magicians—or devils of some sort!

With this family I became acquainted in a most unexpected way. I was standing under their window one day, drinking in the music, when one of the boys caught sight of me and came out. He was Pinny, the flutist, a boy about fifteen, but barefoot like the rest.

"What do you think of the music?" he asked.

"I wish I could play that well in ten years," I told him.

"You can," he said, and explained that for two *rubles* a month his father would teach me to play. Or, if I wanted, he himself would teach me.

"What instrument would you like to play?" he asked. "The fiddle?"

"The fiddle," I said.

"The fiddle," he repeated. "Could you pay a *ruble* and a half a month—or are you as penniless as I am?"

"I can pay," I told him. "But there is one thing. Neither my father nor my mother nor my rabbi must know a thing about it."

"God forbid!" he exclaimed. "Why should anyone find out?" He moved up closer to me and whispered, "Have you got a cigar butt—or a cigarette?" I shook my head. "No? You don't smoke? Well, then, lend me a few *groschen* so I can buy some cigarettes. But don't tell anybody. My father doesn't know that I smoke, and if my mother found out she'd take the money away and buy some bread."

He took the money and said in a friendly voice, "Come on in. You'll get nothing done standing out here."

With great fear, my heart pounding and my legs trembling, I crossed the threshold of this small paradise.

My new friend Pinny introduced me to his father. "This is Sholom—Nochem-Vevik's. A rich man's son . . . He wants to learn to play the fiddle."

Naftaltzi Bezborodka pulled at his earlock, straightened his collar, and buttoned up his coat. Then he began a long and detailed lecture on the subject of music in general and fiddle-playing in particular. He gave me to understand that the fiddle was the best and finest of all instruments—there was no instrument that ranked higher. Else why is the fiddle the chief instrument in an orchestra, and not the trombone or the flute? Because the fiddle is the mother of all instruments . . .

Thus Naftaltzi spoke, accompanying his words with motions of his hands and large nose. I stood gaping at him, swallowing every word that came out.

"The fiddle," Naftaltzi continued, apparently pleased with his lecture, "the fiddle, you understand, is an instrument that is older than all other instruments. The first fiddler in the world was Tubal Cain or Methuselah, I am not sure which. You may know, you study such things in *cheder*. The second fiddler was King David. The third, a man named Paganini, also a Jew. The best fiddlers have always been Jews. I can name you a dozen. Not to mention myself . . . They say I don't play badly, but how can I compare myself to Paganini? Paganini, we are told, sold his soul to the devil for a fiddle. He never would play for the great of the world—the kings and the princes—no matter how much they gave him. He preferred to play for the common people in the taverns and the villages, or even in the woods for the beasts and birds. Ah, what a fiddler Paganini was!"

Suddenly he turned around: "Fellow artists—to your instruments!"

Thus Naftaltzi called out to his band of children, who gathered about him immediately, each with his own instrument. Naftaltzi himself struck the table with his bow, threw a sharp look at each child separately and at all of them at once, and the concert began. They went at it with such fury that I was almost knocked off my feet. Each one tried to outdo the other, but loudest of all played a little boy named Chemeleh, a thin child with a running nose and bare spindly legs. Chemeleh played a strange instrument—some sort of a sack—and when he blew, it gave out an unearthly shriek, like a cat when its tail is stepped on. With his bare foot Chemeleh marked time and all the while watched me out of his small impish eyes and winked at me as if to say, "I am doing well, ain't I?" . . . But hardest of all worked Naftaltzi himself. He both played and conducted, working with his hands, his feet, his nose, his eyes, his whole body; and if anyone made a mistake, he gritted his teeth and yelled out:

"*Forte,* you fool! *Forte, fortissimo!* Count, stupid—count! One, two, three! One, two, three!"

I arranged with Naftaltzi Bezborodka to take three lessons a week, an hour and a half each time, for two *rubles* a month. I begged him over and over to keep this a secret, or I would get into trouble. He gave me his word of honor that he would breathe it to no one.

"We are people," he said gravely, adjusting his collar, "of small means, but when it comes to honor and integrity, we have more than the richest of the rich. By the way—can you spare me a few *groschen?*"

I pulled a *ruble* out of my pocket. Naftaltzi took it from me like a professor—very refined—with the tips of his fingers. Then he called Mother Eve, and hardly looking at her, said, "Here, get something for dinner."

Mother Eve took the money from him with both hands and every one of her fingers, inspected it carefully, and said, "What shall I buy?"

"Anything you want," he said with a show of indifference. "Get a few rolls—two or three herring—a sausage. And don't forget—an onion, some vinegar and oil—and, maybe, a bottle of brandy . . ."

When the food was laid out on the table the crowd fell on it with such gusto as after a fast. Watching them made me so ravenous that when they asked me to join them I couldn't refuse. And I don't know when I enjoyed any food as much as I did that meal.

126

When we were through, Bezborodka winked at the crowd, signaled for them to reach for their instruments, and I was treated to another concert, this time an "original composition." This they played with such verve and spirit that my ears rang and my head swam and I left the house drunk with Naftaltzi Bezborodka's "composition."

All that day in *cheder* the rabbi, the boys and the books all danced before my eyes and the music rang incessantly in my ears. At night I dreamed of Paganini riding the devil. He hit me over the head with his fiddle. I woke screaming, my head splitting, and I began to babble—I don't know what. Later my older sister Pessel told me that I was out of my head. What I said made no sense— crazy words like "composition," "Paganini," "the devil" . . . Another thing my sister told me was that while I was sick someone came to ask about me—somebody from Naftaltzi the musician—a barefoot boy. He was chased away and told never to come back.

"What did that fiddler's boy want from you?" my sister nagged, but I held my tongue.

"I don't know. I don't know a thing. What are you talking about?"

"How does it look?" my mother said. "You are a grown boy already—we are trying to arrange a match for you—and you pick yourself friends like these. Barefoot fiddlers! What have you got to do with musicians anyway? What did Naftaltzi's boy want of you?"

"Which Naftaltzi?" I asked innocently. "What musicians?"

"Look at him!" my father broke in. "He doesn't know a thing. Poor little fellow! At your age I was engaged a long time already, and you are still playing games with children. Get dressed and go to *cheder*. And if you meet Hershel Beltax on the way and he asks what was the matter with you, tell him you had a fever. Do you hear what I said? A fever."

I didn't begin to understand. What did I have to do with Hershel Beltax? And why did I have to tell him about a fever? In a few weeks my question was answered.

Hershel Beltax (he was called that because he and his father and his grandfather had all worked for the tax collector) was a man with a round little belly, a short red beard, small moist eyes and a broad white forehead—the mark of a wise man. He had the reputation in town of being an intelligent man, accomplished and learned—up to a certain point—in the *Torah*. He was a fine writer—that is, he had a clear handwriting. It was said that at one time his writings were known all over the countryside. And besides that he had money and a daughter, an only daughter, with red hair and moist eyes— the exact image of him. Her name was Esther, she was called by a nickname—Flesterl. She was timid and delicate, and terribly afraid of us schoolboys because we teased her all the time. When we met her we sang this song:

> *Esther, Flester,*
> *Where is your sister?*

What was so terrible about that? Nothing, it seemed to me, and yet when Esther heard it she covered her ears and ran off crying. She would hide in her room and not go out on the street for days.

But that was a long time ago when she was a child. Now she was a grown girl with long red braids and went about dressed in the latest fashion. My mother was very fond of her. "Gentle as a dove," she used to say. Sometimes on Saturday Esther used to come to visit my sister and when she saw me she would turn even redder than she was and drop her eyes. And my sister would call me over and start asking me questions—and watch us both to see how we acted.

One day—into the *cheder* walked my father with Hershel Beltax, and behind them trailed Reb Sholom-Shachne, the matchmaker, a man with a curly black beard, a man with six fingers, as people used to say. Seeing such guests, the rabbi, Reb Zorach, grabbed his coat and put on his hat in such a hurry that one of his earlocks was caught behind his ear, and his skullcap stuck out from under his hat, and his cheeks began to flame. We could see that something unusual was about to happen. Lately Reb Sholom-Shachne the matchmaker had been coming to the *cheder* frequently and each time he came he called the rabbi out of the room and there through the doorway we could see them whispering together, shrugging their shoulders, gesturing with their hands—ending up with a sigh.

"Well, it's the same old story. If it's to be, it will be. Regardless."

Now when these guests came in, the rabbi, Reb Zorach, was so confused he didn't know what to do or where to seat them. He grabbed hold of a low bench on which his wife used to salt the meat, and carried it around the room with him, till he finally put it down and sat on it himself. But he quickly jumped up and said to his guests, "Here is a bench. Won't you sit down?"

"That's all right, Reb Zorach," said my father. "We just came in

for a minute. We'd like to hear my son recite something—out of the Bible." And he inclined his head toward Hershel Beltax.

"Surely, why not?" said the rabbi, and picking up the Bible he handed it to Hershel Beltax, with a look that said, "Here—do what you can with it."

Hershel Beltax took the Bible like a man who knew what he was doing, bent his head sideways, shut one eye, shuffled the pages and handed it to me open at the first paragraph of the *Song of Songs*.

"The *Song of Songs?*" said Reb Zorach with a smile, as though to say, "You couldn't find something harder?" "The *Song of Songs,*" says Hershel Beltax, "is not as easy as you think. One has to understand it."

"That's not a lie," said Reb Sholom-Shachne, the matchmaker, with a laugh.

The rabbi beckons to me. I walk up to the table, and begin to chant in a loud voice, with a fine rhythm:

"The *Song of Songs!* A song above all other songs. Other songs have been sung by a prophet, but this song was sung by a prophet who was the son of a prophet. Other songs have been sung by a sage, but this was sung by a sage who was the son of a sage. Other songs have been sung by a king. This was sung by a king who was the son of a king."

While I sang I watched my examiners and saw on the face of each of them a different expression. On my father's face I saw great pride and joy. On the rabbi's face was fear lest I make a mistake. His lips silently repeated each word. Hershel Beltax sat with his head bent sideways, his beard between his lips, one eye shut, and the other raised aloft, listening with a very knowing look. Reb Sholom-Shachne the matchmaker did not take his eyes off Hershel Beltax the whole time. He sat with his body bent forward, swaying back and forth along with me, interrupting me with a sound that was part exclamation, part laugh, part a cough, pointing his fingers at me:

"When I said he knew it I really meant he knew it."

A few weeks later plates were broken, and I became engaged to Hershel Beltax's daughter, Flesterl.

Sometimes it happens that a person ages more in one day than in ten years. When I became engaged I suddenly felt grown up— seemingly the same boy and yet not the same. From the smallest boy to the rabbi himself they all treated me with respect. After all, I was a young man engaged to be married—and I had a watch! No longer did my father scold me—and as for whippings—that was out of the question. How could you whip a young man who wore a gold watch? It would be a shame and a disgrace. Once a boy named Eli who, like me, was engaged to be married, received a whipping in *cheder* because he was caught skating on the ice with some peasant boys. The whole town talked about it, and when his fiancée learned of the scandal she cried so long that her parents broke the engagement. And the young man, Eli, was so heartbroken and so ashamed that he wanted to throw himself into the river. Fortunately, the water was frozen over . . .

Such a calamity befell me, too, but not over a whipping, and not over skating on ice, but over a fiddle. And here is the story:

In our tavern we had a frequent guest, Tchetchek, the bandleader, whom we called Colonel. He was a strapping fellow, tall, with a large, round beard and sinister eyebrows. His speech was a mixture of several languages, and when he spoke he moved his eyebrows up and down. When he lowered his eyebrows his face became black as night, and when he raised them, his face glowed like the sun, because under those thick eyebrows were a pair of eyes that were bright blue and full of laughter. He wore a uniform with gold buttons and that was why we called him Colonel. He came to our tavern frequently—not because he was a heavy drinker, but because my father used to make a raisin wine—"the best—and rarest—Hungarian wine" that Tchetchek could hardly praise enough. He would put his enormous hand on my father's thin shoulder and roar in his queer mixed language:

"Herr Kellermeister, you have the best Hungarian wine in the world. There is no such wine even in Budapest, *predbozhe.*"

Tchetchek was very friendly with me. He praised me for my stories and liked to ask questions like: "Who was Adam? Who was Isaac? Who was Joseph?"

"You mean—*Yosef?*" I would say.

"I mean Joseph."

"*Yosef,*" I corrected him again.

"To us he is Joseph, to you he is *Yosef,*" he would say and pinch my cheek. "Joseph or *Yosef, Yosef* or Joseph, it's all the same, all equal—*wszystko yedno.*"

But when I became engaged Tchetchek's attitude also changed. Instead of treating me like a child he began to talk to me as to an equal, to tell me stories of the army and of musicians. (The Colonel had wonderful stories to tell but no one had time to listen except me.) Once, when he was talking about music, I questioned him, "What instrument does the Colonel play?"

"All instruments," he said, and raised his eyebrows.

"The fiddle too?" I asked, and his face became in my eyes the face of an angel.

"Come to my house some day," he said, "and I will play for you."

"I can only come on the Sabbath. But please, Colonel, no one must know." *"Przed bohem,"* he said fervently and raised his eyebrows.

Tchetchek lived far off beyond the town in a small white cottage with small windows and brightly painted shutters, surrounded by a garden full of bright, yellow sunflowers that carried themselves as proudly as lilies or roses. They bent their heads a little, swayed in the breeze and beckoned to me, "Come to us, young man, come to us. Here is space, here is freedom, here it is bright and fresh, warm and cheerful." And after the stench and heat and dust of the town, the noise and turmoil of the crowded *cheder,* I was glad to come, for here was space and freedom, here it was bright and fresh, warm and cheerful. I felt like running, leaping, yelling, singing, or like throwing myself on the ground with my face deep in the fragrant grass. But that is not for you, Jewish children. Yellow sunflowers, green grass, fresh air, the clean earth, the clear sky, these are not for you . . .

When I came to the gate the first time, I was met by a shaggy, black dog with fiery, red eyes, who jumped at me with such force that I was almost knocked over. Luckily he was tied to a rope. When Tchetchek heard me yell he came running out of the house, without his uniform on, and told the dog to be quiet. Then he took me by the hand and led me up to the black dog. He told me not to be afraid. "Here, pat him—he won't hurt you." And taking my hand he passed it over the dog's fur, calling him odd names in a kindly voice. The dog dropped his tail, licked himself all over and gave me a look that said, "Lucky for you my master is standing here, or you would be leaving without a hand."

Having recovered from my fright, I entered the house with the Colonel and there I was struck dumb; all the walls were covered with guns, and on the floor lay a skin with the head of a lion— or maybe a leopard—with fierce teeth. The lion didn't bother me so much—he was dead. But those guns—all those guns! I didn't enjoy the fresh plums and juicy apples with which my host treated me. I couldn't keep my eyes away from the walls. But later, when Tchetchek took out of its red case a small round fiddle with an odd belly, spread over it his large round beard and placed on it his huge powerful hand and passed the bow over it a few times, and the first melody poured out, I forgot in one instant the black dog, the fierce lion and the loaded guns. I saw only Tchetchek's spreading beard, his overhanging eyebrows, I saw only a round fiddle with an odd belly, and fingers which danced over the strings with such speed that it was hard to imagine where so many fingers came from.

Then Tchetchek himself disappeared—with his spreading beard, his thick eyebrows, and his wonderful fingers—and I saw nothing in front of me. I only heard a singing, a sighing, a weeping, a sobbing, a talking, a roaring—all sorts of strange sounds that I had never heard in my life before. Sounds sweet as honey, smooth as oil, kept pouring without end straight into my heart, and my soul soared far far away into another world, into a paradise of pure sound.

"Would you like some tea?" calls out Tchetchek, putting down the fiddle and slapping me on the back.

I felt as though I had fallen from the seventh heaven down to earth again.

After that I visited Tchetchek every Saturday to listen to his playing. I went straight to the house, not afraid of anyone, and I even became so familiar with the black dog that he would wag his tail when he saw me, and try to lick my hand. But I wouldn't allow that. "Let's be friends at a distance," I said.

At home no one knew where I spent my Saturdays. No one stopped me. After all, I was not a child any more.

And they wouldn't have known until now if a fresh calamity had not occurred—a great calamity which I shall now describe.

Who should care if a young fellow takes a Sabbath walk by himself a short distance out of town? Whose business is it? Apparently there are people who care, and one such person was Ephraim Klotz, a busybody who knew what was cooking in every pot. He made it his business to know. This man watched me closely, followed me, found out where I was going, and later swore with many pious oaths that he had seen me at the Colonel's house eating pork and smoking cigarettes on the Sabbath.

Every Saturday when I was on my way to Tchetchek's I would meet him on the bridge, walking along in a sleeveless, patched, summer coat that reached to his ankles. He walked with his arms folded behind him, his overcoat flapping, humming to himself in a thin voice.

"A good Sabbath," I would say to him.

"Good Sabbath," he would reply. "Where is the young man going?"

"Just for a walk," I said.

"For a walk? Alone?" he repeated, with a meaningful smile . . .

One afternoon when I was sitting with Tchetchek and drinking tea, we heard the dog barking and tearing at his rope. Looking out of the window, I thought I saw someone small and dark with short legs running out of sight. From his way of running I could swear it was Ephraim Klotz.

That night, when I got home, I saw Ephraim Klotz sitting at the table. He was talking with great animation and laughing his odd little laugh that sounded like dried peas pouring out of a dish. Seeing me, he fell silent and began to drum with his short fingers on the table. Opposite him sat my father, his face pale, twisting his beard and tearing hairs out one by one—a sign that he was angry.

"Where are you coming from?" asked my father, with a glance at Ephraim Klotz.

"Where should I be coming from?" I said.

"Where have you been all day?" said my father.

"Where should I be all day? In *shul*."

"What did you do there all day?"

"What should I be doing there? Studying . . ."

"What were you studying?" said my father.

"What should I be studying? The *Gamorah* . . ."

"Which *Gamorah*?" said my father.

At this point Ephraim Klotz laughed his shrill laugh and my father could stand it no more. He rose from his seat and leaning over, gave me two resounding, fiery slaps in the face. My mother heard the commotion from the next room and came running in . . .

"Nochem," she cried, "God be with you! What are you doing? The boy is engaged to be married. Suppose his father-in-law hears of this?"

My mother was right. My future father-in-law heard the whole story. Ephraim repeated it to him himself. It was too good to keep.

The next day the engagement was broken and I was a privileged person no more. My father was so upset that he became ill and stayed in bed for days. He would not let me come near him, no matter how much my mother pleaded for me.

"The shame of it," he said. "The disgrace. That is worst of all."

"Forget about it," my mother begged. "God will send us another match. Our lives won't be ruined by this. Perhaps it was not his lot."

Among those who came to visit my father while he was ill was the bandmaster. When my father saw him, he took off his skullcap, sat up in bed, and extending an emaciated hand, said to him:

"Ah, Colonel, Colonel . . ."

More he could not say because his voice became choked with tears and he was seized with a fit of coughing. This was the first time in my life that I had seen my father cry. My heart ached and my soul went out to him. I stood staring out of the window, swallowing tears. How I regretted the trouble I had caused!

Silently I swore to myself never, never to disobey my father again, never to cause him such grief, never in this world.

No more fiddles.

Some three years after the publication of *Moby Dick,* "The Fiddler" (1854) appeared in *Harper's New Monthly Magazine.* The story alludes to an actual violinist, one Joseph Burke, who, as a child prodigy in Britain and America, made an early sensation before lapsing into forgotten obscurity in Albany, New York. As Helmstone his narrator, Melville was himself deeply concerned with public approval for his work. "The Fiddler" is a parable of artistic reconciliation to the inevitable capriciousness of mass opinion and taste.

The Fiddler

by Herman Melville

So my poem is damned, and immortal fame is not for me! I am nobody forever and ever. Intolerable fate!

Snatching my hat, I dashed down the criticism and rushed out into Broadway, where enthusiastic throngs were crowding to a circus in a side-street near by, very recently started, and famous for a capital clown.

Presently my old friend Standard rather boisterously accosted me.

"Well met, Helmstone, my boy! Ah! what's the matter? Haven't been committing murder? Ain't flying justice? You look wild!"

"You have seen it, then!" said I, of course referring to the criticism.

"Oh, yes; I was there at the morning performance. Great clown, I assure you. But here comes Hautboy. Hautboy—Helmstone."

Without having time or inclination to resent so mortifying a mistake, I was instantly soothed as I gazed on the face of the new acquaintance so unceremoniously introduced. His person was short and full, with a juvenile, animated cast to it. His complexion rurally ruddy; his eye sincere, cheery, and gray. His hair alone betrayed that he was not an overgrown boy. From his hair I set him down as forty or more.

"Come, Standard," he gleefully cried to my friend, "are you not going to the circus? The clown is inimitable, they say. Come, Mr. Helmstone, too—come both; and circus over, we'll take a nice stew and punch at Taylor's"

The sterling content, good-humor, and extraordinary ruddy, sincere expression of this most singular new acquaintance acted upon me like magic. It seemed mere loyalty to human nature to accept an invitation from so unmistakably kind and honest a heart.

During the circus performance I kept my eye more on Hautboy than on the celebrated clown. Hautboy was the sight for me. Such genuine enjoyment as his struck me to the soul with a sense of the reality of the thing called happiness. The jokes of the clown he seemed to roll under his tongue as ripe magnum bonums. Now the foot, now the hand, was employed to attest his grateful applause. At any hit more than ordinary, he turned upon Standard and me to see if his rare pleasure was shared. In a man of forty I saw a boy of twelve; and this too without the slightest abatement of my respect. Because all was so honest and natural, every expression and attitude so graceful with genuine good-nature, that the marvelous juvenility of Hautboy assumed a sort of divine and immortal air, like that of some forever youthful god of Greece.

But much as I gazed upon Hautboy, and much as I admired his air, yet that desperate mood in which I had first rushed from the house had not so entirely departed as not to molest me with momentary returns. But from these relapses I would rouse myself, and swiftly glance round the broad amphitheatre of eagerly interested and all-applauding human faces. Hark! claps, thumps, deafening huzzas; the vast assembly seemed frantic with acclamation; and what, mused I, has caused all this? Why, the clown only comically grinned with one of his extra grins.

Then I repeated in my mind that sublime passage in my poem, in which Cleothemes the Argive vindicates the justice of the war.

Ay, ay, thought I to myself, did I now leap into the ring there, and repeat that identical passage, nay, enact the whole tragic poem before them, would they applaud the poet as they applaud the clown? No! They would hoot me, and call me doting or mad. Then what does this prove? Your infatuation or their insensibility? Perhaps both; but indubitably the first. But why wail? Do you seek admiration from the admirers of a buffoon? Call to mind the saying of the Athenian, who, when the people vociferously applauded in the forum, asked his friend in a whisper, what foolish thing had he said?

Again my eye swept the circus, and fell on the ruddy radiance of the countenance of Hautboy. But its clear honest cheeriness disdained my disdain. My intolerant pride was rebuked. And yet Hautboy dreamed not what magic reproof to a soul like mine sat on his laughing brow. At the very instant I felt the dart of the censure, his eye twinkled, his hand waved, his voice was lifted in jubilant delight at another joke of the inexhaustible clown.

Circus over, we went to Taylor's. Among crowds of others, we sat down to our stews and punches at one of the small marble tables. Hautboy sat opposite to me. Though greatly subdued from its former hilarity, his face still shone with gladness. But added to this was a quality not so prominent before; a certain serene expression of leisurely, deep good sense. Good sense and good humor in him joined hands. As the conversation proceeded between the brisk Standard and him—for I said little or nothing—I was more and more struck with the excellent judgment he evinced. In most of his remarks upon a variety of topics Hautboy seemed intuitively to hit the exact line between enthusiasm and apathy. It was plain that while Hautboy saw the world pretty much as it was, yet he did not theoretically espouse its bright side nor its dark side. Rejecting all solutions, he but acknowledged facts. What was sad in the world he did not superficially gainsay; what was glad in it he did not cynically slur; and all which was to him personally enjoyable, he gratefully took to his heart. It was plain, then—so it seemed at that moment, at least—that his extraordinary cheerfulness did not arise either from deficiency of feeling or thought.

Suddenly remembering an engagement, he took up his hat, bowed pleasantly, and left us.

"Well, Helmstone," said Standard, inaudibly drumming on the slab, "what do you think of your new acquaintance?"

The last two words tingled with a peculiar and novel significance.

"New acquaintance indeed," echoed I. "Standard, I owe you a thousand thanks for introducing me to one of the most singular men I have ever seen. It needed the optical sight of such a man to believe in the possibility of his existence."

"You rather like him, then," said Standard, with ironical dryness.

"I hugely love and admire him, Standard. I wish I were Hautboy."

"Ah? That's a pity now. There's only one Hautboy in the world."

This last remark set me to pondering again, and somehow it revived my dark mood.

"His wonderful cheerfulness, I suppose," said I, sneering with spleen, "originates not less in a felicitous fortune than in a felicitous temper. His great good sense is apparent; but great good sense may exist without sublime endowments. Nay, I take it, in certain cases, that good sense is simply owing to the absence of those. Much more, cheerfulness. Unpossessed of genius, Hautboy is eternally blessed."

"Ah? You would not think him an extraordinary genius then?"

"Genius? What! Such a short, fat fellow a genius! Genuis, like Cassius, is lank."

"Ah? But could you not fancy that Hautboy might formerly have had genius, but luckily getting rid of it, at last fatted up?"

"For a genius to get rid of his genius is as impossible as for a man in the galloping consumption to get rid of that."

"Ah? You speak very decidedly."

"Yes, Standard," cried I, increasing in spleen, "your cheery Hautboy, after all, is no pattern, no lesson for you and me. With average abilities; opinions clear, because circumscribed; passions docile, because they are feeble; a temper hilarious, because he was born to it—how can your Hautboy be made a reasonable example to a heady fellow like you, or an ambitious dreamer like me? Nothing tempts him beyond common limit; in himself he has nothing to restrain. By constitution he is exempted from all moral harm. Could ambition but prick him; had he but once heard applause, or endured contempt, a very different man would your Hautboy be. Acquiescent and calm from the cradle to the grave, he obviously slides through the crowd."

"Ah?"

"Why do you say *ah* to me so strangely whenever I speak?"

"Did you ever hear of Master Betty?"

"The great English prodigy, who long ago ousted the Siddons

and the Kembles from Drury Lane, and made the whole town run mad with acclamation?"

"The same," said Standard, once more inaudibly drumming on the slab.

I looked at him perplexed. He seemed to be holding the master-key of our theme in mysterious reserve; seemed to be throwing out his Master Betty too, to puzzle me only the more.

"What under heaven can Master Betty, the great genius and prodigy, an English boy twelve years old, have to do with the poor commonplace plodder Hautboy, an American of forty?"

"Oh, nothing in the least. I don't imagine that they ever saw each other. Besides, Master Betty must be dead and buried long ere this."

"Then why cross the ocean, and rifle the grave to drag his remains into this living discussion?"

"Absent-mindedness, I suppose. I humbly beg pardon. Proceed with your observations on Hautboy. You think he never had genius, quite too contented and happy, and fat for that—ah? You think him no pattern for men in general? affording no lesson of value to neglected merit, genius ignored, or impotent presumption rebuked?—all of which three amount to much the same thing. You admire his cheerfulness, while scorning his commonplace soul. Poor Hautboy, how sad that your very cheerfulness should, by a by-blow, bring you despite!"

"I don't say I scorn him; you are unjust. I simply declare that he is no pattern for me."

A sudden noise at my side attracted my ear. Turning, I saw Hautboy again, who very blithely reseated himself on the chair he had left.

"I was behind time with my engagement," said Hautboy, "so thought I would run back and rejoin you. But come, you have sat long enough here. Let us go to my rooms. It is only five minutes' walk."

"If you will promise to fiddle for us, we will," said Standard.

Fiddle! thought I—he's a jigembob *fiddler* then? No wonder genius declines to measure its pace to a fiddler's bow. My spleen was very strong on me now.

"I will gladly fiddle you your fill," replied Hautboy to Standard. "Come on."

In a few minutes we found ourselves in the fifth story of a sort of storehouse, in a lateral street to Broadway. It was curiously furnished with all sorts of odd furniture which seemed to have been obtained, piece by piece, at the auctions of old-fashioned household stuff. But all was charmingly clean and cosy.

Pressed by Standard, Hautboy forthwith got out his dented old fiddle, and sitting down on a tall rickety stool, played away right merrily at Yankee Doodle and other off-handed, dashing, and disdainfully care-free airs. But common as were the tunes, I was transfixed by something miraculously superior in the style. Sitting there on the old stool, his rusty hat sideways cocked on his head, one foot dangling adrift, he plied the bow of an enchanter. All my moody discontent, every vestige of peevishness fled. My whole splenetic soul capitulated to the magical fiddle.

"Something of an Orpheus, ah?" said Standard, archly nudging me beneath the left rib.

"And I, the charmed Bruin," murmured I.

The fiddle ceased. Once more, with redoubled curiosity, I gazed upon the easy, indifferent Hautboy. But he entirely baffled inquisition.

When, leaving him, Standard and I were in the street once more, I earnestly conjured him to tell me who, in sober truth, this marvelous Hautboy was.

"Why, haven't you seen him? And didn't you yourself lay his whole anatomy open on the marble slab at Taylor's? What more can you possibly learn? Doubtless your own masterly insight has already put you in possession of all."

"You mock me, Standard. There is some mystery here. Tell me, I entreat you, who is Hautboy?"

"An extraordinary genius, Helmstone," said Standard, with sudden ardor, "who in boyhood drained the whole flagon of glory; whose going from city to city was a going from triumph to triumph. One who has been an object of wonder to the wisest, been caressed by the loveliest, received the open homage of thousands on thousands of the rabble. But today he walks Broadway and no man knows him. With you and me, the elbow of the hurrying clerk, and the pole of the remorseless omnibus, shove him. He who has a hundred times been crowned with laurels, now wears, as you see, a bunged beaver. Once fortune poured showers of gold into his lap, as showers of laurel leaves upon his brow. To-day, from house to house he hies, teaching fiddling for a living. Crammed once with fame, he is now hilarious without it. *With* genius and *without* fame, he is happier than a king. More a prodigy now than ever."

"His true name?"

"Let me whisper it in your ear."

"What! Oh, Standard, myself, as a child, have shouted myself hoarse applauding that very name in the theatre."

"I have heard your poem was not very handsomely received," said Standard, now suddenly shifting the subject.

"Not a word of that, for heaven's sake!" cried I. "If Cicero, traveling in the East, found sympathetic solace for his grief in beholding the arid overthrow of a once gorgeous city, shall not my petty affair be as nothing, when I behold in Hautboy the vine and the rose climbing the shattered shafts of his tumbled temple of Fame?"

Next day I tore all my manuscripts, bought me a fiddle, and went to take regular lessons of Hautboy.

Thomas Bailey Aldrich succeeded William Dean Howells as editor of the *Atlantic Monthly*. Aldrich's most remembered work today is *The Story of a Bad Boy* (1870), based on childhood experiences. "The Little Violinist" (1874), from *Marjorie Daw and Other Stories,* was printed to sell at a fair for the benefit of the Massachusetts Society for the Prevention of Cruelty to Children. This "sketch," as Aldrich called it, counterpoints a child's view of a desirable and romantic fantasy world with a more realistic adult understanding of destructive materialistic exploitation.

The Little Violinist

by Thomas Bailey Aldrich

> Weep with me, all you that read
>   This little story;
> And know, for whom a tear you shed,
>   Death's self is sorry.
>
> BEN JONSON

This story is no invention of mine. I could not invent anything half so lovely and pathetic as seems to me the incident which has come ready-made to my hand.

Some of you, doubtless, have heard of James Speaight, the infant violinist, or Young Americus, as he was called. He was born in London, I believe, and was only four years old when his father brought him to this country, less than three years ago. Since that time he has appeared in concerts and various entertainments in many of our principal cities, attracting unusual attention by his musical skill. I confess, however, that I had not heard of him until last month, though it seems he had previously given two or three public performances in the city where I live. I had not heard of him, I say, until last month; but since then I do not think a day has passed when this child's face has not risen up in my memory—the little half-sad face, as I saw it once, with its large, serious eyes and infantile mouth.

I have, I trust, great tenderness for all children; but I know that I have a special place in my heart for those poor little creatures who figure in circuses and shows, or elsewhere, as "infant prodigies." Heaven help such little folk! It was an unkind fate that did not make them commonplace, stupid, happy girls and boys like our own Fannys and Charleys and Harrys. Poor little waifs, that never know any babyhood or childhood—sad human midges, that flutter for a moment in the glare of the gaslights, and are gone. Pitiful little children, whose tender limbs and minds are so torn and strained by thoughtless task-masters, that it seems scarcely a regrettable thing when the circus caravan halts awhile on its route to make a small grave by the wayside.

I never witness a performance of child-acrobats, or the exhibition of any forced talent, physical or mental, on the part of children, without protesting, at least in my own mind, against the blindness and cruelty of their parents or guardians, or whoever has care of them.

I saw at the theatre, the other night, two tiny girls—mere babies they were—doing such feats upon a bar of wood suspended from the ceiling as made my blood run cold. They were twin sisters, these mites, with that old young look on their faces which all such unfortunates have. I hardly dared glance at them, up there in the air, hanging by their feet from the swinging bar, twisting their fragile spines and distorting their poor little bodies, when they ought to have been nestled in soft blankets in a cosy chamber, with the angels that guard the sleep of little children hovering above them. I hope that the father of those two babies will read and ponder this page, on which I record not alone my individual protest, but the protest of hundreds of men and women who took no pleasure in that performance, but witnessed it with a pang of pity.

There is a Society for the Prevention of Cruelty to Dumb Animals. There ought to be a Society for the Prevention of Cruelty to Little Children; and a certain influential gentleman, who does some things well and other things very badly, ought to attend to it. The name of this gentleman is Public Opinion.

But to my story.

One September morning, about five years and a half ago, there wandered to my fireside, hand in hand, two small personages who requested in a foreign language, which I understood at once, to be taken in and fed and clothed and sent to school and loved and tenderly cared for. Very modest of them—was it not?—in view of the fact that I had never seen either of them before. To all intents and purposes they were perfect strangers to *me*. What was my surprise when it turned out (just as if it were in a fairy legend) that these were my own sons! When I say they came hand in hand, it is to advise you that these two boys were twins, like that pair of tiny girls I just mentioned.

These young gentlemen are at present known as Charley and Talbot, in the household, and to a very limited circle of acquaintances outside; but as Charley has declared his intention to become a circus-rider, and Talbot, who has not so soaring an ambition, has resolved to be a policeman, it is likely the world will hear of them before long. In the meantime, and with a view to the severe duties of the professions selected, they are learning the alphabet, Charley vaulting over the hard letters with an agility which promises well for his career as circus-rider, and Talbot collaring the slippery S's and pursuing the suspicious X Y Z's with the promptness and boldness of a night-watchman.

Now it is my pleasure not only to feed and clothe Masters Charley and Talbot as if they were young princes or dukes, but to look to it that they do not wear out their ingenious minds by too much study. So I occasionally take them to a puppet-show or a musical entertainment, and always in holiday time to see a pantomime. This last is their especial delight. It is a fine thing to behold the businesslike air with which they climb into their seats in the parquet, and the gravity with which they immediately begin to read the play-bill upside down. Then, between the acts, the solemnity with which they extract the juice from an orange, through a hole made with a lead-pencil, is also a noticeable thing.

Their knowledge of the mysteries of Fairyland is at once varied and profound. Everything delights, but nothing astonishes them. That people covered with spangles should dive headlong through the floor; that fairy queens should step out of the trunks of trees; that the poor wood-cutter's cottage should change, in the twinkling of an eye, into a glorious palace or a goblin grotto under the sea, with crimson fountains and golden staircases and silver foliage— all that is a matter of course. This is the kind of world they live in at present. If these things happened at home they would not be astonished.

The other day, it was just before Christmas, I saw the boys attentively regarding a large pumpkin which lay on the kitchen floor, waiting to be made into pies. If that pumpkin had suddenly opened, if wheels had sprouted out on each side, and if the two kittens playing with an onion-skin by the range had turned into milk-white ponies and harnessed themselves to this Cinderella coach, neither Charley nor Talbot would have considered it an unusual circumstance.

The pantomime which is usually played at the Boston Theatre during the holidays is to them positive proof that the stories of Cinderella and Jack of the Beanstalk and Jack the Giant-Killer have historical solidity. They like to be reassured on that point. So one morning last January, when I informed Charley and Talbot, at the breakfast-table, that Prince Rupert and his court had come to town,

> "Some in jags,
> Some in rags,
> And some in velvet gowns,"

the news was received with great satisfaction; for this meant that we were to go to the play.

For the sake of the small folk, who could not visit him at night, Prince Rupert was gracious enough to appear every Saturday afternoon during the month. We decided to wait upon his Highness at one of his *matinées*.

You would never have dreamed that the sun was shining brightly outside, if you had been with us in the theatre that afternoon. All the window-shutters were closed, and the great glass chandelier hanging from the gayly painted dome was one blaze of light. But brighter even than the jets of gas were the ruddy, eager faces of countless boys and girls, fringing the balconies and crowded into the seats below, longing for the play to begin. And nowhere were there two merrier or more eager faces than those of Charley and Talbot, pecking now and then at a brown paper cone filled with white grapes, which I held, and waiting for the solemn green curtain to roll up, and disclose the coral realm of the Naiad Queen.

I shall touch very lightly on the literary aspects of the play. Its plot, like that of the modern novel, was of so subtle a nature as not to be visible to the naked eye. I doubt if the dramatist himself could have explained it, even if he had been so condescending as to attempt to do so. There was a bold young prince—Prince Rupert, of course—who went into Wonderland in search of adventures. He reached Wonderland by leaping from the castle of Drachenfels into the Rhine. Then there was one Snaps, the prince's valet, who did not in the least want to go, but went, and got terribly frightened by the Green Demons of the Chrysolite Cavern, which made us all laugh—it being such a pleasant thing to see somebody else scared nearly to death. Then there were knights in brave tin armor, and armies of fair pre-Raphaelite amazons in all the colors of the rainbow, and troops of unhappy slave-girls, who did nothing but smile and wear beautiful dresses, and dance continually to the most delightful music. Now you were in an enchanted castle on the banks of the Rhine, and now you were in a cave of amethysts and diamonds at the bottom of the river—scene following scene with such bewildering rapidity that finally you did not quite know where you were.

But what interested me most, and what pleased Charley and Talbot even beyond the Naiad Queen herself, was the little violinist who came to the German Court, and played before Prince Rupert and his bride.

It was such a little fellow! He was not more than a year older than my own boys, and not much taller. He had a very sweet, sensitive face, with large gray eyes, in which there was a deep-settled expression that I do not like to see in a child. Looking at his eyes alone, you would have said he was sixteen or seventeen, and he was merely a baby!

I do not know enough of music to assert that he had wonderful genius, or any genius at all; but it seemed to me he played charmingly, and with the touch of a natural musician.

At the end of his piece, he was lifted over the foot-lights of the stage into the orchestra, where, with the conductor's *bâton* in his hand, he directed the band in playing one or two difficult compositions. In this he evinced a carefully trained ear and a perfect understanding of the music.

I wanted to hear the little violin again; but as he made his bow to the audience and ran off, it was with a half-wearied air, and I did not join with my neighbors in calling him back. "There's another performance to-night," I reflected, "and the little fellow isn't very strong." He came out, however, and bowed, but did not play again.

All the way home from the theatre my children were full of the little violinist, and as they went along, chattering and frolicking in front of me, and getting under my feet like a couple of young spaniels (they did not look unlike two small brown spaniels, with their fur-trimmed overcoats and sealskin caps and ear-lappets), I could not help thinking how different the poor little musician's lot was from theirs.

He was only six years and a half old, and had been before the public nearly three years. What hours of toil and weariness he must have been passing through at the very time when my little ones were being rocked and petted and shielded from every ungentle wind that blows! And what an existence was his now—travelling from city to city, practising at every spare moment, and performing night after night in some close theatre or concert-room when he should be drinking in that deep, refreshing slumber which childhood needs! However much he was loved by those who had charge of him, and they must have treated him kindly, it was a hard life for the child.

He ought to have been turned out into the sunshine; that pretty violin—one can easily understand that he was fond of it himself—ought to have been taken away from him, and a kite-string placed in his hand instead. If God had set the germ of a great musician or a great composer in that slight body, surely it would have been wise to let the precious gift ripen and flower in its own good season.

This is what I thought, walking home in the amber glow of the wintry sunset; but my boys saw only the bright side of the tapestry, and would have liked nothing better than to change places with little James Speaight. To stand in the midst of Fairyland, and play beautiful tunes on a toy fiddle, while all the people clapped their hands—what could quite equal that? Charley began to think it was no such grand thing to be a circus-rider, and the dazzling career of policeman had lost something of its glamour in the eyes of Talbot.

It is my custom every night, after the children are snug in their nests and the gas is turned down, to sit on the side of the bed and chat with them five or ten minutes. If anything has gone wrong through the day, it is never alluded to at this time. None but the most agreeable topics are discussed. I make it a point that the boys shall go to sleep with untroubled hearts. When our chat is ended, they say their prayers. Now, among the pleas which they offer up for the several members of the family, they frequently intrude the claims of rather curious objects for Divine compassion. Sometimes it is the rocking-horse that has broken a leg, sometimes it is Shem or Japhet, who has lost an arm in disembarking from Noah's ark; Pinky and Inky, the kittens, and Rob, the dog, are never forgotten.

So it did not surprise me at all this Saturday night when both boys prayed God to watch over and bless the little violinist.

The next morning at the breakfast-table, when I unfolded the newspaper, the first paragraph my eyes fell upon was this:—

"James Speaight, the infant violinist, died in this city late on Saturday night. At the *matinée* of the 'Naiad Queen,' on the afternoon of that day, when little James Speaight came off the stage, after giving his usual violin performance, Mr. Shewell [the stage-manager] noticed that he appeared fatigued, and asked if he felt ill. He replied that he had a pain in his heart, and then Mr. Shewell suggested that he remain away from the evening performance. He retired quite early, and about midnight his father heard him say, *'Gracious God, make room for another little child in Heaven.'* No sound was heard after this, and his father spoke to him soon afterwards; he received no answer, but found his child dead."

The printed letters grew dim and melted into each other, as I tried to re-read them. I glanced across the table at Charley and Talbot eating their breakfast, with the slanted sunlight from the window turning their curls into real gold, and I had not the heart to tell them what had happened.

Of all the prayers that floated up to heaven, that Saturday night, from the bedsides of sorrowful men and women, or from the cots of innocent children, what accents could have fallen more piteously and tenderly upon the ear of a listening angel than the prayer of little James Speaight! He knew he was dying. The faith he had learned, perhaps while running at his mother's side, in some green English lane, came to him then. He remembered it was Christ who said, "Suffer the little children to come unto me".; and the beautiful prayer rose to his lips, "Gracious God, make room for another little child in Heaven."

I folded up the newspaper silently, and throughout the day I did not speak before the boys of the little violinist's death; but when the time came for our customary chat in the nursery, I told the story to Charley and Talbot. I do not think that they understood it very well, and still less did they understand why I lingered so much longer than usual by their bedside that Sunday night.

As I sat there in the dimly lighted room, it seemed to me that I could hear, in the pauses of the winter wind, faintly and doubtfully somewhere in the distance, the sound of the little violin.

Ah, that little violin!—a cherished relic now. Perhaps it plays soft, plaintive airs all by itself, in the place where it is kept, missing the touch of the baby fingers which used to waken it into life!

It has been said that Damon Runyon "may be considered the prose-laureate of the semi-literate American." *Runyonese* has come into the English language as a catchword for the slangy, breezy, journalistic idiom Runyon used so skillfully. But at times this style belies the underlying seriousness of his work. "100 Percent Man" (1923), for example, is in part about racism and prejudice. It also represents a wonderful illustration of the sometimes romantic figures fiddlers cut.

100 Percent Man

by Damon Runyon

One time there drifts into my old home town out West a tall, slim, dark-complected guy, with long black hair, and very dreamy eyes, who tells one and all that his name is Senor José Rodriguez, and that he is a Spaniard, although of course anybody can see that he is nothing but a Mexican.

Now, in those days back in my old home town, Mexicans are not very popular, even when they call themselves Spaniards, and this Senor José Rodriguez is especially unpopular because the dames around town say he is good-looking; as if a Mexican can be good-looking, even when he calls himself a Spaniard.

Furthermore, this Senor José Rodriguez's racket is playing a fiddle, which he calls a violin, although anybody who is not crazy can see right away it is nothing but a fiddle, and such rackets as fiddling are considered very nonsensical by the citizens back in my old home town.

Well, at first there is some talk of running Senor José Rodriguez out of town, but somehow they never get around to the matter, and by and by he is settled down doing odd jobs of fiddling at dances, and church sociables, and even in the Opera House when there is a show in town, and he is called Fiddlin' Joe.

He is pretty much despised by the men folks, but he gets along very good indeed with the dames, who claim he is a romantic proposition, what with his eyes, and his fiddling, and one thing and another. They look at him when he is playing his fiddle, and they heave long breaths, and take on generally, although as far as anybody knows Fiddlin' Joe never tumbles any one of them.

How he comes to drift into my old home town nobody ever knows, but Fiddlin' Joe says it is on account of his health, which is very punk. He says a croaker back East tells him he has the old T.B., a croaker being a way of saying a doctor, and the T.B. a way of saying tuberculosis, and he hears my old home town has a great climate for such, which is very true.

Well, anyway, Fiddlin' Joe stays around two or three years, and by this time everybody is pretty much used to him, and in fact many citizens get so they half speak to him on the street, because no matter what else it may be, my old home time is hospitable if it once gets used to a guy.

Some people, mostly dames, who claim they know about these matters, say Fiddlin' Joe is a real good fiddler, although he sounds like any other fiddler to me. However, I am no judge of fiddling, because I like a harmonica much better but some people claim Fiddlin' Joe is what you might call a real artist at his racket.

Well, anyway, to make a long story longer, as the fellow says, he goes fiddling around town for quite a spell, when along comes the toughest Winter we ever see back in my old home town, with pneumonia, and what-not going on, and the first thing anybody knows Fiddlin' Joe is down very sick.

In fact, old Doc Wilcox says he does not have much chance to live, what with being none too strong to start with, so they put him in St. Mary's Hospital, up near the smelters, to die. It is about this same time the strike starts in the smelters, which are big plants where they handle the ore that comes down from the mines, and naturally everybody forgets all about Fiddlin' Joe.

Well, sir, those are tough times back in my old home town, what

155

with the Winter being so cold and the strikers raising the dickens around the smelters. These strikers are most foreigners, Slavs, Polacks, and the like, who are called roundies back in my old home town, which is a way of saying roundheads, on account of their heads being round.

There are several thousand of these roundies, brought in from the East by the smelter companies, and they all live together in little houses in one section of town near the smelters. Furthermore, they are tough birds, especially when they are on a strike, and one night word goes around that they are rioting something scandalous, and are getting together with clubs and guns, and one thing and another, to march through the rest of the town, and tear it apart.

Well, Sheriff Davis and Marshal Pat Dillon and the other peace officers of my old home town organize a posse of citizens as quick as they can to put a stop to this business, but it looks like a tough spot for one and all on account of there being so many of the roundies.

The word comes down from the smelter district that the roundies are collected in one of the streets up there in regular marching order, all steamed up ready to go, and our citizens fix up a barricade across Santa Fe avenue bridge, which the strikers will have to cross to get to the main part of town.

Then all of a sudden a guy comes down from the smelter district with news of a very strange happening. He says that just as the gang of roundies are about ready to start, all of a sudden a tall, slim, dark-complected guy, with nothing much but a blanket around him, and a fiddle under his arm, bobs up among them, climbs on a barrel, and starts fiddling.

Well, it seems that these roundies all like fiddling pretty much, and the next thing anybody knows they are listening to this fiddler, and forgetting all about tearing my old home town apart. In fact, he fiddles so well and so long that by and by all the steam leaves them and finally they go on home and there is no more trouble than a jack-rabbit.

Of course the fiddler is nobody but Fiddlin' Joe, and naturally the first thing our citizens think of after they find there is to be no fighting is to send up to St. Mary's Hospital to thank him. But old Doc Wilcox meets them at the door and tells them that between the pneumonia and the T.B., and the exposure while fiddling, and one thing and another, Fiddlin' Joe is as dead as a doornail.

That is why you see that little marble statue of a guy playing a fiddle down by the Union Depot back in my old home town, and if you will read what it says on the statue you will find it says:

"Senor José Rodriguez,
100 percent man."

Paul Goodman was a prolific writer of fiction, drama, verse, literary criticism, and social history. Graduating from the City College of New York, he earned a Ph.D. in Humanities at the University of Chicago, and taught at a number of America's leading centers of learning. Fiddlers will observe that some of the musical compositions mentioned in "The Birthday Concert" (1936) are from Goodman's own imagination, not the actual violin literature. This factual lapse, however, does not divert the reader from being profoundly moved by this poignant story of a violinist who has lost his ability to make music.

The Birthday Concert

by Paul Goodman

When I had played the piano part of the Brahms B-flat Sonata,— a work tired for us both, but we forced our feelings.—I quietly spread my folding chair in the wing and sat down, to hear Herman alone perform Handel's E-minor Partita for violin unaccompanied. Quietly, because I knew what the performance would be; not without a gnawing anxiety at heart, nevertheless, for my friend.

It was again his birthday concert. In the crowd were our many friends, of whom some—I saw Alvin in the front row of the balcony and Husky near Exit 10, staring fixedly, like myself—some had been present at the very first one of these concerts, when Herman was seventeen. He would be thirty. (For it was really the eve of his birthday, the idea being for him to play till nearly midnight, and then all of us would go to a restaurant or roadhouse, to celebrate the incoming day.) Loud applause crowned every number; and the warm atmosphere of the lighted hall was a patchwork of the rhythmic noise of handclapping and the strains of the violin.

The louder the applause the sadder I became. There was no longer a moment of music in the violin, neither tone, rhythm, brilliance nor insight; but only notes, bars, a thin technique and nerves. But on pitch. The applause was in honor of a memory. (As for me! the sadder I became the better I played, but I could not teach this to him.) Now, in the wing, during a moment of silence, while Herman raised his bow—a void moment in which one often sees the unvarnished truth—I realized bitterly that I, the accompanist, could now be considered a better musician than my friend— if it is even right to consider such talents as musical. He was done for, *fichu;* he had, as we say, "shot his bolt."

He started to play, a largo introduction, a quick movement. There was not one moment, I say, when the music was played from within.

I could remember a time when each note fell crowded with the composer's mind, as it had been written down; but now the several tones without meaning slipped into cadences without meaning, and these formed no whole.

"But sometimes when I am alone," Herman insisted to me, "sometimes there is one tone that is truly bowed. Here or there, through no doing of mine, one phrase comes to life and is crowded with the composer's mind. Then we slip back. It is through no doing of mine, one way or the other."

At the concert, I could have wept at the hollow tone and the pitiful brilliance. I saw that there was a difference between *this* bad playing, which was a fall from perfection, and just ordinary playing, which would never mount to perfection. In his great days of fire and form, when he was twenty-six and twenty-seven, Herman had refined from his execution—I remember how he did it, week by week—every last dross of personality, of rhetoric and of technique, so that the natural music glowed with a strong and unwavering light, like a flawless candle. But now, therefore, when the music itself was gone, there was nothing left, nothing material to fall back on. It was all framework, no content, either personal or musical. I was somewhat surprised that any sound came forth at all.

"You see, I have lost my touch." He tried to explain where the bowhand was at fault, and how the fingers of his left hand had for some reason become "too cautious." But the change was not in his hands, but in him; what he needed was not a violin lesson, but a revival of the spirit.

With a cadenza and a flourish, he closed the first movement. There was a volley of handclapping, at which he turned toward me in the wing with a wry smile on his face. Then at once, with his head averted from the audience, as if to conceal tears in his eyes— which were not there, however, so far as I could see—he struck up the largo.

I followed him on a miniature score: it was always the same, a faultless reading and not a note of music. We came to the bottom of the page—I turned.

Then, at the top of the next page, in the midst of a delicate phrase, came one note, a B-flat—

As he had said: "Sometimes there is one note truly bowed. Here or there, through no doing of mine, one tone comes to life and is crowded with the composer's mind—" I knew him well, and as soon as he touched this B-flat dotted quarter note, I looked up from the score.

Herman played this note again and again, a fourth time, a fifth time, a sixth, a seventh.

The music had come to a stop, but was returning, like a nicked phonograph record, on the same groove. An uneasy pause! The audience looked up in astonishment. Those who had been tapping the time on the arms of their chairs, found themselves with finger frozen in the air, for the note was in the middle of a bar; those who had allowed their souls to wander off in an internal revery, suddenly found themselves *fixed,* like a butterfly on a pin, in a picture frame.

A pause! as if nothing could advance this whole situation—my stare, the violinist on the platform, the throng of people in the theatre, the social life of the Americans, the imminence of violence, the configuration of the stars—onto its next movement.

> *This uneasy peace*
> *could not cease;*
>
> *we had no power*
> *to break this endless hour by hour;*
>
> *Plato's thoughts knew no way out*
> *but.in the courtyard played about.*

Herman, absorbed, out of his mind, played this B-flat dotted quarter note again and again, a tenth time, an eleventh time and a twelfth time. And everywhere about us, in his mind and in mine too, and in the minds of Alvin and Husky out front, under the influence of this one divine note of true music, there revived all the great moments of music that our friend had ever brought us: the Chaconne, the Vivaldi Concerto in A-flat, the Mozart Sonata in E-minor, the "petite phrase," and the cadenza of Beethoven's Concerto,—an entire world recovered from one memory, for, as Socrates promises Meno,

> *for as all nature is akin, and since the soul has learned all things, nothing prevents one, if he can recollect one single thing, from finding out all the rest—*

all the rest! all blooming from this one quarter note and filling the air with a choral sound,—all the rest, forever and ever, blooming from this one note, from this crotchet.—

No wonder that our friend, lost to the occasion and to the fact of his birthday, played over and over, a thirteenth time, a fourteenth time, this one note that brought back to him, or rather brought him back to, the realms of music where we had been ceasing to live.

As he played the one tone a fifteenth and a sixteenth time—to him each time it seemed with more power and more glory, but it was already only a monotonous scraping—the audience began to murmur, to laugh; several persons rose.

On the seventeenth repetition the string snapped and Herman fell down in a faint.

They rang down the curtain and there was a scene of confusion backstage, reporters taking notes and a dozen admirers crowding round; Morton-Moses, our manager, wanted to know whether or not to refund the money.

I advised him to. "One note of music, even though repeated 17 times, does not make a concert."

Afterwards, the three of us got Herman outside, into my car. He was pretty much recovered, and we started off up Broadway just as if nothing had happened, for so inertia always takes us a few movements further on. I kept stepping on the gas, and the others sat silent in the rear; but Herman talked in jerky sentences.

"It's all over with me as a fiddler; I'm not sorry.

"How would you like to feel that day by day you're losing power? And after a while you don't even care, for to care about it is part of the power."

162

"Oh, this is a good motor," I said, by way of a joke. But I knew the feeling nevertheless, going up a dangerous hill.

"No!" he cried, "an electric current! a telephone—" as if the particular machine made any difference. *"Now the connection is cut off*—you act in the distance. Your arms are far off when you play. Can't hear. Can you hear? Can you hear me, Abe?" he shouted. "Hello! Like a telephone that begins to die away—I joggle the receiver, but I don't have the current."

His left hand was shaking—in tremolo.

I stayed on Broadway as it became Route 9, the Albany Post Road, going north through Riverdale and Yonkers; and all through here I was driving too fast.

"No connection between the body and the mind," said Herman; "and that big audience—they're looking. So I remember the old days, and I try hard; can the feelings be forced? They are absent—"

(Who knows? they are already busy *elsewhere,* and it is only later that we shall find out about it!)

"And what if the power is drained from the line by your own doing? I mean if by—excesses—you so coarsen all feelings that they can't give in any longer to the good music. Heh? What is the use of shouting Hello! hello! But anyway this isn't the reason—not *only* this reason—It's *not* for this reason! It's not for *this* reason! It's not *only* for this reason—"

I veered sharply to the right, up a side road. We had reached Harmon, two miles this side of Croton, and it was nearly midnight. We got out at Nikko's, a roadhouse at the end of the turning. The place was moderately filled with a weeknight crowd, about fifteen couples dancing to Cuban music. We sat down at a table to celebrate and we ordered Old Fashioned cocktails.

Herman began to cry and said: "You see, my birthday always comes in a noisy restaurant, or driving over the sleeping countryside in an automobile. Then I sit back, and count out the year, and my friends confound me with congratulations."

At this, a church bell in the town of Harmon rang out midnight.

"Happy birthday, dear friend," I said to Herman, raising my Old Fashioned, and we all drank, including Herman.

Now the liquor seemed to do him good, for at once he said, in a decided tone quite new to him, hard with conclusions and decisions: "The great fact to remember is this: that it is not through our own doing! These inner changes, from childhood to youth, so on and so on—not through any doing of ours! it is something that happens to us! as much given as anything else. So! the magic powers are lost, the dear habits become impossible. Well! there are some who when their bolt is shot—"

I was startled, to hear from his mouth this same expression that I had myself used.

"—there are some who when their bolt is shot, still try, still try, still try, still try—try—" he faltered and we rose. But he *did* not say it again, and he did not fall down in a faint. He said: "Just as if nothing had happened, I mean as if their bolt *hadn't* been shot! But I, friends, shall look around—" he said it suavely and with a smile on his face, suddenly relieving our tension, lightening the atmosphere, just as if he were making an after-dinner speech, "I shall look around at the new set-up, the new situation in which I have been placed, the new chances given to me and not made by me."

He was like a dead man.

THE RESEMBLANCE BETWEEN A
VIOLIN CASE AND A COFFIN
by Tennessee Williams (1914-   )

Tennessee Williams, one of America's pre-eminent dramatists, is
a documentor of hypersensitive and lonely people usually to be
found in a decadent Southern setting. As in his well-known play
The Glass Menagerie, the focus in the story "The Resemblance
Between a Violin Case and a Coffin" is on a brother and sister
both "coming of age." The violinist, Richard Miles, is the outside
force triggering maturation with its attendant losses—of spontaneity,
innocence, "music." This highly autobiographical story dates from
1950.

The Resemblance
Between a
Violin Case
and a Coffin

by Tennessee Williams

With her advantage of more than two years and the earlier
maturity of girls, my sister moved before me into that country of
mysterious differences where children grow up. And although we
naturally continued to live in the same house, she seemed to have
gone on a journey while she remained in sight. The difference came
about more abruptly than you would think possible, and it was vast,

it was like the two sides of the Sunflower River that ran through the town where we lived. On one side was a wilderness where giant cypresses seemed to engage in mute rites of reverence at the edge of the river, and the blurred pallor of the Dobyne place that used to be a plantation, now vacant and seemingly ravaged by some impalpable violence fiercer than flames, and back of this dusky curtain, the immense cottonfields that absorbed the whole visible distance in one sweeping gesture. But on the other side, avenues, commerce, pavements and homes of people: those two, separated by only a yellowish, languorous stream that you could throw a rock over. The rumbling wooden bridge that divided, or joined, those banks was hardly shorter than the interval in which my sister moved away from me. Her look was startled, mine was bewildered and hurt. Either there was no explanation or none was permitted between the one departing and the one left behind. The earliest beginning of it that I can remember was one day when my sister got up later than usual with an odd look, not as if she had been crying, although perhaps she had, but as though she had received some painful or frightening surprise, and I observed an equally odd difference in the manner toward her of my mother and grandmother. She was escorted to the kitchen table for breakfast as though she were in danger of toppling over on either side, and everything was handed to her as though she could not reach for it. She was addressed in hushed and solicitous voices, almost the way that docile servants speak to an employer. I was baffled and a little disgusted. I received no attention at all, and the one or two glances given me by my sister had a peculiar look of resentment in them. It was as if I had struck her the night before and given her a bloody nose or a black eye, except that she wore no bruise, no visible injury, and there had been no altercation between us in recent days. I spoke to her several times, but for some reason she ignored my remarks, and when I became irritated and yelled at her, my grandmother suddenly reached over and twisted my ear, which was one of the few times that I can remember when she ever offered me more than the gentlest reproach. It was a Saturday morning, I remember, of a hot yellow day and it was the hour when my sister and I would ordinarily take to the streets on our wheels. But the custom was now disregarded. After breakfast my sister appeared somewhat strengthened but still alarmingly pale and as silent as ever. She was then escorted to the parlor and encouraged to sit down at the piano. She spoke in a low whimpering tone to my grandmother who adjusted the piano stool very carefully and placed a cushion on it and even turned the pages of sheet music for her as if she were incapable of finding the place for herself. She was working on a simple piece called *The Aeolian Harp,* and my grandmother sat beside her while she played, counting out the tempo in a barely audible voice, now and then reaching out to touch the wrists of my sister in order to remind her to keep them arched. Upstairs my mother began to sing to herself which was something she only did when my father had just left on a long trip with his samples and would not be likely to return for quite a while, and my grandfather, up since daybreak, was mumbling a sermon to himself in the study. All was peaceful except my sister's face. I did not know whether to go outside or stay in. I hung around the parlor a little while, and finally I said to Grand, Why can't she practice later? As if I had made some really brutal remark, my sister jumped up in tears and fled to her upstairs bedroom. What was the matter with her? My grandmother said, Your sister is not well today. She said it gently and gravely, and then she started to follow my sister upstairs, and I was deserted. I was left alone in the very uninteresting parlor. The idea of riding alone on my wheel did not please me for often when I did that, I was set upon by the rougher boys of the town who called me Preacher and took a peculiar delight in asking me obscene questions that would embarrass me to the point of nausea . . .

In this way was instituted the time of estrangement that I could not understand. From that time on the division between us was ever more clearly established. It seemed that my mother and grandmother were approving and conspiring to increase it. They had never before bothered over the fact that I had depended so much on the companionship of my sister but now they were continually asking me why I did not make friends with other children. I was ashamed to tell them that other children frightened me nor was I willing to admit that my sister's wild imagination and inexhaustible spirits made all other substitute companions seem like the shadows of shades, for now that she had abandoned me, mysteriously and willfully withdrawn her enchanting intimacy, I felt too resentful even to acknowledge secretly, to myself, how much had been lost through what she had taken away . . .

Sometimes I think she might have fled back into the more familiar country of childhood if she had been allowed to, but the grownup ladies of the house, and even the colored girl, Ozzie, were continually telling her that such and such a thing was not proper for her to do. It was not proper for my sister not to wear stockings or to crouch in the yard at a place where the earth was worn bare to bounce a rubber ball and scoop up starry-pointed bits of black metal called jacks. It was not even proper for me to come into her room without knocking. All of these proprieties struck me as mean and silly and perverse, and the wound of them turned me inward.

My sister had been magically suited to the wild country of childhood but it remained to be seen how she would adapt herself to the uniform and yet more complex world that grown girls enter. I suspect that I have defined that world incorrectly with the word uniform; later, yes, it becomes uniform, it straightens out into an all too regular pattern. But between childhood and adulthood there is a broken terrain which is possibly even wilder than childhood was. The wilderness is interior. The vines and the brambles seem to have been left behind but actually they are thicker and more confusing, although they are not so noticeable from the outside. Those few years of dangerous passage are an ascent into unknown hills. They take the breath sometimes and bewilder the vision. My mother and maternal grandmother came of a calmer blood than my sister and I. They were unable to suspect the hazards that we were faced with, having in us the turbulent blood of our father. Irreconcilables fought for supremacy in us; peace could never be made: at best a smoldering sort of armistice might be reached after many battles. Childhood had held those clashes in abeyance. They were somehow timed to explode at adolescence, silently, shaking the earth where we were standing. My sister now felt those tremors under her feet. It seemed to me that a shadow had fallen on her. Or had it fallen on me, with her light at a distance? Yes, it was as if someone had carried a lamp into another room that I could not enter. I watched her from a distance and under a shadow. And looking back on it now, I see that those two or three years when the fatal dice were still in the tilted box, were the years of her beauty. The long copperish curls which had swung below her shoulders, bobbing almost constantly with excitement, were unexpectedly removed one day, an afternoon of a day soon after the one when she had fled from the piano in reasonless tears. Mother took her downtown. I was not allowed to go with them but was told once more to find someone else to play with. And my sister returned without her long copper curls. It was like a formal acknowledgment of the sorrowful differences and division which had haunted the house for some time. I noted as she came in the front door that she had now begun to imitate the walk of grown ladies, the graceful and quick and decorous steps of my mother, and that she kept her arms at her sides instead of flung out as if brushing curtains aside as she sprang forward in the abruptly lost days. But there was much more than that. When she entered the parlor, at the fading hour of the afternoon, it was as momentous as if brass horns had sounded, she wore such beauty. Mother came after her looking flushed with excitement and my grandmother descended the stairs with unusual lightness. They spoke in hushed voices. Astonishing, said my mother. She's like Isabel. This was the name of a sister of my father's who was a famed beauty in Knoxville. She was probably the one woman in the world of whom my mother was intimidated, and our occasional summer journeys to Knoxville from the Delta of Mississippi were like priestly tributes to a seat of holiness, for though my mother would certainly never make verbal acknowledgment of my aunt's superiority in matters of taste and definitions of quality, it was nevertheless apparent that she approached Knoxville and my father's younger sister in something very close to fear and trembling. Isabel had a flame, there was no doubt about it, a lambency which, once felt, would not fade from the eyes. It had an awful quality, as though it shone outward while it burned inward. And not long after the time of these recollections she was to die, quite abruptly and irrelevantly, as the result of the removal of an infected wisdom tooth, with her legend entrusted to various bewildered eyes and hearts and memories she had stamped, including mine, which have sometimes confused her with very dissimilar ladies. She is like Isabel, said my mother in a hushed voice. My grandmother did not admit that this was so. She also admired Isabel but thought her too interfering and was unable to separate her altogether from the excessively close blood-connection with my father, whom I should say, in passage, was a devilish man, possibly not understood but certainly hard to live with . . .

What I saw was not Isabel in my sister but a grown stranger whose beauty sharpened my sense of being alone. I saw that it was all over, put away in a box like a doll no longer cared for, the magical intimacy of our childhood together, the soap-bubble afternoons and the games with paper dolls cut out of dress catalogues and the breathless races here and there on our wheels. For the first time, yes, I saw her beauty. I consciously avowed it to myself, although it seems to me that I turned away from it, averted my look from the pride with which she strolled into the parlor and stood by the mantel mirror to be admired. And it was then, about that time, that I began to find life unsatisfactory as an explanation of itself and was forced to adopt the method of the artist of not explaining but putting the blocks together in some other way that seems more significant to him. Which is a rather fancy way of saying I started writing . . .

My sister also had a separate occupation which was her study of music, at first conducted under my grandmother's instruction but now entrusted to a professional teacher whose name was Miss Aehle, an almost typical spinster, who lived in a small frame house with a porch covered by moonvines and a fence covered by honeysuckle. Her name was pronounced *Ail*-ly. She supported herself and a paralyzed father by giving lessons in violin and piano, neither of which she played very well herself but for which she had great gifts as a teacher. If not great gifts, at least great enthusiasm. She was a true romanticist. She talked so excitedly that she got ahead of herself and looked bewildered and cried out, What was I saying? She was one of the innocents of the world, appreciated only by her pupils and a few persons a generation older than herself. Her pupils nearly always came to adore her, she gave them a feeling that playing little pieces on the piano or scratching out little tunes on a fiddle made up for everything that was ostensibly wrong in a world made by God but disarrayed by the devil. She was religious and ecstatic. She never admitted that anyone of her pupils, even the ones that were unmistakably tone-deaf, were deficient in musical talent. And the few that could perform tolerably well she was certain had genius. She had two real star pupils, my sister, on the piano, and a boy named Richard Miles who studied the violin. Her enthusiasm for these two was unbounded. It is true that my sister had a nice touch and that Richard Miles had a pure tone on the fiddle, but Miss Aehle dreamed of them in terms of playing duets to great ovations in the world's capital cities.

Richard Miles, I think of him now as a boy, for he was about seventeen, but at that time he seemed a complete adult to me, even immeasurably older than my sister who was fourteen. I resented him fiercely even though I began, almost immediately after learning of his existence, to dream about him as I had formerly dreamed of storybook heroes. His name began to inhabit the rectory. It was almost constantly on the lips of my sister, this strange young lady who had come to live with us. It had a curious lightness, that name, in the way that she spoke it. It did not seem to fall from her lips but to be released from them. The moment spoken, it rose into the air and shimmered and floated and took on gorgeous colors the way

that soap bubbles did that we used to blow from the sunny back steps in the summer. Those bubbles lifted and floated and they eventually broke but never until other bubbles had floated beside them. Golden they were, and the name of Richard had a golden sound, too. The second name, being Miles, gave a suggestion of distance, so Richard was something both radiant and far away.

My sister's obsession with Richard may have been even more intense than mine. Since mine was copied from hers, it was probably hers that was greater in the beginning. But while mine was of a shy and sorrowful kind, involved with my sense of abandonment, hers at first seemed to be joyous. She had fallen in love. As always, I followed suit. But while love made her brilliant, at first, it made me laggard and dull. It filled me with sad confusion. It tied my tongue or made it stammer and it flashed so unbearably in my eyes that I had to turn them away. These are the intensities that one cannot live with, that he has to outgrow if he wants to survive. But who can help grieving for them? If the blood vessels could hold them, how much better to keep those early loves with us? But if we did, the veins would break and the passion explode into darkness long before the necessary time for it.

I remember one afternoon in fall when my sister and I were walking along a street when Richard Miles appeared suddenly before us from somewhere with a startling cry. I see him bounding, probably down the steps of Miss Aehle's white cottage, emerging unexpectedly from the vines. Probably Miss Aehle's because he bore his violin case, and I remember thinking how closely it resembled a little coffin, a coffin made for a small child or a doll. About people you knew in your childhood it is rarely possible to remember their appearance except as ugly or beautiful or light or dark. Richard was light and he was probably more beautiful than any boy I have seen since. I do not even remember if he was light in the sense of being blond or if the lightness came from a quality in him deeper than hair or skin. Yes, probably both, for he was one of those people who move in light, provided by practically everything about them. This detail I do remember. He wore a white shirt, and through its cloth could be seen the fair skin of his shoulders. And for the first time, prematurely, I was aware of skin as an attraction. A thing that might be desirable to touch. This awareness entered my mind, my senses, like the sudden streak of flame that follows a comet. And my undoing, already started by Richard's mere coming toward us, was now completed. When he turned to me and held his enormous hand out, I did a thing so grotesque that I could never afterwards be near him without a blistering sense of shame. Instead of taking the hand I ducked away from him. I made a mumbling sound that could have had very little resemblance to speech, and then brushed past their two figures, his and my beaming sister's, and fled into a drugstore just beyond.

That same fall the pupils of Miss Aehle performed in a concert. This concert was held in the parish house of my grandfather's church. And for weeks preceding it the pupils made preparation for the occasion which seemed as important as Christmas. My sister and Richard Miles were to play a duet, she on the piano, of course, and he on the violin. They practiced separately and they practiced together. Separately my sister played the piece very well, but for some reason, more portentous than it seemed at the time, she had great difficulty in playing to Richard's accompaniment. Suddenly her fingers would turn to thumbs, her wrists would flatten out and become cramped, her whole figure would hunch rigidly toward the piano and her beauty and grace would vanish. It was strange, but Miss Aehle was certain that it would be overcome with repeated practice. And Richard was patient, he was incredibly patient, he seemed to be far more concerned for my sister's sake than his own. Extra hours of practice were necessary. Sometimes when they had left Miss Aehle's, at the arrival of other pupils, they would continue at our house. The afternoons were consequently unsafe. I never knew when the front door might open on Richard's dreadful beauty and his greeting which I could not respond to, could not endure, must fly grotesquely away from. But the house was so arranged that although I hid in my bedroom at these hours of practice, I was still able to watch them at the piano. My bedroom looked out upon the staircase which descended into the parlor where they practiced. The piano was directly within my line of vision. It was in the parlor's lightest corner, with lace-curtained windows on either side of it, the sunlight only fretted by patterns of lace and ferns.

During the final week before the concert — or was it recital they called it? — Richard Miles came over almost invariably at four in the afternoon, which was the last hour of really good sunlight in late October. And always a little before that time I would lower the green blind in my bedroom and with a fantastic stealth, as if a sound would betray a disgusting action, I would open the door two inches, an aperture just enough to enclose the piano corner as by the lateral boundaries of a stage. When I heard them enter the front

173

door, or even before, when I saw their shadows thrown against the oval glass and curtain the door surrounded or heard their voices as they climbed to the porch, I would flatten myself on my belly on the cold floor and remain in that position as long as they stayed, no matter how my knees or elbows ached, and I was so fearful of betraying this watch that I kept over them while they practiced that I hardly dared to breathe.

The transference of my interest to Richard now seemed complete. I would barely notice my sister at the piano, groan at her repeated blunders only in sympathy for him. When I recall what a little puritan I was in those days, there must have been a shocking ambivalence in my thoughts and sensations as I gazed down upon him through the crack of the door. How on earth did I explain to myself, at that time, the fascination of his physical being without, at the same time, confessing to myself that I was a little monster of sensuality? Or was that actually before I had begun to associate the sensual with the impure, an error that tortured me during and after pubescence, or did I, and this seems most likely, now, say to myself, Yes, Tom, you're a monster! But that's how it is and there's nothing to be done about it. And so continued to feast my eyes on his beauty. This much is certain. Whatever resistance there may have been from the "legion of decency" in my soul was exhausted in the first skirmish, not exterminated but thoroughly trounced, and its subsequent complaints were in the form of unseen blushes. Not that there was really anything to be ashamed of in adoring the beauty of Richard. It was surely made for that purpose, and boys of my age are made to be stirred by such ideals of grace. The sheer white cloth in which I had originally seen his upper body was always worn by it, and now, in those afternoons, because of the position of the piano between two windows that cast their beams at cross angles, the white material became diaphanous with light, the torso shone through it, faintly pink and silver, the nipples on the chest and the armpits a little darker, and the diaphragm visibly pulsing as he breathed. It is possible that I have seen more graceful bodies, but I am not sure that I have, and his remains, I believe, a subconscious standard. And looking back upon him now, and upon the devout little mystic of carnality that I was as I crouched on a chill bedroom floor, I think of Camilla Rucellai, that highstrung mystic of Florence who is supposed to have seen Pico della Mirandola entering the streets of that city on a milk-white horse in a storm of sunlight and flowers, and to have fainted at the spectacle of him, and murmured, as she revived, *He will pass in the time of lilies!* meaning that he would die early, since nothing so fair could decline by common degrees in a faded season. The light was certainly there in all its fullness, and even a kind of flowers, at least shadows of them, for there were flowers of lace in the window curtains and actual branches of fern which the light projected across him; no storm of flowers but the shadows of flowers which are perhaps more fitting.

The way that he lifted and handled his violin! First he would roll up the sleeves of his white shirt and remove his necktie and loosen his collar as though he were making preparations for love. Then there was a metallic snap as he released the lock on the case of the violin. Then the upper lid was pushed back and the sunlight fell on the dazzling interior of the case. It was plush-lined and the plush was emerald. The violin itself was somewhat darker than blood and even more lustrous. To Richard I think it must have seemed more precious. His hands and his arms as he lifted it from the case, they said the word love more sweetly than speech could say it, and, oh, what precocious fantasies their grace and tenderness would excite in me. I was a wounded soldier, the youngest of the regiment and he, Richard, was my young officer, jeopardizing his life to lift me from the field where I had fallen and carry me back to safety in the same cradle of arms that supported his violin now. The dreams, perhaps, went further, but I have already dwelt sufficiently upon the sudden triumph of unchastity back of my burning eyes; that needs no more annotation . . .

I now feel some anxiety that this story will seem to be losing itself like a path that has climbed a hill and then lost itself in an overgrowth of brambles. For I have now told you all but one of the things that stand out very clearly, and yet I have not approached any sort of conclusion. There is, of course, a conclusion. However indefinite, there always is some point which serves that need of remembrances and stories.

The remaining very clear thing is the evening of the recital in mid-November, but before an account of that, I should tell more of my sister in this troubled state of hers. It might be possible to willfully thrust myself into her mind, her emotions, but I question the wisdom of it: for at that time I was an almost hostile onlooker where she was concerned. Hurt feelings and jealous feelings were too thickly involved in my view of her at that time. As though she were being punished for a betrayal of our childhood companionship,

I felt a gratification tinged with contempt at her difficulties in the duet with Richard. One evening I overheard a telephone call which mother received from Miss Aehle. Miss Aehle was first perplexed and now genuinely alarmed and totally mystified by the sudden decline of my sister's vaunted aptitude for the piano. She had been singing her praises for months. Now it appeared that my sister was about to disgrace her publicly, for she was not only unable, suddenly, to learn new pieces but was forgetting the old ones. It had been planned, originally, for her to play several solo numbers at the recital before and leading up to the duet with Richard. The solos now had to be canceled from the program, and Miss Aehle was even fearful that my sister would not be able to perform in the duet. She wondered if my mother could think of some reason why my sister had undergone this very inopportune and painful decline? Was she sleeping badly, how was her appetite, was she very moody? Mother came away from the telephone in a very cross humor with the teacher. She repeated all the complaints and apprehensions and questions to my grandmother who said nothing but pursed her lips and shook her head while she sewed like one of those venerable women who understand and govern the fates of mortals, but she had nothing to offer in the way of a practical solution except to say that perhaps it was a mistake for brilliant children to be pushed into things like this so early . . .

Richard stayed patient with her most of the time, and there were occasional periods of revival, when she would attack the piano with an explosion of confidence and the melodies would surge beneath her fingers like birds out of cages. Such a resurgence would never last till the end of a piece. There would be a stumble, and then another collapse. Once Richard himself was unstrung. He pushed his violin high into the air like a broom sweeping cobwebs off the ceiling. He strode around the parlor brandishing it like that and uttering groans that were both sincere and comic; when he returned to the piano, where she crouched in dismay, he took hold of her shoulders and gave them a shake. She burst into tears and would have fled upstairs but he caught hold of her by the newel post of the staircase. He would not let go of her. He detained her with murmurs I couldn't quite hear, and drew her gently back to the piano corner. And then he sat down on the piano stool with his great hands gripping each side of her narrow waist while she sobbed with her face averted and her fingers knotting together. And while I watched them from my cave of darkness, my body learned, at least three years too early, the fierceness and fire of the will of life to

176

transcend the single body, and so to continue to follow light's curve and time's . . .

The evening of the recital my sister complained at supper that her hands were stiff, and she kept rubbing them together and even held them over the spout of the teapot to warm them with the steam. She looked very pretty, I remember, when she was dressed. Her color was higher than I had ever seen it, but there were tiny beads of sweat at her temples and she ordered me angrily out of her room when I appeared in the doorway before she was ready to pass the family's inspection. She wore silver slippers and a very grownup-looking dress that was the greenish sea-color of her eyes. It had the low waist that was fashionable at that time and there were silver beads on it in loops and fringes. Her bedroom was steaming from the adjoining bath. She opened the window. Grandmother slammed it down, declaring that she would catch cold. Oh, leave me alone, she answered. The muscles in her throat were curiously prominent as she stared in the glass. Stop powdering, said my grandmother, you're caking your face with powder. Well, it's my face, she retorted. And then came near to flying into a tantrum at some small critical comment offered by Mother. I have no talent, she said, I have no talent for music! Why do I have to do it, why do you make me, why was I forced into this? Even my grandmother finally gave up and retired from the room. But when it came time to leave for the parish house, my sister came downstairs looking fairly collected and said not another word as we made our departure. Once in the automobile she whispered something about her hair being mussed. She kept her stiff hands knotted in her lap. We drove first to Miss Aehle's and found her in a state of hysteria because Richard had fallen off a bicycle that afternoon and skinned his fingers. She was sure it would hinder his playing. But when we arrived at the parish house, Richard was already there as calm as a duckpond, playing delicately with the mute on the strings and no apparent disability. We left them, teacher and performers, in the cloakroom and went to take our seats in the auditorium which was beginning to fill, and I remember noticing a half-erased inscription on a blackboard which had something to do with a Sunday School lesson.

No, it did not go off well. They played without sheet music, and my sister made all the mistakes she had made in practicing and several new ones. She could not seem to remember the composition beyond the first few pages; it was a fairly long one, and those pages she repeated twice, possibly even three times. But Richard was heroic. He seemed to anticipate every wrong note that she struck and to bring down his bow on the strings with an extra strength to cover and rectify it. When she began to lose control altogether, I saw him edging up closer to her position, so that his radiant figure shielded her partly from view, and I saw him, at a crucial moment, when it seemed that the duet might collapse altogether, raise his bow high in the air, at the same time catching his breath in a sort of "Hah!" a sound I heard much later from bullfighters daring a charge, and lower it to the strings in a masterful sweep that took the lead from my sister and plunged them into the passage that she had forgotten in her panic. . . . For a bar or two, I think, she stopped playing, sat there motionless, stunned. And then, finally, when he turned his back to the audience and murmured something to her, she started again. She started playing again but Richard played so brilliantly and so richly that the piano was barely noticeable underneath him. And so they got through it, and when it was finished they received an ovation. My sister started to rush for the cloakroom. But Richard seized her wrist and held her back. Then something odd happened. Instead of bowing she suddenly turned and pressed her forehead against him, pressed it against the lapel of his blue serge suit. He blushed and bowed and touched her waist with his fingers, gently, his eyes glancing down . . .

We drove home in silence, almost. There was a conspiracy to ignore that anything unfortunate had happened. My sister said nothing. She sat with her hands knotted in her lap exactly as she had been before the recital, and when I looked at her I noticed that her shoulders were too narrow and her mouth a little too wide for real beauty, and that her recent habit of hunching made her seem a little bit like an old lady being imitated by a child.

At that point Richard Miles faded out of our lives for my sister refused to continue to study music, and not long afterwards my father received an advancement, an office job as a minor executive in a northern shoe company, and we moved from the South. No, I am not putting all of these things in their exact chronological order, I may as well confess it, but if I did I would violate my honor as a teller of stories . . .

As for Richard, the truth is exactly congruous to the poem. A year or so later we learned, in that northern city to which we had moved, that he had died of pneumonia. And then I remembered the case of his violin, and how it resembled so much a little black coffin made for a child or a doll . . .

A fourth generation American of Swiss ancestry, Herbert Kubly was born and brought up on a Wisconsin farm. Upon graduation from the University of Wisconsin in 1937, he was for a time a newspaper reporter and art critic. Pursuing his special interest in music, he served as music editor of *Time* magazine in the late 'forties. His non-fiction *American in Italy* won the 1956 National Book Award. "The Wasp" appeared in a collection of short stories titled *Varieties of Love* (1958).

The Wasp

by Herbert Kubly

A bottle of port reflected the room like a mirror; in it the flames of the hearth danced like rubies. On the table beside the bottle was a letter, the only mail that day for "Herr Professor Anton Erne, Limnatstrasse, Zurich."

The professor, a frail man a half-century old, stood beside the table, gazing at the letter. It was a heavy gray card in a gray linen envelope. He did not touch it. There was no need; its ten short lines were burned deeply into his brain.

The professor was thinking of another note, one that had come three months ago from the Herr Professor of the Knabenschule. "Thirty peasants I must teach to read notes," the high-school professor had written. "For a genius who already knows more than I, I have no time. So I send him to you." The note had irritated Professor Erne. He did not take pupils. It was only ten days before his yearly winter journey to the south. There were plenty of good violin teachers in Zurich searching for talented students. It was presumptuous of the high-school teacher to put Professor Erne in the position of having to refuse one. Herr Erne decided to write the teacher and tell him not to send the boy.

But he came. It was a warm October afternoon. The boy carried a wooden violin case and wore black corduroy shorts. He was strong and fair with wide blue eyes; his legs were sturdy and pink. He was out of breath, because he had been playing football, he explained.

"Football!" Herr Erne exclaimed. "The professor sends me a football player."

"I am on the class team," the boy said. He was too shy to smile; his remote gaze searched a mysterious object over Herr Erne's shoulder.

"And the violin, what do you do with that?"

"I play it," the boy said, as if the question were a natural one.

"We shall hear," Herr Erne said, quite certain that a football athlete's playing would be adequate excuse to send him away. The boy opened the case and took out an inexpensive mahogany-colored instrument. It was a child's violin, which the boy had outgrown. With slow seriousness he tightened the bow and tuned the strings. The ear, Herr Erne noted, was good. The boy raised the violin to his chin and began to play. It was a simple piece by Bach and the instrument had a common undistinguished tone but the cadenzas flowed with clarity and precision. Herr Erne watched the fingers, which were rather stubby, moving precisely, keeping firm control of the strings. Even from such a soulless little fiddle they were able to produce warmth and beauty. Herr Erne marveled that such playing could come from so dreary a box. Unable to stand any more, he went to his cabinet, took out a golden Stradivarius and handed it to the boy. He held it reverently.

"Play!" Herr Erne ordered excitedly. "Play!"

The boy tuned carefully and bowed some chords. "What shall I play?" he, asked.

"Whatever you like, but play."

He did. It was a simple Mozart minuet but he knew it well and played it with authority. The rich tones of the violin stirred him on until the room sang with Mozart melodies. Herr Erne could hardly contain himself. The little pieces glowed like candlelight on crystal, and then suddenly they stopped.

"Play, play!" Herr Erne ordered.

"I do not know any more," the boy said.

"Then play them over." He did and Herr Erne listened closely, watching for faults in fingering, for errors in bowing. There were some but they were slight.

"What's your name?" he asked the boy, the professor's note already forgotten.

"Fuchs," the boy replied.

"Fuchs!" Herr Erne repeated. "Fox! What kind of a name is that?"

"It is my school name," he said. "They call me that because I play football like a fox. My name is Dietrich Taugerwald."

"How old are you?"

"I will be seventeen in March," he said.

"Who taught you to play?"

"The professor at school."

"No other teacher?"

The boy shook his head. "Last year at the Academy I heard Yehudi Menuhin play a violin like this," he said.

"One day you shall play this one," Herr Erne said. He took the Stradivarius and returned it to the cabinet. He brought out another instrument, an old and beautiful Cremona. "Now you shall play on this." He placed it in the boy's hands. "Can you come every day?" he asked.

"Except on days when I play football. . . ."

"Football! Football!" Herr Erne said angrily. "Are we in America?"

"It would be hard for them to play without me," Fuchs said innocently. Herr Erne softened, planning to wean the boy gradually from football. "You will start tomorrow and come every day that you can," he said.

After the boy left, Herr Erne went out to a music shop to buy some practice lessons and a score for the G Major Violin Concerto. It was a work of youth, written when Mozart was nineteen years old. Herr Erne was feeling younger than he had in years. He forgot about the south. The frost had not yet nipped the red geraniums in his window boxes and there was no need to think of winter. He spent the evening marking bowing instructions on the concerto.

The first lesson next day was a formal affair. Fuchs was shy and serious. Watching his earnest manner with the violin, Herr Erne felt something familiar about the clean, sharp profile on the raised head, the finely modeled body, the remote expression of the eyes. It was possible, of course, to have seen the boy in Zurich but Herr

Erne did not think so. The association was vague, reaching somewhere beyond time and space, to another life or perhaps another world. Certainly another land. As the days passed the memory became sharper but offered no further clues. There were times when Herr Erne felt uneasy with Fuchs, for the boy absorbed his every word and move as if storing it away in a dark reservoir of thought. Herr Erne wished he could know his pupil better. But he had no way to approach him. Except for the occasional and distasteful subject of football, they had nothing but music to talk about.

It was necessary to discuss the details of payment for lessons. Herr Erne would have taught Fuchs without charge but the boy's mother sent a message that she wished to pay. Inquiring of the high-school professor, Herr Erne learned that Frau Taugerwald was a widow of moderate means so he asked the four francs an hour charged by spinster pedagogues in the town. At the end of one week he would gladly have paid the boy double the four francs to come. After three lessons it was obvious to Herr Erne that Fuchs should not continue practicing on the small violin, so he offered to lend him the Cremona.

Fuchs hesitated. "I do not think that I should have it," he said.

Explaining that it would be harmful for him to continue with the small violin, Herr Erne persuaded him to take the instrument. The next day he received his second note from Frau Taugerwald, asking if the violin was valuable. Herr Erne answered her that it was only a good imitation. He knew he need not fear for the instrument in Fuch's care.

With the fine violin upon which to work, Fuchs progressed rapidly. In three days he learned the first movement of the Mozart. Weeks passed.

The weather turned cold, the storm windows went up, the fire in the grate was never allowed to go out. Fuchs, still wearing the corduroy pants, did not seem to mind the cold. Nor was Herr Erne especially aware of the changing weather. Except on the fretful days when the boy played football, he did not even think of the south. It was only when Fuchs did not come that the professor longed restlessly for the neat old house in the Sicilian lemon grove, for the mockingbirds singing through January, the scent of ripening fruit in February and the perfume of wisteria in March. His thoughts went back to the brown boys Fuchs's own age swimming in the grottoes of the sea and how he used to play his violin for two fishermen named Marino and Bruno while they beat out the rhythm with their bare feet. The fishermen probably spoke of him as they guarded their nets on the dark sea at night, wondering why *Antonio Svizzera* was not among them. With their southern love for death, Marino and Bruno doubtlessly would have the professor in his grave.

Always Fuchs would return, bringing his radiance of youth and music, and Herr Erne would forget his longing for the sun. One such day, watching the distant dreams in the young eyes, Herr Erne in a flash of memory realized the source of the boy's mysterious familiarity. It was a statue in Rome, the Belvedere Apollo. There was more to it than the physical resemblance between boy and statue. It was a glimpse into eternity, an unswerving faith in the goodness of life and the indestructibility of beauty that the boy shared with the statue. Like the statue, Fuchs never smiled. Herr Erne knew that to reach the artist behind the inscrutable mask, he must bring a smile to the boy's solemn face. He longed to become his friend.

Then something happened to melt away the cool reserve between them. The days had been gray, too cold and wet for football. They were playing the Mozart concerto. Suddenly, for the first time in a week, the sun flashed through the window. As light filled the room, Fuchs played a false note. Stopping to correct it, Herr Erne saw that the boy was distracted by something at the window. A wasp, stirred by the unexpected warmth, was staggering unsteadily from his burrow between the panes. He rested on the glass, absorbing the warmth, languidly stretching his legs. "He thinks it is spring," Fuchs said. "He is tired of being cold."

Herr Erne resented the insect for stealing precious minutes from the shining hour of his day. As the wasp came slowly to life, its drab form glowed with a golden radiance, the dark wings turned to topaz. Fuchs went to the window. Sensing his fascination for the wasp, Herr Erne laid a friendly hand on the boy's shoulder and together they watched the strange rites of the wasp in the sun.

There was an excitement about the lesson that day which there had never been before. Sharing his attention with the wasp did not impair Fuch's playing, rather it electrified him and in compensation for a slurred note or two there was strength and vibrancy in his fingers. The violin sang. They turned often to see if the wasp was still there. They admired his body (where, Fuchs asked, was the heart?) and they marveled at the tiny thread of a waist which bound the two graceful ellipses (was it one thin nerve, Fuchs wondered, or a host of them spreading like a net as in his own spinal column?).

While Fuchs speculated on where the wasp lived and what he ate, Herr Erne brought out the crystal bottle of port and filled two glasses. They watched until the afternoon settled into twilight and the wasp crawled back into his cavern in the molding. "Perhaps he is alone," Fuchs said. "It is sad to be alone in winter."

"Yes," Herr Erne said, "it is sadder to be alone in winter than in summer." He realized what he and the boy both knew, that it was sad to be alone in any season.

The friendship which began that day, Herr Erne considered a gift from the wasp. The wasp had broken through the conventions of pedagoguery and the third of a century that separated them. On cheerless days when neither port wine nor flaming logs could illuminate the gloom, the wasp did not awaken and the lessons were as sober and gray as the winter. But on sunny days quite promptly at three o'clock the wasp appeared. When the sun shone Fuchs came early, flushed and breathless, his legs nipped pink by the wind, a voluminous hand-knit scarf wound around his neck. He would stay until the wasp returned with the sinking sun to its lair. The wasp became a munificent genie, more than repaying the minutes stolen from music so that the shining hour became two and three. Fuchs brought a book on insects from his school library and they studied a diagram to see how the wasp was constructed; another time Herr Erne serenaded the wasp with "The Flight of the Bumblebee" and Fuchs's face lit with a feckless sort of gaiety. Still Herr Erne had never heard him laugh.

After the concerto they would play duets, gay little dances in which it seemed to Herr Erne the boy's dexterity often excelled his own. Then, violins laid away, they would drink wine, perhaps with some nuts or cakes; and they would talk, sometimes until the lamps in the street shone into the room. At first Herr Erne had even politely listened to football gossip but that ended with the real winter. Then they talked more easily of the school play in which Fuchs was rehearsing the role of Marc Antony.

There was one sunny afternoon when the wasp did not come out. Anxiously they watched for it, stopping often in the lesson to see if it was there. When it did not appear a sadness descended on them. They had their wine; to fill the silence Fuchs asked Herr Erne to tell him the story of his life and Herr Erne did, beginning with the boyhood of a prodigy, the priest who wrote to a bishop and the miracle of moving from a snowy village in the Engadine to the studio of a master in Paris. Fuchs listened with shimmering eyes and trembling lips as Herr Erne told of concerts at which women swept the

185

prodigy into their arms and men cried "Bravo!" He did not tell Fuchs how the boy was pushed too hard, how the prodigy, too adored, had no time to mature, how, when the curls which covered his ears were clipped, the public no longer came to the concerts. He said nothing of the frantic years of trying to catch up and the final tragic realization at thirty that it was too late. He said nothing of the occasional charity performances at which critics were always kind. Some day, Herr Erne thought, I will tell you the whole story but not until the time when you will need its lesson. He told instead of the boy's golden moment of glory when he played for Kreisler.

"It is fantastic," Fuchs said. "What did he say?"

" 'You must work hard,' he said to me. 'God does not descend easily. You must work hard.' " Herr Erne spoke to Fuchs as Kreisler had spoken to the boy in Paris.

On another day Fuchs asked, "Why do you live alone?"

Eager to arouse his pupil's sympathy, Herr Erne answered sadly, "When I was twenty I fell in love with a dancer. We were married in London. I always played when she danced. In Vienna she became sick. I begged her not to dance, but she was proud. From the orchestra I could watch her, dancing in her fever as she had never danced before. She floated in the air and when she finished she came to rest as gently as a hummingbird on a rose. The people stood up to cheer. When I ran to the stage I found my hummingbird was dead."

Tears welled up in Fuchs's eyes. Herr Erne, a lifelong bachelor, realized he had gone too far, that from now on, in the presence of the boy, he would have to live forever with the fantasy of his eloquence. "I have never married again," he said. Herr Erne turned to the window, hoping for the absent friend to interrupt his absurd narrative. The wasp was not there. "You must tell me the story of your life," he said, to distract the boy.

Fuchs thought for a moment. "I am too young to have a story," he said. "I will tell you, instead, the story of my family."

He told of a missionary grandfather, a zealous Calvinist who sacrificed his wife's life in the jungle rather than return with her to Switzerland for medical treatment; and of the missionary's jungle-born son who journeyed to the south to prosper in Capetown. Before the last war the son, by then in his fifties, came to Switzerland for the first time and married a Zurich schoolteacher in her forties. Two years after their marriage their only child was born. "I did not know my father very well," Fuchs said. "He was as old as my friends' grandfathers. Three years ago he died."

Upon her husband's death the mother returned to teaching in a girls' school. Fuchs saw her only on evenings and holidays. Fuchs had no companionship, not even from the schoolboys with whom he played football, who gave him the name Fox. On his summer holidays he bicycled alone through the forests of Valais and Graubunden; Herr Erne could see him, a young Siegfried of the conifers, dappled by sunlight shining through the birches and pines.

"Next summer perhaps you will go with me," Fuchs said hesitantly, not quite certain whether it was a proper suggestion. Herr Erne confessed he had never ridden a bicycle, which Fuchs thought very strange. "Then we will walk," he said. "Have you ever been on Görnergrat?"

Herr Erne hadn't. "There is a lodge there for students to sleep," Fuchs said, and then remembered, "But you are too old."

Herr Erne winced at the boy's candor. Sensing the pain he had inflicted, Fuchs quickly added, "It is only for students under twenty-five years."

"We will find another place where old men are permitted to sleep," Herr Erne said, smiling again.

The sunlight now slanted obliquely across the room and still the wasp had not appeared. To fill the silence, Fuchs began to recite lines from his play, his gentle voice growing stronger in emotion. Herr Erne could not believe that something so remote as the death of Julius Caesar would touch a boy so deeply. "My heart is in the coffin there with Caesar and I must pause till it comes back to me." Tears shone in his eyes.

"Are you sad for Caesar?" Herr Erne asked.

"I sorrow for Marc Anthony who has lost a friend," Fuchs said.

No matter how hard Herr Erne tried to redeem the afternoon, it continued oppressive and melancholy. Then what Herr Erne wanted so earnestly was suddenly accomplished easily by the patron of their friendship.

"Look!" Fuchs pointed to the window where the wasp was peering sleepily from his cavern, unable to decide whether or not to venture forth. They watched him, wondering what he would do.

Herr Erne tapped the ivory tip of his bow on the glass and said sharply, "Come, Wolfgang! Come! The sun shines."

It was the name that did it. Fuchs's face crinkled merrily. As if responding to the call, the wasp staggered out. Fuchs started to laugh. Like music his laughter filled the dying afternoon with joy.

Herr Erne's heart glowed as he poured a second glass of wine. Fuchs raised the window and with the tip of his finger carefully planted a drop of wine in front of the wasp. The wasp explored it with his sharp tongue and—they hoped—warmed his soul with it. They played Mozart for the wasp and made a party for him, but he did not stay long. The sun went down and he staggered back.

"Wolfgang has taken too much wine," Fuchs said, laughing still. For the rest of the afternoon they called the wasp Wolfgang. Herr Erne, dreading the moment when he would be alone, tried to prolong the jollity. Feeling drunk, he suddenly succumbed to an impulse to do what he had planned vaguely for a shining day in the future.

"I am going to give you the violin," he said.

Fuchs did not at once understand. "You have already given it to me and I am thankful," he said.

"I give it to you for good," Herr Erne said. "It is yours to keep."

The effect when the boy realized what was happening was not as Herr Erne expected. The laughter passed like sun and a cloud followed it over the inscrutable face. The eyes filled with tears and the lips quivered silently. Finally the boy was able to say, "I could not accept it."

"You can," Herr Erne said. "You can and you must." Still wanting to revive the gaiety he added, "You see it is a gift from Wolfgang and if you do not accept it, Wolfgang will be angry enough to sting us both. I will order a medallion with the words, 'To Fuchs from Wolfgang.'"

Moving like one in a dream, Fuchs wrapped the violin and its bow in their flannel coverings and laid them gently in the case. Then without warning, he threw his arms about Herr Erne's shoulders, his dry lips touched Herr Erne on the cheek. Falling back into his shy reserve, he said, "Now I must go tell my mother." He took up the case and his cap and muffler. A moment later Herr Erne saw him through the window, carrying the violin case with the same love Herr Erne had once seen a thin southern child carrying a new loaf of bread.

Fuchs's spontaneous gesture of gratitude and affection left Herr Erne weak and trembling. He poured some more port, filling the glass too full. The red wine flowed over his hand as he drank like a man newly delivered from the desert. His mind wandered to the house in Sicily and he was overwhelmed with longing for the sea. Suddenly a thought came to him.

Why not? The winter school holiday was upon them, six cold stormy weeks. He would take Fuchs to Sicily with him and there would be no interruption in the daily lessons. It pleased him to think of exposing Fuchs's gentle northern spirit to the southern sun, watching it unfold in the fullness of Mediterranean warmth. Six weeks of music and plaintive fishermen's songs sung by Marino to the guitar. They would eat the best in Marino's nets, cooked in a bed of coals by the side of the sea. Herr Erne decided to inquire at once about trains and tickets. They would go as soon as school closed so as not to waste a day of sun and sea. When they returned the bleak heart of winter would be over.

Anxiously Herr Erne awaited the next day. The night was a fitful sequence of feverish dreams and excited plans. In the morning he awoke to a winter storm. Before he could leave his room, the housekeeper received a telephone message that Fuchs had a cold and would not come for his lesson. The bleak day had no climax, no memorable hour to bring it to life. Herr Erne thought he would never see the end of it.

The next day was the same, no Fuchs and no sunlight, only gray cold, snow and rain. On the third day, snow still eddied over the Limnat and Herr Erne longed more than ever for the garden in Sicily and the warm sunlight in the open door. That morning the postman brought the heavy envelope with the handwriting flourishes, lying so boldly before him on the table.

He had torn at it anxiously. "Dear Herr Erne," the note said, "Yesterday I took the violin to the *Knabenschule* and learned from the Herr Professor its true value. I do not understand why you should offer such a valuable gift which, of course, it is impossible for my son to accept. I have discussed the extraordinary situation with Dietrich and I am sorry to inform you that we have decided together that it would be unwise for him to continue further study with you. He will return the violin tomorrow. I am yours sincerely, Frau Ida Taugerwald."

For an hour Herr Erne sat with the letter in his hand, reading and rereading it, imagining the pages written between the lines, trying to fathom what secret thought the mother had crystallized into such stern words. What had she said to Fuchs, this woman who had borne a son when it was too late to be a mother? She who had never been able to give her son friendship, how had she robbed him of the understanding and compassion which Herr Erne was able to offer? What could she give him in return but guilt and shame? How would she destroy a talent which might one day have become a Paganini?

He wondered if Fuchs would come and hoped he wouldn't. If he were away when Fuchs delivered the violin he would not have to see him, not have to face his questioning eyes. Yet Herr Erne could not help but wish that some redemption were still possible. Clenching a wet fist over the letter, he knew that parting from Fuchs without seeing him would be unbearable. He waited for the afternoon.

On the brooding river only the black swans were visible; the white ones were lost in swirls of snow. Nothing was so gloomy as Zurich in a winter storm, nothing such a trap for the human spirit. Herr Erne thought of the mockingbirds in Sicily and of Marino and Bruno and all the others who would die without ever feeling snow.

He picked up a tiny pair of scissors and began to nip at his nails. When his fingers twitched with pain, he put them down and opened the air-sealed glass instrument cabinet. He selected a Guarnerius and plucked fitfully at its strings. He raised the bow and rosin wafted forth like frost. A scherzo failed to light up the room and an adagio only deepened the gloom. The lovely throat of the violin was stained with the blood from his cuticles. He returned the instrument to its padded niche and locked the cabinet.

The day dragged on with the intolerable slowness of empty time. In the afternoon he sat idly by the fire. The panes were steamed over and he opened the window an inch or two to dry them. He remembered that for three days the wasp had failed to come out and he began to associate with the wasp's absence all the sorrow that had befallen him. He waited quietly like a mourner by a corpse.

At three o'clock he heard the bell, the steps on the stairs, the familiar shuffling of snow from boots. Fuchs appeared, scarf about his neck, cap and violin in hand, snowflakes clinging to his glistening hair. He greeted Herr Erne without expression and extended the leather case.

"Will you play it once more?" Herr Erne asked. Fuchs looked at him questioningly, and then without a word he opened the case and took out the violin. He held the instrument like one clasping an old friend for the last time. His love was centered on the violin; there was nothing left for the teacher.

"Perhaps if you are cold you would like some wine first," Herr Erne said.

"Thank you," Fuchs replied. He drank the glass quickly. He was restless and tense; his fingers on the strings were unsteady and nervous. The Mozart, which he had played so well before, went badly as if both hands and violin were too cold. Herr Erne stood by the window listening. For the tenth time that day he picked up the scissors and clipped nervously at his nails. Fuchs was distracted by the nipping of the scissors.

"Your tempo is choppy and you have forgotten the notes. You

are playing very badly today."

Fuchs began again. His fingers moved heavily, the bow scraped ponderously on the strings. The heart that made the violin sing was gone. As he played, clouds broke in the gray sky outside and a patch of sun lit up the room. His eyes filled and he stopped playing.

"Try it again," Herr Erne demanded. "You have forgotten everything."

The boy started once more. This time he pushed doggedly through without stopping. Herr Erne paid him little attention. He was looking at the window, watching the wasp stagger forth to greet the sun. Reaching the edge of the slightly raised window, the wasp tentatively explored his way over the molding, bent his body around the corners, entering, for the first time, the room which he had so enriched.

You are late, Herr Erne thought, you are come too late to the feast. Fuchs, turning his face toward his teacher, saw the wasp. He kept on playing. In his wretchedness he scratched a chord. Herr Erne cringed at the impure ugly sound. Fuchs tried again. When he scraped a second time, Herr Erne shuddered and raised the tiny scissors to the window. He opened the pointed tips over the thread waist of the wasp and held them there a second. Then he clipped the wasp in two.

Fuchs dropped his bow. His face was white; his eyes were wide with horror. The two halves of the wasp clung spastically to the glass for a second and then fell, one after the other, to the rug on the floor. Outside the clouds covered the sun and the room darkened.

The eyes that had once rested on him with love, now settled on Herr Erne with cold hatred. Loathing covered the handsome face like a shadow. With great care, Fuchs laid the violin in its case. Then, without a backward glance, he ran from the room. Herr Erne heard the clatter of boots down the stairs and a minute later he saw a black figure against the white landscape. It stopped by a tree and doubled over; the port wine stained the snow like blood.

Herr Erne folded the mittens and cap inside the scarf. He would send them to Frau Taugerwald in the morning. He wished he might also send the violin, but he knew there was no use; even if the gift were acceptable, the boy would have no more need of it. Now that Herr Erne had assisted the good Frau Taugerwald in turning flesh back into stone, now that he had freed himself of winter, he could depart at once for Sicily. His thoughts turned to the Mediterranean and the blossoming lemon groves. But he felt no joy. His heart was weary and heavy with loneliness.

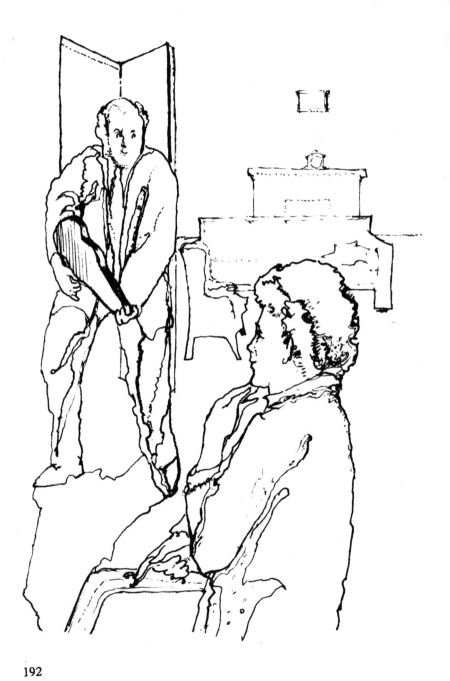

Barry Targan was born and reared in Atlantic City, and educated at Rutgers (B.A.), the University of Chicago (M.A.), and Brandeis (Ph.D.). Fiction, poetry, and essays by Targan have appeared widely in such magazines as *Esquire, The Saturday Review*, and *The New Republic*. He has taught writing and literature at a number of colleges and universities. Targan's first collection of short stories, the title story of which is reprinted here, won the coveted Iowa Short Fiction Award for 1975. Targan is regularly recognized in *The Best American Short Story* series.

Harry Belten and the Mendelssohn Violin Concerto

by Barry Targan

If a thing is worth doing, surely it is worth doing badly

Alice Belten labored up the thin wooden outer stairway leading to Josephine Goss's tiny apartment above Fulmer's dress shop. She opened the weather-stained door, streamed into the limited sitting room, and cried, "Oh, Josie. I think my Harry's going crazy." From the day thirty-one years before, when Alice and Harry had married, Josephine Goss, Alice's best friend, had suspected that Harry Belten was crazy. Thirty-one years' knowledge of him fed the suspicion. Her friend's announcement came now as no surprise.

"The violin again?" she asked, but as though she knew.

"Yes," Alice said, almost sobbing, "but worse this time, much worse. Oh God!" She put her hands to her head. "Why was I born?"

"Well, what is it?" Josephine asked.

"Oh God," Alice moaned.

"*What is it?*" Josephine lanced at her.

Alice snapped her head up, to attention. "A concert. He's going to give a concert. He's going to play in front of people."

Josephine slumped a little in her disappointment. "Is that all? He's played in front of people before, the jerk. Do you want some tea?" she asked in a tone which considered the subject changed.

"No, I don't want any tea. Who could drink? Who could eat? It's not the same. This time it's for *real*. Don't you understand?" Alice waved her hands upward. "This time he thinks he's Heifetz. He's renting an orchestra, a hall. He's going to a big city. He's going to advertise. Oh God! Oh God!" She collapsed into the tears she had sought all day.

Josephine revived. "Well I'll be. . . ." She smiled. "So the jerk has finally flipped for real. Where's he getting the money?"

"A mortgage," Alice managed. "A second mortgage." Although not relieved, she was calming. "Harry figures it'll cost about three thousand dollars."

"Three thousand dollars!" Josephine shouted. It was more serious than she had thought. "Does he stand to make anything?"

"No."

"No?"

"Nothing."

"Nothing? Nothing? Get a lawyer," she said and she rose to do it.

Harry Belten sold hardware and appliances for Alexander White, whose store was located in the town of Tyler, population four thousand, southwest New York—the Southern Tier. He had worked for Alexander White for thirty-two years, ever since he came up from the Appalachian coal country of western Pennsylvania on his way to Buffalo and saw the little sign in the general-store window advertising for a clerk. Harry had had the usual young-man dreams of life in the big city, but he had come up in the Depression. He had figured quickly on that distant afternoon that a sure job in Tyler was better than a possible soup line in Buffalo, so he stopped and he stayed. Within a year he had married Alice Miller, the young waitress and cashier at what was then Mosely's filling station, bus depot, and restaurant—the only one in Tyler. Two years later Alice was pregnant and gave birth in a hot August to a son, Jackson (after Andrew Jackson, a childhood hero of Harry's). Two years after that Harry started to pay for a house. That was in 1939. He didn't have the down payment, but in 1939, in or around Tyler, a bank had to take some risk if it wanted to do any business at all. And Harry Belten, after six years in Tyler and at the same job, was considered by all to be, and in fact was, reliable.

His life had closed in upon him quickly. But, he sometimes reflected, he would not have arranged it to be anything other than what it was.

In 1941 Harry Belten bought a violin and began to learn to play it. Once a week, on Sunday afternoon, he would take the short bus ride over to neighboring Chamsford to Miss Houghton, a retired schoolteacher who gave music lessons to an occasional pupil. A couple of jokes were made about it in Tyler at the time, but the war was starting and all interest went there. Alice was pregnant again, and in 1942 gave birth to a daughter, Jane. Harry started working part time in a ball-bearing factory in Buffalo. He drove up with four other men from Tyler three times a week. Mr. White didn't object, for there wasn't much to sell in the hardware line anymore, and besides, it was patriotic. Through it all Harry practiced the violin. Hardly anyone knew and no one cared, except maybe Josephine Goss, who never tired of remembering that Harry's violin playing and the Second World War started together.

"Harry," Alexander White called out from his little cubbyhole office in the back of the store, "could you come back here a minute please?"

"Right away, Alex," Harry answered. He took eighty cents out of a dollar for nails, handed the customer his change, and walked to the back of the store. "Keep an eye on the front," he said to Martin Bollard, who was stacking paint cans, as he passed him. While not technically a manager—besides himself and White there were only two others—Harry was by far the senior clerk. Frequently he would open and close the store, and more than once, when the boss took a vacation or had an operation, he had run the entire business, from ordering stock to making the bank deposits and ledger entries. Over the accumulating years White had sometimes reminded himself that you don't find a Harry Belten every day of the week or around some corner.

Harry squeezed into the office and sat down in the old ladder-back chair. "What can I do for you, Alex?"

"Oh, nothing . . . nothing," the older man said. He was looking at a household-supplies catalog on the desk, thumbing through it.

After a few seconds he said, "You know these new ceramic-lined garbage pails? You think we should try a gross?"

"Too many," Harry said. "We don't sell a gross of pails in a year."

"Yeah, yeah. That's right, Harry. It was just that the discount looked so good." He thumbed the catalog some more. "Harry," he started again, "yesterday at lunch down at Kiwanis I heard a couple of guys saying you was going to give a violin concert?"

"Yes sir, Alex. That's correct. As a matter of fact," he continued, "I'd been meaning to talk to you about it." Harry rushed on into his own interest and with an assurance that left his employer out. He made it all seem so "done," so finished, so accomplished. "You see, I figure I'll need a year to get ready, to really get ready. I mean I know all the fingerings and bowings of the pieces I'll be playing. But what I need is *polish*. So I've contacted a teacher— you know, a really top professional teacher. And, well, my lessons are on Monday afternoons starting in a month. The end of April that is." Alexander White looked sideways and up at Harry.

"Harry," he said slowly, smilingly, "the store isn't closed on Mondays. It's closed on Wednesday afternoons. Can't you take your lessons on Wednesday?"

"No," Harry said. "Karnovsky is busy on Wednesday. Maybe," he offered, "we could close the store on Monday and open on Wednesday instead?" White gave a slight start at such a suggestion. "Anyway, I've got to have off Monday afternoons. Without pay, of course." Alexander White shook his hand in front of his eyes and smiled again.

"Harry, when did you say the concert was? In a year, right? And you said just now that you knew all the fingers and bows?"

"Fingerings and bowings," Harry corrected.

"Fingerings and bowings. Yeah. You said so yourself all you need was polish. Okay. Good! But Harry, why a *year*? I mean how much polish do you need for Tyler anyway?"

"Oh," Harry said, "the concert isn't going to be in Tyler. Oh no sir." Harry was igniting. It was something that Alexander White did not behold easily: this fifty-one-year-old man—his slightly crumpled face, the two deep thrusts of baldness on his head, the darkening and sagging flesh beneath the eyes—beginning to burn, to be lustrous. "This isn't going to be like with the quartet that time or like with Tingle on the piano. No sir, Alex. This is *it*! I'm giving the concert in Oswego."

"Uuuh," White grunted as though he had been poked sharply above the stomach.

"I'm renting the Oswego Symphony Orchestra—two days for rehearsals, one day for the performance," Harry continued.

"Uuuh. Aaah," White grunted and wheezed again, nodding, his eyes wincing and watering a little.

"Are you okay, Alex?" Harry asked.

"Harry!" Martin Bollard shouted from the front of the store. It meant that there were customers waiting.

"Be right there," Harry shouted back. He stood to leave and started to squeeze his way out. "And I'm renting the auditorium there," he said over his shoulder and was gone back to work.

"Eeeh. Uuuh," White grunted in conclusion, his breath escaping him. The corners of his mouth turned down. He had blanched and the color had not come back. He said softly to himself, "Then it's true," and waited as if for refutation from a spirit more benign than Harry's demonic one. "But Harry," he rose up, "you're not that kind of fiddler!"

"Mr. Belten, in all candor, you are not a concert-caliber violinist." Karnovsky was speaking. His English was perfect, tempered by a soft, prewar Viennese lilt which could bring delicate memories of music and a time past. Harry had just finished playing a Spanish dance by Sarasate. He put his violin down on top of the piano and turned to the old, gentle man. It was the first time Karnovsky had heard him play.

"I know," Harry said. "I know. But I don't want to be a concert violinist. All I want to do is to give this one concert." Somewhere Karnovsky sighed. Harry went on. "I know all the notes for all the pieces I'm going to play, all the fingerings and bowings. What I need now is polish."

"Mr. Belten, what you need is . . ." but Karnovsky did not finish. "Mr. Belten, there is more to concertizing than all the notes, all the fingerings and bowings. There is a certain . . ." and again he did not finish. "Mr. Belten, have you ever heard Heifetz? Milstein? Stern? Either on records or live?" Harry nodded. "Well that, Mr. Belten, that kind of polish you aren't . . . I'm not able to give you." Karnovsky ended, embarrassed by his special exertion. He was a small man, bald and portly. His eyebrows flickered with every nuance of meaning or emotion, either when he spoke or when he played. He stood now before Harry, slightly red, his eyes wide. Harry soothed him.

"Ah, Mr. Karnovsky, that kind of playing no man can give to another. I don't ask so much from you. Just listen and suggest. Do to me what you would do to a good fiddler." Karnovsky could not look at him longer this way. He turned around.

"What do you propose to play for your concert, Mr. Belten?" Suspicions began to rise in Karnovsky's mind.

"I thought I'd start with the Vivaldi *Concerto in A Minor.*" Karnovsky nodded. "The Chausson *Poème,* then the two Beethoven *Romances,* then something by Sarasate. . . ." Karnovsky's head continued to bob. "And finish up with the Mendelssohn." Karnovsky could not help it. He spun around on Harry.

"The *Mendelssohn?*"

"Yes."

"The Mendelssohn? The Mendelssohn *Violin Concerto?* You are going to play the Mendelssohn? You know the Mendelssohn?"

"Yes," Harry said, "Yes. Yes." He was himself excited by the excitement of the older man, but in a different way.

"How do you know the Mendelssohn?" Karnovsky asked him. His tone was tougher. A fool was a fool, but music was music. Some claims you don't make. Some things you don't say.

"I've studied it," Harry answered.

"How long?" Karnovsky probed. "With whom?"

"Eighteen years. With myself. Ever since I learned how to play in all the positions, I've worked on the Mendelssohn. Every day a little bit. Phrase by phrase. No matter what I practiced, I always saved a little time for the Mendelssohn. I thought the last forty measures of the third movement would kill me. It took me four-and-a-half years." Harry looked up at Karnovsky, but that innocent man had staggered back to the piano bench and collapsed. "It's taken a long time," Harry smiled. No matter what else, he was enjoying talking about his music.

"Eighteen *years?*" Karnovsky croaked from behind the piano.

"Eighteen years," Harry reaffirmed, "and now I'm almost ready." *But is the world?* Karnovsky thought to himself. His own wryness softened him toward this strange and earnest man.

"It's fifteen dollars an hour, you know," he tried finally.

"Right," Harry said. Karnovsky fumbled in his pocket and withdrew a white Life-Saver. He rubbed it in his fingers and then flipped it like a coin in the air. He caught it in his hand and put it into his mouth. Outside, March rain slicked the grimy streets.

"Okay," he muttered. "Like we agreed before you . . . when we spoke . . . on the . . ." The eyebrows fluttered. "Go," he said. "Get the fiddle. We begin." Harry obeyed.

"Then you're really going through with it?" Alice asked.

"Of course," Harry said, swallowing quickly the last of his Jell-O. He pushed his chair back and stood up.

"Where are you going?" Alice asked.

"I've got something Karnovsky showed me that I want to work on. It's terrific." He smiled. "Already I'm learning stuff I never dreamed of." He started to leave.

"Harry," Alice said, getting up too, "first let's talk a little, huh?"

"Okay," he said, "talk."

"Come into the living room" she said, and walked into it. Harry followed. They both sat down on the sofa. Alice said, "Harry, tell me. Why are you doing it?"

"Doing what?" he asked.

"Throwing three thousand bucks out the window, is what," Alice said, her voice beginning to rise, partly in offended surprise at his question, at his innocence.

"What are you talking about, 'throw out the window'? What kind of talk is that. Is lessons from Louis Karnovsky throwing money away? Is performing the Mendelssohn *Violin Concerto* with a full, professional orchestra behind you throwing money away? What are you talking about? Drinking! That's throwing money away. Gambling! That's throwing money away. But the Mendelssohn *Violin Concerto?* Jeezzz," he concluded turning away his head, not without impatience.

Alice sat there trying to put it together. Something had gotten confused, switched around. It had all seemed so obvious at first. But now it was she who seemed under attack. *What had drinking to do with anything?* she wondered. *Who was doing what wrong?* She gave it up to try another way.

"Do you remember when you and the other guys played together and sometimes put on a show . . . concert . . . in the Grange Hall?"

Harry smiled and then laughed. "Yeah," he said. "Boy, were we a lousy string quartet." But it was a pleasant memory and an important one, and it released him from both his excitement and his scorn.

Shortly after the war some gust of chance, bred out of the new mobility enforced upon the land, brought to Tyler a cellist in the form of a traveling salesman. His name was Fred Miller and he represented a company which sold electric milking machines, their necessary supporting equipment, and other dairy sundries. It was not the first merchandise Fred Miller had hawked across America; it proved not to be the last—only one more item of an endless linkage of products which seemed to gain their reality more from such as he than from their own actual application. Who, after all, can believe in the abstraction of an electric milking machine, of plastic dolls, of suppositories, of Idaho? But Fred Miller was real, full of some American juice that pumped vitality into whatever he touched. And he had brought his cello with him.

After they played, over beer and sandwiches, Fred Miller would tell them about America and about music. "Once," he would begin, "when I was selling automobile accessories [or brushes or aluminum storm windows or animal food] in Denver, one night after supper I was outside the hotel when looking up the street I saw on the movie marquee, instead of the usual announcement of 'Fair star in a country far,' the single word 'Francescatti.' " (The other three would look at each other knowingly.) "Of course, I hurried to the theatre." And then he would take them through the music, through the performance, piece by piece, gesture by gesture, play by play.

"And there he was, not more than twenty bars away from his entrance, big as life and cool as day, wiping his hands on his hankerchief, that forty-grand Strad sticking out from under his chin. *And then he starts to mess with the bow.* Yep. He's got both hands on the bow tightening the hairs. It's a bar to go. It's two beats away. You're sure he's missed it and *wham.* Faster than the speed of light he's whacked that old bow down on the cleanest harmonic A you've ever heard, and it's off to the races, playing triple stops all the way and never missing nothing. Hand me a beer, will you, Harry?" And only then would the three of them breathe.

There was the one about when Milstein lost his bow and it almost stabbed a lady in the eighth row. Or the Heifetz one, where he didn't move anything but his fingers and his bow arm, not even his eyes, through the entire Beethoven *Concerto.* There was Stern and Rosand and Oistrakh and Fuchs and Ricci and Piatigorsky and Feuermann and Rose and the Juilliard and the Hungarian and the Budapest and Koussevitsky and Toscanini and Ormandy and the gossip and the feuds and the apocryphal. All of music came to Tyler on those Thursday nights mixed gloriously with the exotic names of Seattle and Madison and Butte and Tucson and with the rubber, steel, plastic, and edible works of all our hands and days.

One Tuesday Fred Miller came into the hardware store to tell

Harry that he was leaving. The electric-milking-machine business hadn't made it and he was off to Chicago to pick up a new line. There wasn't even time for a farewell performance. For a few weeks after, Harry, Tingle, and the reconstructed viola player from Bath had tried some improvised trios, but the spirit had gone out of the thing. Harry would sometimes play to Tingle's piano accompaniment or to Music Minus One records. But mostly he played alone.

"Harry," Alice broke in upon him gently, for she sensed where he had been, "Harry, all I'm trying to say is that for people who don't have a lot of money, three thousand dollars is a lot of money to spend . . . on anything!"

"I'll say," Harry agreed, getting up. "I'll be five years at least paying this thing off." He walked away to the room at the back of the house in which he had practiced for twenty-four years. Alice sat, miserable in her dumbness, frustrated and frightened. Something was catching and pulling at her which she couldn't understand. What was she worried about? When he had spent the eight hundred dollars on the new violin, she had not flinched. She had taken the six hundred dollars of hi-fi equipment in her wifely stride, indeed, had come to like it. All their married life they had lived in genteel debt. She looked then as she had in other anxious times for reference and stability to the bedrock of her life, but what she found there only defeated her further: the children were grown and married, the boy, even, had gone to college; all the insurance and the pension plans were paid to date; the second mortgage on the house—which would pay for all of this concertizing—would only push back the final ownership slightly, for the house, on a thirty-year mortgage to begin with, had only four more years to go. The impedimenta of existence were under control.

As Alice sat in the midst of this, the phone rang. She rose to answer it. What was the problem? Was there a problem? Whose problem? It was all so hard. Alice could have wept.

"Hello, Alice." It was Josephine Goss.

"Yes."

"I've been talking to the lawyer." Josephine sounded excited in the way people do who act after obliterating ages of inaction have taught them to forget the taste—giddy, high-pitched, trying to outrun the end of it. "He says you can't do anything legal to stop Harry unless he really is crazy, and if he really is crazy, you've got to be able to prove it."

"So?" Alice said, bracing for the lash of her friend's attitude her questions always earned.

"*So?* So you got to get him to a psychiatrist, so that's what." All at once Alice was deeply frightened, only to discover in the center of her fear the finest speck of relief. Terrible as it was to contemplate, was this the answer? Was this why nothing made sense with Harry anymore? Was he really mad?

From the back of the house Harry's violin sounded above it all.

Harry came out of the storeroom with an armload of brooms. "Well, if it ain't Pangini himself," Billy Rostend shouted out.

"Paganini," Harry corrected him, laughing, "the greatest of them all." He put the brooms down. "What can I do for you, Billy?"

"I came for some more of that off-white caulking compound I bought last week. But what I'd really like is to know what is all this about you giving a concert in Oswego. You really going to leave all us poor people and become a big star?"

"Not a chance," Harry said. "How many tubes do you want?"

"Eight. But no kidding, Harry, what's the story?" Alexander White put down the hatchet he had been using to break open nail kegs to listen. The shy, ubiquitous Tingle, a frequent visitor to the store, slipped quietly behind a rack of wooden handles for picks and axes. Martin Bollard and Mrs. George Preble, who had been talking closely and earnestly about an electric toaster at the front of the store, paused at the loudness of Billy's voice and at the question too. There were many in Tyler who wanted to know the story.

"No story," Harry answered him. "I've got this feeling, you see, that I've always wanted to give a real, big-time concert. And now I'm going to do it. That's all. It's that simple." He had been figuring on a pad. "That'll be $3.12, Billy. Do you want a bag?" Billy became conspiratorial. He dropped his voice to a whisper, but it was sharp and whistling.

"Come on, Harry, what gives?" It was more a command than a question, the kind of thing living for three decades in a small town permits, where any sense of secret is affront.

"It's nothing more than what I just told you, Billy. It's something I've always wanted to do, and now I'm going to do it."

"Yeah!" Billy spat at him. "Well, I'll believe that when I believe a lot of other things." He scooped up the tubes of caulking aⁿd slammed out of the store. Mrs. George Preble followed, either unnerved by the encounter or bent on gossip, without buying the toaster. Harry looked at Martin Bollard and shrugged his shoulders, but what could Martin say, who also wanted answers to the question Billy had asked. Only the wraithlike Tingle, glancing quickly about himself twice, looked at Harry, smiled, and then was gone.

"Harry, could I see you a minute," Alexander White called to him.

In back, in the little office, White explained to Harry that "it" was all over the town, indeed, all over the entire area of the county that had contact with Tyler. He explained to Harry that business was a "funny thing" and that people were "fickle." He explained that if a man didn't like you he would drive (county roads being so good now) ten miles out of his way to do his business elsewhere. After more than thirty years people didn't distinguish between Harry Belten and White's Hardware. What Harry did reflected on the business. And what Harry was doing, whatever it was, wasn't good for it. Harry listened carefully and attentively, as he always had. In thirty-two years he had never sassed the boss or had a cross word with him. He wasn't going to start now. Whatever was bugging Alexander White and the town of Tyler was something they were going to have to learn to live with until April twenty-eight, eight months away.

"Yes, sir," Harry said. After almost a minute, when Alexander White didn't say anything more, Harry went back to work. And Alexander White went back to opening nail kegs, smashing vigorously and repeatedly at the lids, splintering them beyond necessity.

When Harry came into Karnovsky's studio and said hello, Karnovsky's expressive eyebrows pumped up and down four times before he said a thing. The grey-and-yellow sallowness of the old man's skin took on an illusory undercast of healthy pink from the blood that had risen.

"Mr. Belten, from the beginning I have felt strangely about our relationship. I never minced words. I told you from the beginning that you didn't have it to be a concert violinist. That the idea of you concertizing, beginning to concertize, you, a man your age, was . . . was . . . *crazy!*" Harry had never seen the gentle Karnovsky sputter before. It affected him deeply. "But okay, I thought," Karnovsky continued, "so who cares. So a man from the Southern Tier wants to put on a performance with the local high-school orchestra or something. So okay, I thought. So who cares." He was using his arms to form his accusation the way that a conductor forms a symphony. Karnovsky brought his orchestra to a climax. "But now I find that you have engaged the Oswego Symphony Orchestra and are going to perform in . . . in public! *You are doing this thing for real!*" Not in years, perhaps never before, had Karnovsky shouted so loudly. The sound of his reaching voice surprised him, shocked him, and he fell silent, but he continued to look at Harry, his eyebrows bounding.

After a moment Harry asked, "Am I committing some crime? What is this terrible thing I am about to do?"

Karnovsky hadn't thought about it in those terms. Six weeks earlier he had told Bronson, his stuffy colleague at the university where he was Professor of Violin, about Harry. A frustrated Heifetz, he had called him. He had also used the word "nut," but gently and with humor. So it was that when at lunch that very day, Bronson had told him that his Harry Belten had hired a professional orchestra and had rented a hall in the middle of the downtown of a large city, Karnovsky felt unjustly sinned against, like the man who wakens belatedly to the fact that "the joke's on him." He considered, and reasonably, the effect that this might have upon his reputation. To be linked with this mad venture was not something you could easily explain away to the musical world. And Karnovsky had a reputation big enough to be shot at by the droning snipers who, living only off of wakes, do what they can to bring them about. Finally, there was the central offense of his musicianship. After fifty-five years of experience as performer and teacher, he knew what Harry's performance would sound like. It wouldn't be unbearably bad, but it didn't belong where Harry was intent on putting it. Maybe, he thought, that would be the best approach.

"Mr. Belten, the musicians will laugh at you. Anyone in your audience—if you even have an audience—who has heard a professional play the Mendelssohn will laugh at you."

"So." Harry shrugged it off. "What's so terrible about that? They laughed at you once."

"What?" Karnovsky started. "What are you talking about?"

"In 1942, when you played the Schoenberg *Violin Concerto* for the first time in Chicago. Worse than laugh at you, they booed and shouted and hissed, even. And one lady threw her pocketbook and it hit you on the knee. I read about it all in *Grant's History of Music Since 1930.*"

Who could help but be softened? Karnovsky smiled. "Believe me, that performance I'll never forget. Still, in Italy in 1939, in Milan, it was worse. Three guys in the audience tried to get up on the stage, to kill me I guess, at least from the way they were screaming and shaking their fists. Thank God there were some police there. I was touring with the Schoenberg *Concerto* then, so I guess they had heard about the trouble it was causing and that's why the police were there." He was warming to his memory and smiling broadly now. *It is a good thing,* he thought, *to have a big, good thing to remember.*

"So what's the difference?" Harry asked.

"What?" Karnovsky came back to the room slowly.

"They laughed at you. They'll laugh at me. What's the difference?"

Repentantly softened, Karnovsky gently said, "It wasn't me they were laughing at, it was the music." He looked away from Harry. "With you it will be you."

"Oh, of course," Harry agreed. "What I meant was what is the difference to the performer?" Harry really wanted to know. "Does the performer take the cheers for himself but leave the boos for the composer? In Italy they were going to kill *you,* not Schoenberg."

Karnovsky had moved to the large window and looked out, his back to Harry. March had turned to May. He heard Harry unzip the canvas cover of his violin case.

"No lesson," he said without turning. He heard Harry zip the case closed again. "Next week," he whispered, but Harry heard and left. Karnovsky stood before the window a long time. Auer had Heifetz, he thought. Kneisel had Fuchs. And I got Harry Belten.

"You're home early," Alice called out.

"Yeah. It's too hot to sell, too hot to buy. White closed up early." He had the evening paper under his arm and in his hand the mail.

"Oh, the mail," Alice said. "I forgot to get it. Anything?"

Harry was looking. He saw a letter addressed to him from the Oswego Symphony, opened it and read.

"Ha!" he shouted, flinging his hand upward.

"What is it?" Alice came over to him.

"It's from the Oswego Symphony. They want to cancel the agreement. They say they didn't know I was going to use the orchestra to give my own public performance." Harry hit the letter with his fist. "They want out. Listen." Harry read from the letter.

". . . given the peculiar nature of the circumstances surrounding your engagement of the orchestra and considering that it is a civically sponsored organization which must consider the feelings and needs both present and future of the community, I am sure that you will be sensitive to the position in which we find ourselves. It has taken many years to establish in the minds and hearts of our people here a sense of respect and trust in the orchestra, and while this is not to say that your intended performance would violate that trust, yet it must be obvious to you that it would perhaps severely qualify it. It goes without saying that upon receipt of the contract, your check will be returned at once along with a cash consideration of fifty dollars for whatever inconvenience this will have involved you in."

Somewhere in the middle of the first ponderous sentence, Alice had gotten lost. "Harry," she asked, "What does it mean?"

"Wait," Harry said as he read the letter again. And then he laughed, splendidly and loud. "It means," he gasped out to her, "that they are offering me my first chance to make money from the violin—by *not* playing." He roared. "Well, the hell with them!" he shouted up at the ceiling. "A contract is a contract. We play!" And he thundered off to his music room to write a letter saying so.

"Harry," Alice called after him. "Harry," she trailed off. But he was gone. She had meant to tell him that the children were coming that night for supper. And she had meant to tell him that Tingle had quietly left at the front door that morning a bundle of large maroon-and-black posters announcing the debut of Harry Belten in Oswego. But, then, it seemed that it was not important to tell him, that until all of this was settled one way or another she would not be able to tell what was important or what was not. Under her flaming flesh, she felt heavy, sodden, cold.

Throughout supper he regaled them with his excitement. Although neither of his children had become musicians, Jackson had learned the piano and Jane the violin. But once past high school they had left their instruments and their skill in that inevitable pile of lost things heaped up by the newer and for a time more attractive urgencies. College had engulfed the boy, marriage and babies the girl. As children they had made their music and had even liked it, but the vital whip of love had never struck them. Still, they had lived too long in that house and with that man not to be sympathetic to his joy. It was, then, wrenchingly difficult when, after supper, after the ice cream on the summer porch which he and his father had built, Jackson told his father that everyone was concerned by what they thought was Harry's strange behavior. Would he consent to be examined?

"Examined?" Harry asked.

"By a doctor," his son answered.

The daughter looked away.

"What's the matter?" Harry looked around surprised. "I feel fine."

"By a different kind of doctor, Dad."

"Oh," Harry said, and quickly understood. "By a . . . uh . . . a psychiatrist?"

"Yes." Jackson's voice hurried on to add, to adjust, to soften. "Dad . . . it's not that we. . . ."

But Harry cut him off. "Okay," he said.

They all turned and leaned toward him as though they expected him to fall down.

"Daddy?" his daughter began, putting her hand out to him. She didn't think that he had understood. She wanted him to be certain that he understood what was implied. But he forestalled her, them. "It's okay," he said, nodding. "I understand. A psychiatrist. Make the arrangements." And then, to help them out of their confused silence and their embarrassment, he said, "Look. I really may be nuts or something, but not," he added, "the way everybody thinks." And with the confidence of a man who knows a thing or two about his own madness, he kissed them all good night and went to bed.

By the middle of September all kinds of arrangements had been made or remained to be made. First of all, there was the Oswego Symphony. A series of letters between Mr. Arthur Stennis, manager of the orchestra, and Harry had accomplished nothing. It was finally suggested that Harry meet with the Board of Directors personally. A date, Tuesday afternoon, September 21, was set. Then there was the psychiatrist. For convenience, an appointment had been made for Tuesday morning. The psychiatrist was in Rochester. Harry's plan was to have his lesson as usual Monday afternoon, sleep over in Buffalo, drive to Rochester and the psychiatrist the following morning, and then on to Oswego and the Board of the Symphony in the afternoon; home that night and back to work on Wednesday. That was the way he explained it to Alexander White at the store.

After lunch on the twentieth of September Harry prepared to enter upon his quest. He knew it was off to a battle that he went, so he girded himself and planned. And it was the first time he would be sleeping away from home without his wife since he took his son camping fourteen years before. He was enjoying the excitement.

"Is everything in the suitcase?" he asked Alice.

"Yes," she said.

"Are you sure?"

"Yes, yes. I've checked it a dozen times." She held up the list and read it off. "Toothbrush, shaving, underwear, shirt, handker-chief."

"Tie?"

"Tie."

"Okay," he said. "Tonight I'll call you from the Lake View Hotel and tomorrow after the doctor I'll call you too. I won't call after the meeting. I'll just drive right home." He picked up the suitcase and walked toward the door. "Wish me luck," he said.

"Oh, Harry," Alice called and ran to him. She kissed him very hard on his cheek and hugged him to her. "Good luck," she said.

Harry smiled at the irony. "With whom?" he asked.

"With . . . with *all* of them," she said, laughing and squeezing his arm.

At the door he picked up his violin case and, hoisting it under his arm in exaggerated imitation of an old-time movie gangster, turned and sprayed the room. "Rat-a-tat-tat."

They both laughed. Harry kissed his wife and left the house, his weapon ready in his hand.

The psychiatrist was fat and reddish, his freckles still numerous and prominent. He sat behind an expensive-looking desk-like table and smoked a large, curved pipe. Harry thought that he looked like a nice man.

"Good morning, Mr. Belten," he said, gesturing for Harry to be seated. "Please, be comfortable."

"That pipe smells wonderful," Harry said. The doctor wrote on a legal-size yellow pad on the desk. "Did you write that down?" Harry asked.

The doctor looked up and smiled. "Not exactly. I wrote down something about what you said."

"Oh," Harry nodded.

"Mr. Belten, do you know why you're here?" the psychiatrist asked.

"Certainly," Harry answered. "For you to see if I'm crazy."

"Not exactly. In fact, not at all." The word "crazy" made the doctor's ears redden. "Your family felt that your behavior in the past six months exhibited a definite break with your behavior patterns of the past and felt that, with your consent, an examination now would be useful in determining any potential developments of an aberrated nature. Are you laughing?" he asked Harry, a bit put off.

"I was just thinking, my family felt that, all that?"

The doctor laughed too.

"Doctor, do you know why my family felt whatever it was you said they felt and wanted me examined? I'll tell you, One: Because they can't understand why I want to give this big, public concert. Two: Because it's costing me three thousand dollars, which for me is a lot of money. And three: Because my wife's best friend, who has always disliked me for no good reason, put the bug into my wife."

"Suppose you tell me about it," the doctor said.

Although not certain what the doctor meant by "it" Harry told him plenty. He told him about Alexander White and the hardware business and about Tyler, about Fred Miller and about Miss Houghton, the old violin teacher, and about Karnovsky, the new one, and about the teachers in-between. He told him about Josephine Goss and about his children, about his wife and about the gentle Tingle and about when he bought the new violin. It took a long time to tell all the things that Harry was telling. The doctor was writing rapidly.

"Are you writing down things about that too?" Harry asked.

The doctor paused and looked up at Harry. "Do you want to see what I'm writing?" he asked.

"No," Harry said. "I trust you."

The doctor leaned forward. "Good," he said. "Now, what do you mean by 'trust me'?"

"I mean," Harry answered, "that you'll see I'm not craz . . . not . . . ah . . ." he gave it up with a shrug . . . "*crazy* and that you'll tell my family that and they'll feel better and won't try to stop me from giving the concert."

The doctor leaned back heavily. His pipe had gone out. "Mr. Belten, I can tell you right now that you're not *crazy*—as you put it—and that I have nothing to do with stopping you from giving your concert. Even if I thought you were *crazy* I couldn't stop you. It would have to go through the courts, there would have to be a trial. . . ."

"Fine," Harry interrupted. He stood up. "Just tell them that nothing's wrong with me."

"I didn't say that," the doctor said.

Harry sat down. "What do you mean?" he asked.

"Well." The doctor lit his pipe at length. "Sometimes people can be 'sane' and still 'have something wrong with them.'" He was uncomfortable with Harry's phrasing but decided to use it for the sake of clarity. "By helping the individual to find out what that thing is, we help him to lead a . . . a . . . *happier* life."

"Oh, I get it." Harry brightened. "We find out why I want to give the concert so that when I do give it I'll enjoy it even more?"

"Not exactly." The doctor smiled, but something in what Harry had said lurked dangerously over him. He stiffened slightly as he said, "By finding out why you want to give it maybe we discover that isn't so important after all, that maybe, finally, you don't really need to give it, that you would be just as happy, maybe happier, by *not* giving it." He continued, his pipe steaming, "There are all kinds of possibilities. It might easily be that your apparent compulsion to give this concert is in reality a way of striking back at the subconscious frustrations of a small life, a way of grasping out for some of the excitement, some of the thrill that you never had."

"Sure," Harry said. "Now that you put it that way, I can see where it could be that too." Harry smiled. "That's pretty good." The doctor smiled. "Still, I don't see where that means that I *shouldn't* have the thrill, the excitement of giving the concert. Maybe after the concert I won't have anymore—what did you call them— 'subconscious frustrations.' Maybe the best thing for me *is* to give the concert."

There was a long silence. The doctor let his pipe go out and stared at Harry. At last he said, "Why not?"

It didn't take the Board, or more precisely, Mr. Arthur Stennis, manager of the orchestra and secretary to the Board, more than ten minutes to come to the point. To wit: even though they (he) had executed a contract with one Harry Belten, the Board felt that the reputation of the orchestra had to be protected and that there were sufficient grounds to charge misrepresentation on his part and take the whole thing to court if necessary, which action could cost Harry Belten a small fortune. Why didn't he take their generous offer (now up to two hundred dollars) for returning the contract and forget the whole thing?

"Because," Harry explained again, "I don't want the money. I want to give a concert with a professional orchestra." But that simple answer, which had alienated others, did not aid him here.

He looked around him at the other eight members of the Board. Five were women, all older than Harry, all looking identical in their rinsed-grey hair and in those graceless clothes designed to capture women in their age. They all wore rimless glasses and peered out at Harry, silently, flatly, properly. No help there, he thought. There was the conductor, Morgenstern, a good minor-leaguer. He had said nothing and had not even looked at Harry from the time both had entered the room. Next to him was the treasurer, elected to the Board but, Harry knew, strictly a hired hand. He would take no opposite side. Finally there was Mr. Stanley Knox, eighty-three years old and one of the wealthier men in Oswego, improbably but defiantly present. Although Harry had never seen this ancient man before that afternoon, he knew instinctively that he knew him well. Stanley Knox wore the high-button boot of the past. The too-large check of his unlikely shirt, the width of his tie, the white, green-lined workman's suspenders which Harry glimpsed under the Montgomery Ward suit marked Stanley Knox for what he basically was: for all that counted, just one more of Harry's customers. He had dealt with Stanley Knoxes for more than thirty years. Had he learned anything in all that time that would matter now? Yes.

"It isn't fair," Harry said.

"It might not seem fair to you," Stennis countered, "but would it be fair to the people of Oswego?" He looked around the table in that kind of bowing gesture which suggested that he spoke for them all.

But Harry pursued. "You start by being fair to one man at a time." He paused for that to work. Then he continued. "But *besides* me," he said, waving himself out of the picture, "it isn't fair to the musicians. You talk about the good of the orchestra, but you take bread out of the musicians' mouths. Do you think *they* would mind playing with me?"

"What does each man lose?" Stanley Knox asked of anyone. His eyes were rheumy and his teeth chattered in his head.

"For two rehearsals and the performance, between thirty and forty dollars a man," Harry answered.

Stanley Knox looked at Stennis. "Hee, hee," he began. His head lolled for a moment and then straightened. "That's a lot of money for a man to lose."

"Mr. Knox," Stennis explained in the tone affected for the young and the senile, "the thirty dollars lost now could mean much more to the individual members of the orchestra in the years to come. The thirty dollars now should be looked at as an investment in the future, a future of faith and trust that the Oswego Symphony will bring to its people the *best* in music *all* of the time." He said the last looking, glaring, at Harry.

The old man leaned forward in his chair, shaking, and said,

"Forty bucks now is forty bucks now." His spittle flew around him. He slapped his open palm down upon the sleek conference table. And then he asked Stennis, "Have you ever heard him play?" Stennis told him no. "Then how do you know he's so bad?" The old ladies, who had been watching either Harry or Stanley Knox, now turned to Stennis. It was the first sign that Harry had a chance.

Then Stennis said, too prissily, too impatiently, "Because at fifty-one years of age you *don't* start a career as a concert violinist. You *don't* start giving concerts."

But that was exactly the wrong thing to say.

"Get your fiddle and play for us," the old man said to Harry. Harry got up and walked to the back of the room where his violin case rested on a table. He took the violin out of the case. Behind him he could hear Stennis squawk:

"Mr. Knox. This is *still* a Board meeting and we are *still* subject to the rules of parliamentary procedure."

"Shut up, Stennis," Stanley Knox said. Harry came forward and played. After he finished a pleasant little minuet of Haydn's he saw the old ladies smiling.

"Very nice," Stanley Knox said.

Stennis interrupted him, feverishly. "But Haydn minuets don't prove anything. My twelve-year-old *daughter* can play that, for God's sake."

Stanley Knox paid him no heed. "Do you know *Turkey in the Straw?*"

Harry nodded and played. Stennis was frantic. As Harry finished, he stood up. "Mr. Knox. I must insist on order." He looked around him for support, and, much as they were enjoying the music, the old ladies nodded, reluctantly, in agreement—Board business was, after all, Board business.

But Stanley Knox slapped the table for his own order. "Quiet," he commanded. "Let the boy play. Play *The Fiddler's Contest*," he ordered Harry.

"*Mr. Knox!*" Stennis shouted.

"*Quiet!*" Knox shouted back. "Let the boy play."

Harry played.

Stennis hit his hand to his head and rushed noisily from the room.

One by one the old ladies tiptoed out, and then the treasurer left, and then Morgenstern, who walked by Harry and neither looked at him nor smiled nor frowned. Harry played on.

"Let the boy play," Stanley Knox roared, pounding the table. "Let the boy play."

By the time Alexander White ate lunch on Monday, April 24, Harry was halfway to Buffalo and his last lesson with Karnovsky. "Well, this is the week," he had cheerfully observed for White that morning. "It sure is," his wearied boss had replied. Although it was spring and the busier time of the year in the hardware business, he had suggested that Harry take off Tuesday as well as the other three and a half days of the week. Harry had objected that he didn't mind working Tuesday. "I know," White told him. "It's me. I object. Go. Get this thing over with." So Harry went. Now Alexander White sat in the Tyler Arms coffee shop-restaurant on Route 39 eating a chicken-salad sandwich. It was two in the afternoon, but he couldn't have gotten away sooner. Louis Bertrand came into the shop and walked over to where Alexander White was sitting.

"Mind if I join you, Alex?" he asked.

"No, no. Sit down," White said, gesturing to the seat opposite him. But even before Bertrand had settled creakingly down onto the cane chair, White regretted it.

"So Harry's gone and left you," he observed lightly.

For a fact, White thought, everything travels fast in a small town. "No, no. He had three-and-a-half days off so I gave him the fourth too. Let him get it out of his system. Thank God when this week is over." He went to bite into the other half of his sandwich but found that he didn't want it. He sipped at his coffee several times. Thank God when this week is over, he thought.

"But will it be over? Will he get it out of his system?"

"What? What do you mean? You don't think he's going to become a musician, do you? A gypsy?" With his voice Alexander White turned the idea down. He knew his man.

"Why not?" Louis Bertrand asked.

"Why not? Why not? Because a man lives and works in a place all his life, he doesn't just like that leave it. Because . . . because he likes it here, the people, his job and everything. And besides, he couldn't afford it even if he wanted to."

"Couldn't he?"

In all the weeks, in all the months that Alexander White had been engulfed and upset by the impinging consequences of Harry's action, he had never been frightened because he had never imagined conclusions more complex than the return to normal which he expected to take place after the concert. But now, for the first time, he imagined more largely.

"What does that mean?" he asked Louis Bertrand steadily and hard.

"I don't say it means anything." He looked away from White over to where George Latham, owner of the Tyler Arms, was sitting drinking coffee. He raised his voice to attract an ally. There had been something in Alexander White's tone. "But when a clerk starts spending three thousand bucks on nothing and takes off a week just like that and buys fancy violins, well . . . ." George Latham had come over and so had George Smiter, who had just entered. Bertrand looked up at them.

"Well *what?*" White demanded.

"Now take it easy, Alex," George Latham soothed him. "Lou didn't mean anything."

"*The hell he didn't.* Are you accusing Harry of something? Are you saying he's been stealing from me?" No one had said it and none of them thought that it was so, but anger breeds its kind, and mystery compounds it. It wasn't long before they were all arguing heatedly, not to prove a point but to attack an enigma. All except Alexander White, who found out that in thirty-two years men could be honest and loyal and even courageous, and that in the face of that exciting truth violin concerts or what have you for whatever reasons didn't matter much. Uncertain of Harry's compelling vision, unnerved by the ardor of his dream, certain only of the quality of the man and what that demanded of himself, he defended Harry and his concert stoutly. He was surprised to hear the things he was saying, surprised that he was saying them. But he felt freed and good.

In the Green Room Karnovsky paced incessantly.

"Relax," Harry said to him. Karnovsky looked up to see if it was a joke. Harry was tuning his violin.

"I'm relaxed," he said. "I'm relaxed. Here. Give me that," he commanded Harry and grabbed the violin away from him. He began to tune it himself, but it was in tune. He gave it back to Harry. "And don't forget, in the *tutti* in the second movement of the Vivaldi, you have got to come up *over* the orchestra, *over* it."

An electrician knocked at the door. "How do you want the house lights?" he asked Harry.

"What?" Harry said, turning to Karnovsky.

"Halfway," Karnovsky said to the electrician, who left. "Never play in a dark house," he explained to Harry. "You should always be able to see them or else you'll forget that they're there and then the music will die. But don't look at them," he rushed to add.

Harry laughed. "Okay," he said. Then he heard the merest sound of applause. The conductor had taken his place. Harry moved for the door.

"Good luck," Karnovsky said from back in the room.

"Thanks," Harry said. And then, turning, he asked, "You care?"

"I care," Karnovsky said slowly. "I care."

In the great auditorium, built to seat some five thousand, scattered even beyond random were, here and there, a hundred twenty-seven people. Most had come from Tyler, but at least thirty were people who would come to a hear a live performance, especially a live performance of the Mendelssohn, anywhere, anytime. In their time they had experienced much. But what, they wondered this night as Morgenstern mounted the podium, was this? Certainly it was Morgenstern and indeed that was the orchestra and there, walking gaily out upon the stage, was a man with a violin in his hand. The house lights were sinking, as in all the concerts of the past. But where were the people? What was going on? Some four or five, unnerved by the hallucinated spectacle, stood up and raced out of the auditorium. But it was only after Harry had been playing (the Vivaldi) for three or four minutes, had wandered for ten measures until he and the orchestra agreed upon the tempo, had come in flat on two successive entrances, and had scratched loudly once, that the others—the strangers—began to get nervous. Now a fine anxiety sprang up in them. Their minds raced over the familiar grounds of their expectations—the orchestra, the conductor, the hall, the music—but nothing held together and no equation that they could imagine explained anything. One woman felt in herself the faint scurryings of hysteria, the flutters of demonic laughter, but she struggled out of the hall in time. Among the other strangers there was much nudging of neighbors and shrugs of unknowing. Then, each reassured that he was not alone in whatever mad thing it was that was happening, they sank down into the wonder of it all. And Harry got, if not good, better. He played through the rest of the first half of the concert pleasantly enough and without incident.

There was no intermission. The time for the Mendelssohn had come.

The Mendelssohn *Concerto in E minor for Violin and Orchestra, Op. 64* was completed September 16, 1844, and was first performed by the celebrated virtuoso Ferdinand David in Leipzig, March 13, 1845. From its first performance and ever after it was and is greatly received in its glory. Every major violinist since David has lived long enough to perform it well. And of concerti for the violin it is preeminent, for it combines a great display of violin technique with lyric magnificence, holding the possibiltes of ordered sound at once beyond and above satisfying description. Nowhere in all the vast world of violin literature does the instrument so perfectly emerge as a disciple of itself. No one performs the Mendelssohn *Violin Concerto* publicly without entering into, at least touching upon, its tradition.

After a measure and a half, the violin and the orchestra engage each other and stay, throughout the piece, deeply involved in the other's fate. But the music is for the violin after all, so it is important that the violinist establish at once his mastery over the orchestra, determine in his entrance the tempo and the dynamic pattern that the orchestra must bow to. This Harry did. But he did not do much more. Playing with a reasonable precision and, even, polish; with, even, a certain technical assurance which allowed his tone to bloom, he played well enough but not grandly. As he concluded the first movement he thought to himself, with neither chagrin nor surprise, "Well, Belten. You're no Heifetz," and at the end of the lovely, melancholy second movement, "You're no Oistrakh, either." It was really just as he expected it would be. He was enjoying it immensely.

In the Mendelssohn *Violin Concerto* there are no pauses between the three movements. Part of the greatness of the piece lies in its extraordinary sense of continuity, in its terrific pressure of building, in its tightening, mounting pace (even the cadenza is made an integral part of the overall development). Because there are no pauses and because of the length of the piece and because of the great physical stress put upon the instrument by the demands of the music, there is an increased possibility for one of the strings to lose that exact and critical degree of tautness which gives it—and all the notes played upon it—the correct pitch. If such a thing happens, then the entire harmonic sense of the music is thrown into jeopardy.

Deep into the third movement, at the end of the recapitulation in the new key, Morgenstern heard it happen. He glanced quickly over at Harry. And Glickman, the concertmaster, heard it. He glanced up at Morgenstern. And Karnovsky heard it too. In the many times that he himself had performed the Mendelssohn, this same thing had happened to him only two terrible times. He remembered them like nightmares, perfectly. There was only one thing to do. The performer must adjust his fingering of the notes played on the weakened string. In effect, he must play all the notes on that one string slightly off, slightly wrong, while playing the notes on all the other three strings correctly. Karnovsky tightened in his seat while his fingers twitched with the frustrated knowledge that he could not give to Harry up on the stage. He was suffocating in his black rage at the injustice about to overtake this good man. That the years of absurd dreaming, the months of aching practice should be cast away by the failure of a miserable piece of gut strangled Karnovsky almost to the point of fainting.

Even before Morgenstern had looked at him (and with the first real emotion Harry had seen on that man's face), Harry had heard the pitch drop on the D string. Only his motor responses formed out of his eighteen years of love carried him through the next three speeding measures as terror exploded in him. He had time to think two things: *I know what should be done,* and *Do it.* He did it. It almost worked.

Harry Belten played the worst finale to the Mendelssohn *Violin Concerto* probably ever played with a real orchestra and before the public, any public. But it was still recognizably the Mendelssohn, it was not too badly out of tune, and if he was missing here and there on the incredibly difficult adjustments to the flatted D string, there were many places where he wasn't missing at all. Besides Karnovsky, Morgenstern, and Glickman, nobody in the tiny audience in the Coliseum knew what was going on. What they knew was what they heard: to most, sounds which could not help but excite; to the more knowledgeable, a poor performance of a great piece of music. But what Karnovsky knew made him almost weep in his pride and in his joy. And then, in that wonder-filled conclusion, violin and orchestra welded themselves together in an affirming shout of splendor and success. The Mendelssohn *Concerto in E minor for Violin and Orchestra, Op. 64,* was over.

In all his life Harry did not remember shaking as he was shaking now as Morgenstern and then the concertmaster grasped his hand in the traditional gesture made at concert's end. His sweat was thick upon him. He turned, smiling, to the world. Out of the great silence someone clapped. One clap. It rang like a shot through the empty hall, ricocheting from high beam to vacant seat and back. And then another clap. And then a clapping, an uncoordinated, hesitant buzz of sound rising up into the half gloom of the hollow dome. Then someone shouted out, "Hey, Harry. That was terrific."

"Yeah," fourteen rows back a voice agreed, "terrific." Two on either distant side of the auditorium whistled shrilly their appreciation. Someone pounded his feet. Joe Lombardy remembered a picture he had seen on TV once where after a concert they had shouted *bravo*.

"Bravo," he shouted. He was on his feet, waving to the stage. "Hey, Harry. Bravo." He looked around him to bring in the others. "Bravo," he shouted again. Others joined, almost chanting: "Bravo. Bravo. Bravo. Bravo." And the sounds flew upward like sparks from fire glowing and dying in the dark.

"Encore," Joe Lombardy, remembering more, shouted out. "Encore," he screamed, pleased with himself. "Encore," he knifed through the thinly spread tumult.

"Encore," the others yelled. "Encore. Encore." What there was there of Tyler cheered.

Alice Belten, sitting between her two children, holding their hands, her eyes full, laughing, was at ease. She looked up at the man on the stage. He threw her a kiss. And she kissed him back.

Then Harry Belten tuned his violin, placed it under his chin, and played his encore. And then he played another one.

Paganini, Bull, Vieuxtemps, Joachim, Wieniawski, Sarasate